The Unabridged Collected Works

Of

Michael Molinos
And
Francois Fenelon

The Unabridged Collected Works

Of

Michael Molinos
And
Francois Fenelon

Edited By

Glenn Kahley

ISBN: 978-0-9788914-0-4

For my wife Lisa and my daughter Hannah

TABLE OF CONTENTS

PREFACE XI

MICHAEL MOLINOS

The Spiritual Guide 1
Daily Communion 127

FRANCOIS FENELON

Spiritual Progress 153
Maxims of The Saints 241
Spiritual Letters 269
Fenelon Biography 323

PREFACE

About Michael Molinos

Michael Molinos, a Spaniard of a rich and honorable family, entered, when young, into priest's orders, but would not accept any preferment in the Church. He possessed great natural abilities, which he dedicated to the service of his fellow creatures, without any view of emolument to himself. Although his course of life was pious and uniform, he did not exercise those austerities which are common among the religious orders of the Church of Rome. Being of a contemplative turn of mind, he pursued the track of the mystical divines, and having acquired great reputation in Spain, and being desirous of propagating his sublime mode of devotion, he left his own country, and settled at Rome. Here he soon connected himself with some of the most distinguished among the literati, who so approved of his religious maxims, that they concurred in assisting him to propagate them; and, in a short time, he obtained a great number of followers, who, from the sublime mode of their religion, were distinguished by the name of Quietists.

In 1675, Molinos published a book entitled The Spiritual Guide, to which were subjoined recommendatory letters from several great personages. One of these was by the archbishop of Reggio; a second by the general of the Franciscans; and a third by Father Martin de Esparsa, a Jesuit, who had been divinity-professor both at Salamanca and Rome. No sooner was the book published than it was greatly read, and highly esteemed, both in Italy and Spain; and this so raised the reputation of the author that his acquaintance was coveted by the most respectable characters. Letters were written to him from numbers of people, so that a correspondence was settled between him, and those who approved of his method in different parts of Europe. Some secular priests, both at Rome and Naples, declared themselves openly for it, and consulted him, as a sort of oracle, on many occasions. But those who attached themselves to him with the greatest sincerity were some of the fathers of the Oratory; in particular three of the most eminent, namely, Caloredi, Ciceri, and Petrucci. Many of the cardinals also courted his acquaintance, and thought themselves happy in being reckoned among the number of his friends. The most distinguished of them was the Cardinal d'Estrees, a man of very great learning, who so highly approved of Molinos' maxims that he entered into a close connection with him. They conversed together daily, and notwithstanding the distrust a Spaniard has naturally of a Frenchman, yet Molinos, who was sincere in his principles, opened his mind without reserve to the cardinal; and by this means a correspondence was settled between Molinos and some distinguished characters in France.

While Molinos was thus laboring to propagate his religious mode, Father Petrucci wrote several treatises relative to a contemplative life; but he mixed in them so many rules for the devotions of the Roman Church, as mitigated that censure he might have otherwise incurred. They were written chiefly for the use of the nuns, and therefore the sense was expressed in the most easy and familiar style. Molinos had now acquired such reputation, that the Jesuits and Dominicans began to be greatly alarmed, and determined to put a stop to the progress of this method. To do this, it was necessary to decry the author of it; and as heresy is an imputation that makes the strongest impression at Rome, Molinos and his followers were given out to be heretics. Books were also written by some of the Jesuits against Molinos and his method; but they were all answered with spirit by Molinos. These disputes occasioned such disturbance in Rome that the whole affair was taken notice of by the Inquisition. Molinos and his book, and Father Petrucci, with his treatises and letters, were brought under a severe examination; and the Jesuits were considered as the accusers. One of the society had, indeed, approved of Molinos' book, but the rest took care he should not be again seen at Rome. In the course of the examination both Molinos and Petrucci acquitted themselves so well, that their books were again approved, and the answers which the Jesuits had written were censured as scandalous.

Petrucci's conduct on this occasion was so highly approved that it not only raised the credit of the cause, but his own emolument; for he was soon after made bishop of Jesis, which was a new declaration made by the pope in their favor. Their books were now esteemed more than ever, their method was more followed, and the novelty of it, with the new approbation given after so vigorous an accusation by the Jesuits, all contributed to raise the credit, and increase the number of the party. The behavior of Father Petrucci in his new dignity greatly contributed to increase his reputation, so that his enemies were unwilling to give him any further disturbance; and, indeed, there was less occasion given for censure by his writings than those of Molinos. Some passages in the latter were not so cautiously expressed, but there was room to make exceptions to them; while, on the other hand Petrucci so fully explained himself, as easily to remove the objections made to some parts of his letter.

The great reputation acquired by Molinos and Petrucci occasioned a daily increase of the Quietists. All who were thought sincerely devout, or at least affected the reputation of it, were reckoned among the number. If these persons were observed to become more strict in their lives and mental devotions, yet there appeared less zeal in their whole deportment at the exterior parts of the Church ceremonies. They were not so assiduous at Mass, nor so earnest to procure Masses to be said for their friends; nor were they so frequently either at confession, or in processions.

Though the new approbation given to Molinos' book by the Inquisition had checked the proceedings of his enemies; yet they were still inveterate against him in their hearts, and determined if possible to ruin him. They insinuated that he had ill designs, and was, in his heart, an enemy to the Christian religion: that under pretence of raising men to a sublime strain of devotion, he intended to erase from their minds a sense of the mysteries of Christianity. And because he was a Spaniard, they gave out that he was descended from a Jewish or Mahometan race, and that he might carry in his blood, or in his first education, some seeds of those religions which he had since cultivated with no less art than zeal. This last calumny gained but little credit at Rome, though it was said an order was sent to examine the registers of the place where Molinos was baptized.

Molinos finding himself attacked with great vigor, and the most unrelenting malice, took every necessary precaution to prevent these imputations being credited. He wrote a treatise, entitled "Frequent and Daily Communion," which was likewise approved by some of the most learned of the Roman clergy. This was printed with his Spiritual Guide, in the year 1675; and in the preface to it he declared that he had not written it with any design to engage himself in matters of controversy, but that it was drawn from him by the earnest solicitations of many pious people. The Jesuits, failing in their attempts of crushing Molinos' power in Rome, applied to the court of France, when, in a short time, they so far succeeded that an order was sent to Cardinal d'Estrees, commanding him to prosecute Molinos with all possible rigor. The cardinal, though so strongly attached to Molinos, resolved to sacrifice all that is sacred in friendship to the will of his master. Finding, however, there was not sufficient matter for an accusation against him, he determined to supply that defect himself. He therefore went to the inquisitors, and informed them of several particulars, not only relative to Molinos, but also Petrucci, both of whom, together with several of their friends, were put into the Inquisition.

When they were brought before the inquisitors, (which was the beginning of the year 1684) Petrucci answered the respective questions put to him with so much judgment and temper that he was soon dismissed; and though Molinos' examination was much longer, it was generally expected he would have been likewise discharged: but this was not the case. Though the inquisitors had not any just accusation against him, yet they strained every nerve to find him guilty of heresy. They first objected to his holding a correspondence in different parts of Europe; but of this he was acquitted, as the matter of that correspondence could not be made criminal. They then directed their attention to some suspicious papers found in his chamber;

but Molinos so clearly explained their meaning that nothing could be made of them to his prejudice. At length, Cardinal d'Estrees, after producing the order sent him by the king of France for prosecuting Molinos, said he could prove against him more than was necessary to convince them he was guilty of heresy. To do this he perverted the meaning of some passages in Molinos' books and papers, and related many false and aggravating circumstances relative to the prisoner. He acknowledged he had lived with him under the appearance of friendship, but that it was only to discover his principles and intentions: that he had found them to be of a bad nature, and that dangerous consequences were likely to ensue; but in order to make a full discovery, he had assented to several things, which, in his heart, he detested; and that, by these means, he saw into the secrets of Molinos, but determined not to take any notice, until a proper opportunity should offer of crushing him and his followers.

In consequence of d'Estree's evidence, Molinos was closely confined by the Inquisition, where he continued for some time, during which period all was quiet, and his followers prosecuted their mode without interruption. But on a sudden the Jesuits determined to extirpate them, and the storm broke out with the most inveterate vehemence. The Count Vespiniani and his lady, Don Paulo Rocchi, confessor to the prince Borghese, and some of his family, with several others, (in all seventy persons) were put into the Inquisition, among whom many were highly esteemed for their learning and piety. The accusation laid against the clergy was their neglecting to say the breviary; and the rest were accused of going to the Communion without first attending confession. In a word, it was said, they neglected all the exterior parts of religion, and gave themselves up wholly to solitude and inward prayer. The Countess Vespiniani exerted herself in a very particular manner on her examination before the inquisitors. She said she had never revealed her method of devotion to any mortal but her confessor, and that it was impossible they should know it without his discovering the secret; that, therefore it was time to give over going to confession, if priests made this use of it, to discover the most secret thoughts entrusted to them; and that, for the future, she would only make her confession to God. From this spirited speech, and the great noise made in consequence of the countess's situation, the inquisitors thought it most prudent to dismiss both her and her husband, lest the people might be incensed, and what she said might lessen the credit of confession. They were, therefore, both discharged, but bound to appear whenever they should be called upon.

Besides those already mentioned, such was the inveteracy of the Jesuits against the Quietists, that, within the space of a month, upwards of two hundred persons were put into the Inquisition; and that method of devotion which had passed in Italy as the most elevated to which mortals could aspire, was deemed heretical, and the chief promoters of it confined in a wretched dungeon. In order, if possible, to extirpate Quietism, the inquisitors sent a circular letter to Cardinal Cibo, as the chief minister, to disperse it through Italy. It was addressed to all prelates, informed them, that whereas many schools and fraternities were established in several parts of Italy, in which some persons, under the pretence of leading people into the ways of the Spirit, and to the prayer of quietness, instilled into them many abominable heresies, therefore a strict charge was given to dissolve all those societies, and to oblige the spiritual guide to tread in the known paths; and, in particular, to take care that none of that sort should be suffered to have the direction of the nunneries. Orders were likewise given to proceed, in the way of justice, against those who should be found guilty of these abominable errors.

After this a strict inquiry was made into all the nunneries of Rome, when most of their directors and confessors were discovered to be engaged in this new method. It was found that the Carmelites, the nuns of the Conception, and those of several other convents, were wholly given up to prayer and contemplation, and that, instead of their beads, and the other devotions to saints, or images, they were much alone, and often in the exercise of mental prayer; that when they were asked why they had laid aside the use of their beads and their ancient forms, their answer was that their directors had advised them so to do. Information of this being given to the Inquisition, they sent orders that all books written in the same strain with those of Molinos and Petrucci should be taken from them, and that they should be compelled to return to their original form of devotion. The circular letter sent to Cardinal Cibo, produced but little effect, for most of the Italian bishops were inclined to Molinos' method. It was intended that this, as well as all other orders from the inquisitors, should be kept secret; but notwithstanding all their care, copies of it were printed, and dispersed in most of the principal towns in Italy. This gave great uneasiness to the inquisitors, who used every method they could to conceal their proceedings from the knowledge of the world. They blamed the cardinal, and accused him of being the cause of it; but he retorted on them, and his secretary laid the fault on both.

During these transactions, Molinos suffered great indignities from the officers of the Inquisition; and the only comfort he received was from being sometimes visited by Father Petrucci. Though he had lived in the highest reputation in Rome for some years, he was now as much despised as he had been admired, being generally considered as one of the worst of heretics. The greater part of Molinos' followers, who had been placed in the Inquisition, having abjured his mode, were dismissed; but a harder fate awaited Molinos, their leader. After lying a considerable time in prison, he was at length brought again before the inquisitors to answer to a number of articles exhibited against him from his writings. As soon as he appeared in court, a chain was put round his body, and a wax light in his hand, when two friars read aloud the articles of accusation. Molinos answered each with great steadiness and resolution; and notwithstanding his arguments totally defeated the force of all, yet he was found guilty of heresy, and condemned to imprisonment for life. When he left the court he was attended by a priest, who had borne him the greatest respect. On his arrival at the prison he entered the cell allotted for his confinement with great tranquility; and on taking leave of the priest, thus addressed him: "Adieu, father, we shall meet again at the Day of Judgment, and then it will appear on which side the truth is, whether on my side, or on yours." During his confinement, he was several times tortured in the most cruel manner, until, at length, the severity of the punishments overpowered his strength, and finished his existence. The death of Molinos struck such an impression on his followers that the greater part of them soon abjured his mode; and by the assiduity of the Jesuits, Quietism was totally extirpated throughout the country.

About Francois Fenelon

The French archbishop, theologian, and man of letters François de Salignac de la Mothe Fénelon held liberal views on politics and education that put him at odds with church and state. Nevertheless, his pedagogical concepts and literary works exerted a lasting influence on French culture.

Descended from a long line of nobility, Fénelon was born on Aug. 6, 1651, at his family's château in Périgord, France. He began his higher studies in Paris in about 1672 at Saint-Sulpice seminary. Ordained a priest in 1676, he was appointed director of Nouvelles Catholiques (New Catholics), a college for women who instructed converts from French Protestantism. From his experiences there he wrote his first important work, Traité de l'éducation des filles (1687; Treatise on the Education of Girls). Although conservative, the treatise submitted innovative concepts on the education of females and criticized the coercive methods of his day.

In 1689, with the support of the renowned bishop Jacques-Bénigne Bossuet, Fénelon was named tutor to Louis, duke of Bourgogne, grandson and heir to Louis XIV. For the prince's education, Fénelon composed his best-known work, Les Aventures de Télémaque (1699), in which Telemachus' search for his father, Odysseus, symbolically expresses Fénelon's fundamental political ideas. He was elected to the French Academy in 1693.

Fénelon lost favor at court when he turned to Madame Guyon, the leading exponent of the Quietist school of prayer, for guidance in his spiritual life. Quietism is a doctrine of Christian spirituality that holds that perfection consists in passivity (quiet) of the soul and suppression of human effort so that divine action may have full play.

When Madame Guyon's teaching and personal life were attacked by Bossuet and other influential people at court, Fénelon responded with Explication des maximes des saints sur la vie intérieure (1697; Explanation of the Sayings of the Saints on the Interior Life). Fénelon not only lost Bossuet's friendship but also exposed himself to Bossuet's public denunciation. As a result, Fénelon's Maximes des saints was condemned by the pope, and he was exiled to his diocese. He died on Jan. 7, 1715, in Cambrai, France.

MICHAEL MOLINOS

THE SPIRITUAL GUIDE

An account of the following book

There is nothing more difficult, than to please all People, not more easy and common than to censure Books that come abroad in the World. All Books, without exception, that see the light, run the common Risk of both these inconveniences, though they may be sheltered under the most sublime Protection, what will become of this little Book then, which has no Patronage? The Subject whereof being mystical, and not well-seasoned; carries along with it the common censure, and will seem insipid? Kind Reader, if you understand it not, be not therefore apt to censure the same. The Natural Man may hear and read these Spiritual Matters, but he can never comprehend them, as Saint Paul said; The Natural Man receives not the things of the Spirit of God. If you condemn it, you condemn your self to the number of the wise men of this World, of who St. Denis says, that God imparts not this Wisdom to them, as he does to the simple and humble, though in the opinion of Men they be ignorant. Mystical knowledge proceeds not from Wit, but from Experience; it is not invented, but proved; not read, but received; and is therefore most secure and efficacious, of great help and plentiful in fruit; it enters not into the Soul by Ears, nor by the continual Reading of Books, but by the free Infusion of the Holy Ghost, whose Grace with most delightful intimacy, is communicated to the simple and lowly. There are some Learned Men, who have never read these Matters, and some Spiritual Men that hitherto have hardly relished them and therefore both condemn them, the one out of Ignorance, and the other for want of Experience. Besides, it is certain, that he who has not the experience of this sweetness, cannot pass a Judgment upon these Mysterious Secrets; nay, rather he'll be Scandalized (as many are) when he hears of the Wonders which the Divine Love is wont to work in Souls, because he finds no such Rarities in his own. Who shall limit the goodness of God, whose Arm is not shortened, but that he can do now what he has wrought at other times? God calls neither the strongest nor the richest for their Merit; but calls rather the weakest and most wretched, that his infinite mercy may shine forth the more. This Science is not Theoretical, but Practical, wherein Experience surpasses the most refined and ingenious Speculation. Hence it was that Saint Teresa admonished her Ghostly Father, that he should not confer about Spiritual Matters, but with Spiritual Men; Because, said she, if they know but one way, or if they have stopped mid-way, there is no success to be expected. It will soon appear that he has no experience of this practical and mystical Science, who shall condemn the Doctrine of this Book, and who has not read Saint Dennis, Saint Austin, Saint Gregory, Saint Bernard, Saint Thomas, Saint Bonaventure, and many other Saints and Doctors approved by the Church, who like expert men, approve, commend, and teach the Practice of this Doctrine. It is to be taken notice of, that the Doctrine of this Book instructs not all sorts of Persons, but those only who have the Senses and Passions well mortified, who have already advanced and made progress in Prayer, and are called by God to the inward way, who encourages and guides them, freeing them from the obstacles which hinder the course to perfect Contemplation. I have taken care to have the Style of this Book devote, chaste, and useful, without the ornament of polite Sentences, ostentation of Eloquence, or Theological Niceties, my only scope was to teach the Naked Truth, with humility, sincerity and perspicuity. It is not to be wondered at that new Spiritual Books are every day published in the World, because God has always new Light to communicate, and Souls stand always in need of these Instructions. All things have not been said, nor every thing written, hence it is that there will be Writing to the end of the World. Wonderful were the Lights that God Almighty communicated to his Church by means of the Angelical Doctor St. Thomas, and at the hour of his Death, he himself said that the Divine Majesty had at that instant communicated to him so much light, that all he had before written came short of it. God has, then, and always will have new Lights to communicate, without any diminution to his own Infinite Wisdom. The many and grievous pains and difficulties of the inward way ought not to make a Soul despond, because it is but reasonable that a thing of great value should cost dear. Be of good comfort, and believe, that not only those which are here represented, but many others also will be overcome with the Grace of God and internal Fortitude. It was never my design to treat of Contemplation, nor in defense of it, as many have done who have learnedly and speculatively published whole Books, full of efficacious Reasons, Doctrines and Authorities of Saints and of the Holy Scripture, for confuting the Opinion of those who without any ground have condemned, and do condemn it. The Experience of many Years (by reason of the many Souls who have trusted to my insufficiency, for their conduct in the inward way, to which they have been called) hath convinced me of the great necessity they are in of having the obstacles taken out of their way, the inclinations, affections and allurements removed, which wholly hinder the course and obstruct the way to perfect Contemplation. This whole Practical Book tends chiefly to this end, because it is not enough to ascertain the inward way of Contemplation, if the obstacles be not taken out of the way of those Souls that are called and assured, which hinder their progress and spiritual flight; For which end I have made use rather of what God out of his infinite mercy has inspired into me, and taught me, than of any thing that the speculative reading of Books has suggested unto me, or furnished me with. Sometimes (though very seldom) I quote the Authority of some practical and experienced Author, to show that the Doctrine which is here taught is not singular and rare. It has been my first scope then, not to ascertain the inward way but to disentangle and unpester it; My next has been to instruct the Spiritual Diverters, that they may not stop those Souls in their course which are called by these secret Paths to internal Peace and Supreme Felicity. God of his infinite Mercy grant, that an end so much desired may be obtained. I hope in God, that some of those Souls, whom his Divine Majesty calls to this knowledge, will find profit from what I have written; for whose sake I shall reckon my pains very well employed. This has been the only But of my desire, and if God (as certainly he will) accept and approve those pure desires, I shall be content and have my reward.

Two Ways to God

By two ways one may go to God, the first by Meditation and Discourse or Reasoning; the second by pure Faith and Contemplation.

There are two ways of going to God, the one by Consideration and Mental Discourse, and the other by the Purity of Faith, an indistinct, general and confused knowledge. The first is called Meditation, the second Internal Recollection, or acquired Contemplation. The first is of Beginners, the second of those whom are proficient. The first is sensible and material, the second more naked, pure and internal.

When the Soul is already accustomed to discourse of Mysteries, by the help of imagination, and the use of corporal Images; being carried from Creature to Creature, and from Knowledge to Knowledge (though with very little of that which it wants) and from these to the Creator; Then God is wont to take that Soul by the hand (if rather he calls it not in the very beginning, and leads it without ratiocination by the way of pure Faith) making the Intellect pass by all considerations and reasoning, draws it forward, and raises it out of this material and sensible state, making it under a simple and obscure knowledge of Faith, wholly aspire to its Bridegroom upon the wings of Love, without any farther necessity of the persuasions and information of the Intellect, to make it love him, because in that manner the Soul's love would be very scanty, much dependent on Creature, stinted to drops, and these too but falling with pauses and intervals.

By how much less it depends on Creatures, and the more it relies on God alone, and his secret documents, by the mediation of pure Faith, the more durable, firm, and strong will that Love be. After the Soul has already acquired the knowledge which all the meditations and corporal Images of Creatures can give her; it, now, the Lord raise her out of that state, by stripping her of ratiocination, and leaving her in divine darkness, to the end she may march in the straight Way, and by pure Faith, let her be guided, and not love with the scantiness and tenacity that these direct; but let her suppose that the whole World, and all that the most refined conceptions of the wisest understandings can tell her, are nothing, and that the goodness and beauty of her beloved, infinitely surpasses all their knowledge, being persuaded that all Creatures are too rude to inform her, and to conduct her to the true knowledge of God.

She ought then to advance forward with her love, leaving all her understanding behind. Let her love God as he is in himself, and not as her imagination says he is, and frames him to her; And if she cannot know him as he is in himself, let her love him without knowing him under the obscure veils of Faith; in the same manner as a Son who has never seen his Father, but fully believing those who have given him information of him, loves him, as if he had already seen him.

The Soul, from which Mental Discourse is taken, ought not to strain her self, nor solicitously seek for more clear and particular knowledge, but even without the supports of sensible consolations or notices, with poverty of spirit, and deprived of all that the natural appetite requires; continue quiet, firm and constant, letting the Lord work his work, though she may seem to be alone, exhausted and full of darkness: and though this appear to her to be idleness, it is only of her own sensible and material activity, not of God's, who is working true knowledge in her.

Finally, the more the Spirit ascends, the more it is taken off of sensible Objects. Many are the Souls who have arrived and do arrive at this gate, but few have passed or do pass it, for want of the experimental guide, and those who have had, and actually have it, for want of a true subjection and entire submission.

They'll say that the Will, will not love; but be inactive, if the Intellect understand not clearly and distinctly, it being a received Maxim, that that which is not known, cannot be loved. To this it is answered, that although the Intellect understand not distinctly by ratiocination, Images and Considerations, yet it understands and knows by an obscure, general and confused Faith; which knowledge, although so obscure, indistinct, and general, and being supernatural, has nevertheless a more clear and perfect cognition of God, than any sensible and particular notice, that can be formed in this life, because all corporal and sensible representation is infinitely distant from God.

We know God more perfectly (says St. Denis - Mystic) by Negatives, than by Affirmatives. We think more highly of God, by knowing that he is incomprehensible, and above all our capacity, than by conceiving him under any image or created beauty, according to our rude understanding. A greater esteem and love then will flow from this confused, obscure and negative, than from any other sensible and distinct way; because that is more proper to God, and abstracted from creatures; and this, on the contrary, the more it depends on creatures, the less it has of God.

Defining Meditation and Contemplation

Declaring what Meditation and Contemplation are, and the difference that is betwixt them.

St. John Damascene and other Saints say, that Prayer is a sallying out or elevation of the Mind to God. God is above all creatures, and the Soul cannot see him, nor converse with him, if it raise not it self above them all. This friendly conversation, which the Soul has with God, that's to say, in Prayer, is divided into Meditation and Contemplation.

When the Mind considers the Mysteries of our holy Faith with attention, to know the truth of them, reasoning upon the particulars, and weighing the circumstances of the same, for the exciting of affections in the Will; this mental discourse and pious Act is properly called Meditation.

When the Soul already knows the truth (either by a habit acquired through reasoning, or because the Lord has given it particular light) and fixes the eyes of the Mind on the demonstrated truth, beholding it sincerely with quietness and silence, without any necessity of considerations, ratiocinations, or other proofs of conviction, and the will loves it, admiring and delighting it self therein; This properly is called the Prayer of Faith, the Prayer of Rest, Internal Recognition or Contemplation. Which St. Thomas with all the mystical Masters says, is a sincere, sweet, and still view of the eternal truth without ratiocination, or reflexion. But if the Soul rejoices in, or eyes the effects of God in the creatures, and amongst them, in the humanity of our Lord Christ, as the most perfect of all, this is not perfect Contemplation, as St. Thomas affirms, since all these are means for knowing of God as he is in himself: And although the humanity of Christ be the most holy and perfect means for going to God, the chief instrument of our salvation, and the channel through which we receive all the good we hope for, nevertheless the humanity is not the chief good, which consists in seeing God; but as Jesus Christ is more by his divinity than his humanity, so he that thinks and fixes his contemplation always on God (because the divinity is united to the humanity) always thinks on, and beholds Jesus Christ, especially, the contemplative man, in whom Faith is more sincere, pure and exercised.

As often as the end is obtained, the means cease, and when the Ship arrives in the Harbor the voyage is over. So if the Soul after it has been toiled and carried by means of meditation, arrives at the stillness, tranquility, and rest of Contemplation, it ought then to cut off all reasoning, and rest quiet with an amorous attention, and simple Vision of God; seeing and loving him, sweetly rejecting all the imaginations that present themselves, calming the Mind in that Divine Presence, recollecting the Memory, and fixing it wholly on God, being contented with a general and confused knowledge, which is had by the Mediation of Faith, applying the whole Will to love him, wherein consists all their fruit of enjoyment.

St. Denis says, As for you, most dear Timothy, in applying your self to Mystical Speculations, abstract from the Senses and Operations of the Intellect; from all sensible and intelligible Objects, and Universally from all things that are, and are not; and in an unknown and inexpressible Way, as much as lies in the power of Man, raise your self to the Union of him, who is above all Nature and Knowledge.

It concerns us then, to forsake all created, sensible, intelligible and affected Beings; and in short, every thing that is, and is not, that we may cast our selves into the loving Bosom of God, who will restore to us as much as we have left, increasing in us strength and power to love him more ardently, whose love will maintain it self within this Holy and Blessed Silence, which is of more worth than all Acts joined together.

St. Thomas says, It is the least thing, that the Understanding can know of God in this Life, but much what the Will can have of Love.

When the Soul attains to this state, it ought wholly to retreat within it self, in its own pure and profound Center; where the Image of God is, there is amorous attention, silence, the forgetfulness of all things, the application of the Will, with perfect resignation, hearing and talking with God hand to hand, and in such manner, as if there was no other but them two in the World.

Good reason have the Saints to say, that Meditation operates with toil, and with fruit; Contemplation without toil, with quiet, rest, peace, delight, and far greater fruit. Meditation sows, and Contemplation reaps; Meditation seeks, and Contemplation finds; Meditation chews the Food, Contemplation tastes and feeds on it.

Two Kinds of Contemplation

What is the Difference betwixt the Acquired and Active Contemplation, and the Infused and Passive. With the Signs whereby it is known, when God will have the Soul to pass from Meditation, to Contemplation.

There are moreover two ways of Contemplation: The one is Imperfect, Active and Acquired; The other Infused and Passive. The Active (whereof we have treated hitherto) is that which may be attained to by our Diligence, assisted with Divine Grace; we gathering together the Faculties and Senses, and preparing our selves by every way that God would have. So says Boias and Arnaia. St. Bernard recommends this Active

Contemplation. In like manner St. Thomas inculcates this acquired contemplation. Very clear Words to stop the Mouth of those who condemn acquired contemplation.

How much the nearer a man approaches his own Soul, or the Soul of another to God, so much the more acceptable is the Sacrifice to God; from whence it is inferred (concludes the same Saint) that the application of a man's own Soul, or the procuring that of another's to Contemplation, is more acceptable to God, than the applying of the same to Action. It cannot be said, that the Saint speaks here of infused Contemplation, because it is not in the power of man, to apply himself to the infused, but to the acquired.

Though it be said, that we may with the Lord's help, set our selves to acquired contemplation; nevertheless, no man ought of his own Head to be so bold, as to pass from the state of Meditation to this, without the counsel of an expert Director, who shall clearly know whether his Soul be called by God to this inward way; or for want of a Director, the Soul it self is to know it by some Book, that treats of these Matters, sent to him by Divine Providence, for discovering that, which without knowing what it was, he experimentally felt within his own Heart. But though by means of the light which that Book gives him he may obtain assurance enough, to leave Meditation for the quiet of contemplation, yet his Soul will still retain an ardent desire of being more perfectly instructed.

And to the end it may receive good Instruction in order to that point, I'll here give it the Signs whereby it shall know that call to contemplation. The first and chief is, an inability to meditate, and if the Soul meditate, it will perform it with much disquiet and irksomeness, provided that proceed not from the indisposition of Nature, or a melancholy Humor, or a Dryness, springing from the want of Preparation.

It will be known not to be any of these defects, but rather a true call, when that Soul passes a Day, a Month; nay, and many Months, without being able to discourse in Prayer. The Lord guides the Soul by Contemplation (says the holy Mother Teresa) and the Mind finds it self much disabled from meditating the

Passion of Christ, since Meditation is nothing else but a seeking of God; the Soul once finding him, and retaining the Custom of seeking him of new, by the operation of the Will, it will not be baffled with the Intellect.

The second Sign is, that though it is wanting in sensible Devotion, yet it covets Solitude, and avoids conversation. The third, that the reading of godly Books is usually tedious to it, because they speak not of the Internal Sweetness that is in its Heart, though it know it not. The fourth, that though it find it self destitute of ratiocination, yet it has a firm purpose of persevering in Prayer. The fifth is, that it will experience a sense (with great confusion) of it self, abhorring guilt, and entertaining a higher esteem of God.

The other Contemplation is perfect and infused. Wherein (as Saint Teresa says) God speaks to a man, sequestrating his intellect, questioning his thought, and seizing (as they say) the word in his mouth; so that if he would, he cannot speak, but with great pain. He understands, that without the noise of words, the Divine Master is instructing him, suspending all his powers and faculties, because if at that time they should operate, they would do more hurt than good. These rejoice, but know not how they rejoice; the Soul is inflamed with love, and conceives not how it loves; it knows that it enjoys what it desires, and knows not the manner of that enjoyment; well it knows, that that is not enjoyment which the intellect longs for. The Will embraces it, without understanding how; but being unable to understand any thing, perceives it is not that good, which can be merited by all the labors put together which are suffered upon earth for gaining it. It is a gift of the Lord of the Soul, and of Heaven, who in the end gives as he is, and to whom he pleases as he pleases: Such is his Majesty in this, that it does every thing, and his operation is above our nature. All this we have from holy Mother, in her Way to Perfection. From whence it follows, that this Contemplation is infused, and freely given by the Lord to whom he pleases.

The Way to Inward Peace

The Burden of this Book consisting in rooting out the Rebellion of our own Will, that we may attain to internal Peace.

The way of inward Peace, is in all things to be conformed to the pleasure and disposition of the Divine Will. Such as would have all things succeed and come to pass according to their own fancy, are not come to know this way, and therefore lead a harsh and bitter life, always restless and out of humor without treading the way of Peace, which consists in a total conformity to the will of God.

This conformity is the sweet yoke that introduces us into the regions of internal Peace and serenity. Hence we may know, that the rebellion of our Will is the chief occasion of our disquiet; and that because we will not submit to the sweet yoke of the Divine Will, we suffer so many streights and perturbations. O Soul! if we submitted our own to the Divine Will, and to all his Disposition, what tranquility should we feel! what sweet peace! what inward serenity! what supreme felicity and earnest of bliss!. This then is to be the burden of this Book: May it please God to give me his Divine Light, for discovering the secret Paths of this Inward Way, and chief Felicity of perfect Peace.

The First Book

Chapter One

To the end God may rest in the Soul, the Heart is always to be kept peaceable in whatsoever Disquiet, Temptation and Tribulation.

You should know, that your Soul is the Center, Habitation, and the Kingdom of God. That therefore, to the end the Sovereign King may rest on that Throne of your Soul, you ought to take pains to keep it clean, quiet, void and peaceable; clean from guilt and defects; quiet from fears; void of affections, desires, and thoughts; and peaceable in temptations and tribulations.

You ought always then to keep your Heart in peace; that you may keep pure that Temple of God, and with a right and pure intention, you are to work, pray, obey and suffer, without being in the least moved, whatever it pleases the Lord to send unto you. Because it is certain, that for the good of your Soul, and for thy spiritual profit, he will suffer the envious enemy to trouble that City of Rest, and Throne of Peace, with temptations, suggestions and tribulations, and by the means of creature, with painful troubles and grievous persecutions.

Be constant, and cheer up your heart in whatsoever disquiet these tribulations may cause to you. Enter within it, that you may overcome it; for therein is the Divine Fortress, which defends, protects, and fights for you. If a man has a safe Fortress, he is not disquieted, though his enemies pursue him; because, by retreating within it, these are disappointed and overcome. The strong Castle, that will make thee triumph over all your enemies, visible and invisible, and over all their snares and tribulations, is within your own Soul, because in it resides the Divine Aid and

Sovereign Succor. Retreat within it and all will be quiet, secure, peaceable and calm.

It ought to be your chief and continual exercise, to pacify that Throne of your Heart that the Supreme King may rest therein. The way to pacify it, will be, to enter into your self by means of internal recollection; all your protection is to be Prayer and a loving recollection in the Divine Presence. When you see yourself more sharply assaulted, retreat into that region of Peace, where you will find the Fortress. When you are more faint-hearted, go to this refuge of Prayer, the only Armor for overcoming the enemy, and mitigating tribulation: you should not be at a distance from it in a Storm, to the end you may, as another Noah, experience tranquility, security and serenity, and to the end you will may be resigned, devote, peaceful and courageous.

Finally, be not afflicted nor discouraged to see your self faint-hearted, he returns to quiet you, that still he may stir you, because this Divine Lord will be alone with you, to rest in your Soul, and form therein a rich Throne of Peace; that within your own heart, by means of internal recollection, and with his heavenly Grace, you may look for silence in tumult, solitude in company, light in darkness, forgetfulness in pressures, vigor in despondency, courage in fear, resistance in temptation, peace in war, and quiet in tribulation.

Chapter Two

Though the Soul perceive it self deprived of Discourse, or Ratiocination, yet it ought to persevere in Prayer, and not be afflicted, because that is its greater Felicity.

You find yourself, as all other Souls that are called by the Lord to the inward way, full of confusion and doubts, because in Prayer you have failed in Discourse: It will seem to you that God does no more assist you as formerly, that the exercise of Prayer is not in your power; that you lose time, while hardly and with great trouble you cannot make one single Ejaculation as you desire to do.

How much confusion, and what perplexities, will that want of enlarging yourself in mental Discourse raise in you? And if in such a juncture you have not a ghostly Father, expert in the Mystical Way, you will certainly conclude that your Soul is out of order, and that for the security of your Conscience, you stand in need of a general confession; and all that will be got by that care, will be the shame and confusion of both. O how many Souls are called to the inward way, and the spiritual Fathers for want of Understanding their case, instead of guiding and helping them forwards, stop them in their Course, and ruin them.

You should be persuaded, that you may not draw back, when you want expansion and discourse in Prayer; that it is your greatest happiness, because it is a clear sign, that the Lord will have you to walk by Faith and Silence in his Divine Presence, which is the most profitable and easiest Path; in respect, that with a simple view, or amorous attention to God, the Soul appears like a humble Supplicant before its Lord, or as an innocent Child, that casts it self into the sweet and safe Bosom of its dear Mother. Thus did Gerson express it, Though I have spent Forty Years in Reading and Prayer, yet I could never find any thing more efficacious, nor compendious, for attaining to Mystical Theology, than that our Spirit should become like a young Child and Beggar in the presence of God.

That kind of Prayer is not only the easiest, but the most secure; because it is abstracted from the operations of the Imagination, that is always exposed to the Tricks of the Devil, and the extravagancies of Melancholy, and Ratiocination, wherein the Soul is easily Distracted, and being wrapped up in speculation, reflects on it self.

When God had a mind to instruct his own Captain Moses, and give him the two Tablets of the Law, written in Stone, he called him up to the Mountain, at what time God being there with him, the Mount was Darkened and environed with thick Clouds, Moses standing idle, not knowing what to think or say. Seven days after God commanded Moses, to come up to the top of the Mountain, where he showed him his Glory, and filled him with great Consolation.

So in the Beginning, when God intends after an extraordinary manner, to guide the Soul into the School of the divine and loving Notices of the internal Law, he makes it go with Darkness, and Dryness, that he may bring it near to himself, because the Divine Majesty knows very well, that it is not by the means of ones one Ratiocination, or Industry, that a Soul draws near to him, and understands the Divine Documents; but rather by silent and humble Resignation.

The Patriarch Noah gave a great instance of this; who after he had been by all men reckoned a Fool, floating in the middle of a raging Sea, wherewith the whole World was overflowed, without Sails and Oars; and environed with wild Beasts, that were shut up in the Ark, walked by Faith alone, not knowing nor understanding what God had a mind to do with him.

What most concerns you, O redeemed Soul, is Patience, not to desist from the Prayer you are about, though you can not enlarge in Discourse. Walk with firm Faith, and a holy Silence, dying in yourself, with all your natural Industry, trusting that God who is he who is, and changes not; neither can err, intends nothing by your good. It is clear that he who is at dying, must needs feel it, but how well is time employed, when the Soul is dead, dumb, and resigned in the presence of God, there without any clutter or distraction, to receive the Divine Influences.

The Senses are not capable of divine Blessings; hence if you would be Happy and Wise; be Silent and Believe; Suffer and have Patience; be Confident and Walk on; it concerns you far more to hold your Peace, and to let yourself be guided by the hand of God, than to enjoy all the Goods of this World. And though it seem to you, that you do nothing at all, and are idle being so Dumb and Resigned; yet it is of infinite fruit.

Consider the blinded Beast that turns the Wheel of the Mill, which though it see not, neither know what it does, yet does a great Work in grinding the Corn, and although it taste not of it; yet its Master receives the fruit, and tastes of the same. Who would not think, during so long a time that the Seed lies in the Earth, but that it were lost? Yet afterwards it is seen to spring up, grow and multiply. God does the same with the Soul, when he deprives it of Consideration and Ratiocination: While it thinks it does nothing, and is, in a manner undone, in time it comes to is self again, improved, disengaged, and perfect, having never hoped for so much favor.

Take care then that you afflict not yourself, nor draw back, though you can not enlarge yourself, and discourse in Prayer; suffer, hold your peace, and appear in the presence of God; persevere constantly, and trust to his infinite Bounty, who can give unto you constant Faith, true light, and divine Grace. Walk as if you were blindfolded, without thinking or reasoning; put yourself into his kind and paternal hands, resolving to do nothing but what his divine Will and Pleasure is.

It is the common opinion of all the holy Men who have treated of the Spirit, and of all the Mystical Matters: That the Soul cannot attain to perfection and an union with God, by means of Meditation, and Ratiocination: Because that is only good for beginning the spiritual Way, to the end one may acquire a habit of Knowledge, of the beauty of Virtue, and ugliness of Vice: which habit in the opinion of Saint Teresa, may be attained to in Six Months time and according to Saint Bonaventure.

O how are, in a manner infinite numbers of Souls to be pitied, who from the beginning of their Life to the end, employ themselves in mere Meditation, constraining themselves to Reason, although God Almighty deprive them of Ratiocination, that he may promote them to another State, and carry them on a more perfect kind of Prayer, and so for many years they continue imperfect, and in the beginning, without any progress or having as yet made one step in the way of the Spirit; beating their Brains about the frame of the Place, the choice of the Minutes, Imaginations, and strained Reasoning, seeking God without, when in the mean time, they have him within themselves.

Saint Austin complained of that, in the time when God led him to the Mystical Way, saying to his Divine Majesty, I, Lord, went wandering like a strayed Sheep, seeking you with anxious Reasoning without, while you were within me, I wearied myself much in looking for you without while you have your habitation within me; If I long and breathe after you, I went round the Streets and Places of the City of this World, seeking you and found you not; because, in vain I sought without for him, what was within my self.

The Angelical Doctor Saint Thomas, for all he was so circumspect in his Writings, may seem yet to jeer those, who go always in search of God, without by means of Ratiocination, when they have him present within themselves. There is great Blindness, and excessive Folly in some, says Saint Ocuse, who always seek God, continually sigh after God, often long for God, invocate and call upon God daily in Prayer; they themselves (according to the Apostle) being the living Temple of God, and his true Habitation, since their Soul is the Seat and Throne of God, where he continually rests. Who then, but a Fool, will look for an Instrument abroad, when he knows he has it fast shut up within Doors? Or who can refresh himself with the Food he desires, and yet not taste it? Such exactly is the Live of some just men, always seeking, and never enjoying, and therefore all their Works are imperfect.

It is certain, that Our Lord Christ taught Perfection to all, and ever will have all to be Perfect, particularly the Ignorant and Simple. He clearly manifested this Truth, when for his Apostles, he chose the Smallest and most Ignorant, saying to his Eternal Father, I thank you, O Father, Lord of Heaven and Earth, because you have hid these things from the Wise and Prudent, and have revealed them unto Babes. And it is certain, that these cannot acquire Perfection, by acute Meditations, and subtle Reasoning, though they be as capable as the most Learned, to attain to Perfection, by the affections of the Will, wherein principally it consists.

Saint Bonaventure, teaches us not to form Conceptions of any thing, no not of God, because it is Imperfection to make Representations, Images, and Ideas, how subtle or ingenious so ever, either of the Will, or of the Goodness, Trinity, and Unity; nay, of the Divine Presence it self: In respect that, though all these Representations appear Deiform, yet are they not God, who admits of no Image, nor Form. We must not here think any thing of Creature, of Angles, nor of God himself, because that

Wisdom and Perfection, is not acquired by nice and quaint Meditation, but by the desire and affection of the Will.

The holy man cannot speak more clearly; and you would disquiet yourself, and leave off Prayer, because you do not know, or can not tell how to enlarge therein, though you may have a good Will, good Desire, and pure Intention? If the young Ravens forsaken of the old, because seeing them without Black Feathers, they think them Spurious, are by the Dew of Heaven fed that they may not perish; what will he do to redeem Souls, though they cannot speak nor reason, if they believe, trust, and open their Mouths to Heaven, declaring their wants: It is not more certain that the Divine Bounty will provide for them, and give them their necessary Food?

Manifest it is, that it is a great Martyrdom, and no small Gift of God, for the Soul, finding it self deprived of the sensible Pleasures it had, to walk by holy Faith only, through the dark, and desert Paths of Perfection, to which, notwithstanding, it can never attain but by this painful, though secure means. Wherefore endeavor to be constant, and not draw back, though Discourse be wanting to you in Prayer, believe at that time firmly, be quietly silent, and patiently persevere if you would be happy, and attain to the Divine Union, eminent rest, and to the Supreme Internal Peace.

Chapter Three

The Soul is not to afflict itself, nor intermit Prayer, because it sees itself encompassed with dryness.

You should know that there are two sorts of Prayer, the one tender, delightful, amicable, and full of sentiments; the other obscure, dry, desolate, tempted, and darksome. The first is of Beginners, the second of Proficients, who are in the progress to Perfection. God gives the first to gain Souls, the second to purify them. With the first he uses them like Children; with the second he begins to deal with them as with strong men.

This first Way may be called the Animal Life, and belongs to them who go in the tract of the sensible Devotion, which God uses to give to Beginners, to the end that being endowed with that small relish, as the natural man is with the sensible Object, they may addict themselves to the spiritual Life. The second is called the Life of men, and belongs to those, who not minding sensible Pleasures, fight and war against their own Passions, that they may conquer and obtain Perfection, the proper employment of men.

Assure yourself, that dryness or aridity is the Instrument of your Good, because it is nothing else but a want of sensibility, that Remora, which puts a stop to the flight of almost all Spiritual Men, and makes them even draw back, and leave off Prayer: as may be seen in many Souls, which only persevere while they taste sensible Consolation.

Know that the Lord makes use of the Veil of Dryness, to the end we may not know what he is working in us, and so be humble; because if we felt and knew what he is working in our Souls, satisfaction and presumption would get in, imagining that we were doing some good thing, and reckoning our selves very near to God; which would be our undoing.

Lay this down as a firm ground in your Heart, that for walking in the inward Way, all sensibility should first be removed; and that the means God uses for that is dryness. By that also he takes away reflection, or that view, whereby the Soul Eyes what it is doing, the only impediment that obstructs the advancing forward, and God communicating himself, and operating in it.

You should not afflict yourself, nor think that you reap no fruit, because in coming from a Communion or Prayer, you do not have the experience of many sentiments, since that is a manifest Cheat. The Husbandman Sows in one time and Reaps in another: So God, upon occasions, and in his own due time, will help them to resist Temptations, and when least you expect it, will give you holy purposes, and more effectual desires of serving him. And to the end , you may not suffer yourself to be transported, by the violent suggestion of the Enemy, who will enviously persuade you, that you do nothing, and that you lose time, that so you may neglect Prayer: I'll declare to you some of the infinite fruits, that your Soul reaps from that great dryness.

The first is to persevere in Prayer, from which fruit springs many other advantages.

A. You will find a loathing of the things of the World, which by little and little tends to the stifling of the bad desires of your past Life, and the production of other new ones of serving God.

B. You will reflect upon many failings on which formerly you did not reflect.

C. You will find, when you are about to commit any evil, an advertency in your Heart, which restrains you from the execution of it, and at other times from Speaking. Lamenting, or Revenging yourself; that'll take you off from some little earthy Pleasure, or from this or the other Occasion, or Conversation, into which formerly you were running in great Peace and Security, without the least Check or Remorse of Conscience.

D. After that through frailty, you have fallen in to some light fault, you will feel a Reproof for it in your Soul, which will exceedingly afflict you.

E. You will feel within yourself, desires of suffering, and of doing the will of God.

F. An inclination to Virtue, and greater ease in overcoming yourself, and conquering the difficulties of the Passions, and Enemies that hinder you in the way.

G. You will know yourself better, and be confounded also in yourself, feel in you a high esteem of God above all created Beings, a contempt of Creatures, and a firm Resolution not to abandon Prayer, though you know that it will prove to you a most cruel Martyrdom.

H. You will be sensible of greater Peace in your Soul, love to Humility, confidence in God, submission, and abstraction from all Creatures; and finally the Sins you have omitted since the time that you exercised yourself in Prayer, are so many signs, that the Lord is working in your Soul, (though you do not know it) by means of dry Prayer; and although you feel it not while you are in prayer, you will feel it in his due time, when he shall think it fit.

All these and many other fruits are like new Buds that spring from the Prayer, which you would give over, because it seems to you to be dry, that you see no Fruit of it, nor reap no advantage there from. Be constant and persevere with Patience, for though you do not know it, your Soul is profited thereby.

Chapter Four

Treating of the same thing, declaring how many ways of Devotion there are, and how the sensible Devotion is to be disposed; and that the Soul is not idle, though it reason not.

There are to be found two sorts of Devotion, the one essential and true; the other accidental and sensible. The essential, is a promptitude of mind to do well, fulfill the commands of God, and to perform all things belonging to his service, though, through humane frailty, all be not actually done as is desired. This is true Devotion, though it be not accompanied with pleasure, sweetness, delight, nor tears, but rather it is usually attended with temptation, dryness, and darkness.

Accidental and sensible Devotion is, when good desires are attended with a pleasant softness of heart, tenderness of tears, or other sensible affections. This is not to be sought after, nay, it is rather more secure to wean the will from it, and to set light by it; because besides that it is usually dangerous, it is a great obstacle to progress, and the advancement in the internal way. And therefore we ought only to embrace the true and essential Devotion, which is always in our power to come by, seeing every one doing his duty may with the assistance of the Divine Grace acquire it. And this may be had with God, with Christ, with the Mysteries, with the Virgin, and with the Saints.

Some think that when Devotion and sensible Pleasure are given them, they are Favors of God, that thence forward they have him, and that the whole life is to be spent in breathing after that delight; but it is a cheat, because it is no more, but a consolation of nature, and a pure reflexion, wherewith the Soul beholds what it does, and hinders the doing, or possibility of doing any thing, the acquisition of the true light, and the making of one step in the way of perfection. The Soul is a pure Spirit and is not felt; and so the internal acts, and of the will, as being the acts of the Soul and spiritual, are not sensible: Hence the Soul knows not if it lives, nor, for most part, is sensible if it acts.

From this you may infer, that that Devotion and sensible Pleasure, is not God, not Spirit, but the product of Nature; that therefore you should set light by, and despise it, but firmly to persevere in Prayer, leaving yourself to the conduct of God, who will be to you light in aridity and darkness.

Think not that when you are dry and darksome in the presence of God, with faith and silence, that you do nothing, that you lose time, and that you are idle, because not to wait on God, according to the saying of St. Bernard is the greatest idleness: And elsewhere he says, that idleness of the Soul is the business of the businesses of God.

It is not to be said, that the Soul is idle; because though it operate not Actively, yet the Holy Ghost operates in it. Besides, that it is not without all activity, because it operates, though spiritually, simply, and intimately. For to be attentive to God, draw near to him, to follow his internal inspirations, receive his divine influences, adore him in his own intimate center, reverence him with the pious affections of the will, to cast away so many and so fantastical imaginations, and with softness and contempt to overcome so many temptations: all these, I say, are true acts though simple, wholly spiritual, & in a manner imperceptible, through the great tranquility, wherewith the Soul exerts them.

Chapter Five

The Soul is not to be disquieted, that is sees it self encompassed with darkness, because that is an instrument of its greater felicity.

There are two sorts of darkness: some unhappy, and others happy: the first are such as arise from sin, and are unhappy, because they lead the Christian to an eternal precipice. The second are those which the Lord suffers to be in the Soul, to ground and settle it in virtue; and these are happy, because they enlighten it, fortify it, and cause greater light therein, so that you should not grieve and disturb yourself, nor be disconsolate in seeing yourself obscure and darksome, judging that God has failed you, and the light also that you formerly had the experience of; you should rather at that time persevere constantly in Prayer, it being a manifest sign, that God of his infinite mercy intends to bring you into the inward path, and happy way of Paradise. O how happy will you be, if you embrace it with peace and resignation, as the instrument of perfect quiet, true light, and of all your spiritual good.

Know then that the straightest, most perfect and secure way of proficients, is the way of darkness: because in them the Lord placed his own Throne; And He made darkness his secret place. By them the supernatural light which God infuses into the Soul, grow and increases. Amidst them wisdom and strong love are begotten, by darkness the soul is annihilated, and the species, which hinder the right view of the divine truth, are consumed. By this means God introduces the Soul by the inward way into the Prayer of Rest, and of perfect contemplation, which so few have the experience of. Finally; by darkness the Lord purges the senses and sensibility, which hinder the mystical progress.

See now if darkness be not to be esteemed and embraced. What you should do amidst them, is to believe, that you are before the Lord, and in his Presence; but you should do so, with a sweet and quiet attention; not desire to know any thing, nor search after delicacies, tenderness or sensible devotions, nor do any thing but what is the good will and pleasure of God; Because otherwise you will only make circles, all your life time, and not advance one step toward perfection.

Chapter Six

To the end the Soul may attain to the supreme internal peace, it is necessary, that God purge it after his way, because the exercises and mortifications that of it self it sets about, are not sufficient.

So soon as you shall firmly resolve to mortify your external senses, that you may advance towards the high mountain of perfection, and union with God; His divine Majesty will set his hand to the purging of your evil inclinations, inordinate desires, vain complacency, self-love and pride, and other hidden vices, which you do not know, and yet reign in the inner parts of your Soul, and hinder the divine union.

You will never attain to this happy state, though you tire yourself out with the external acts of mortifications and resignation, until this Lord purge you inwardly, and discipline you, after his own way, because he alone knows how secret faults are to be purged out. If you persevere constantly, he'll not only purge you from affections and engagements to natural and temporal goods, but in his own time also he will purify you with the supernatural and sublime, such as are internal communications; inward raptures and ecstasies, and other infused graces, on which the Soul rests and enjoys itself.

God will do all this in your Soul by means of the cross, and dryness, if you freely give your consent to it by resignation, and walking through those darksome and desert ways. All you have to do, is to do nothing by your own choice alone. The subjection of your liberty, is that which you should do, quietly resigning yourself up in every thing whereby the Lord shall think fit internally and externally to mortify you: because that is the only means, by which your Soul can become capable of the divine influences, while you suffer internal and external tribulation, with humility, patience, and quiet; not the penances, disciplines and mortifications, which you could impose upon yourself.

The husbandman sets a greater esteem upon the plants which he sows in the ground, than those that spring up of themselves, because these never come to seasonable maturity. In the same manner God esteems and is better pleased with the virtue, which he sows and infuses into the Soul (as being sunk into its own nothingness, calm and quiet, retreated within its own center, and without any election) than all the other virtues which the Soul pretends to acquire by its own election and endeavors.

It concerns you only then, to prepare your heart, like clean paper, wherein the divine wisdom may imprint characters to his own liking. O how great a work will it be for your Soul to be whole hours together in Prayer, dumb, resigned, and humble, without acting, knowing, or desiring to understand any thing.

With new efforts you will exercise yourself, but in another manner than hitherto, giving your consent to receive the secret and divine operations, and to be polished, and purified by this Lord, which is the only means whereby you will become clean & purged from your ignorance and dissolutions. Know, however, that you are to be plunged in a bitter sea of sorrows, and of internal and external pains, which torment will pierce into the most inward part of your Soul and Body.

You will experience, that the creatures will forsake you, nay, those too from which you hoped for most favor and compassion in your straights; the brooks of your faculties will be so dried up, that you will not be able to form any ratiocination, nay, nor so much as to conceive a good thought of God. Heaven will seem to you to be of brass, and you will receive no light from it. Nor will the thought comfort you, that in times past so much light and devote consolation have rained into your Soul.

The invisible enemies will pursue you with scruples, lascivious suggestions, and unclean thoughts, with incentives to impatience, pride, rage, cursing and blaspheming the Name of God, his Sacraments, and holy Mysteries. You will find a great luke-warmness, loathing, and weary for the things of God; and obscurity and darkness in your understanding; a faintness, Confusion and narrowness of heart; such a coldness and feebleness of the will to resist, that a straw will appear to you a beam. Your desertion will be so great, that you will think there is no more a God for you, and that you are rendered incapable of entertaining a good desire: so that you will continue shut up betwixt two walls, in constant streights and anguish, without any hopes of ever getting out of so dreadful an oppression.

But fear not: all this is necessary for purging your Soul, and making it know its own misery, and sensibly perceive the annihilation of all the passions, and disorientate appetites, wherewith it rejoiced itself. Finally, to the end the Lord may refine and purify you after his own manner with those inward torments, will you not cast the Jonas of sense into the sea, that thereby you may procure it? With all your outward disciplines and mortifications, you will never have true light, nor make one step towards perfection: so that you will stop in the beginning, and your Soul will not attain to the amiable rest, and supreme internal peace.

Chapter Seven

The Soul ought not to be disquieted, nor draw back in the spiritual way, because it finds it self assaulted by temptations.

Our own nature is so base, proud and ambitious, and so full of its own appetites, its own judgments and opinions, that if temptations restrained it not, it would be undone without remedy. The Lord then seeing our Misery and perverse inclination, and thereby moved to compassion, suffers us to be assaulted by divers thoughts against the Faith, horrible temptations, and by violent and painful suggestions of impatience, pride, gluttony, luxury, rage, blasphemy, cursing, despair, and an infinite number of others, to the end we may know our selves and be humble. With these horrible temptations, that infinite goodness humbles our pride, giving us in them the most wholesome medicine.

All our righteousness are as filthy rags, through the stains of vanity, conceitedness, and self-love. It is necessary they be purified with the fire of tribulation and temptation, that so they may be clean, pure, perfect and agreeable to the eyes of God.

Therefore the Lord purifies the Soul which he calls, and will have for himself, with the rough file of temptation, with which he polishes it from the rust of pride, avarice, vanity, ambition, presumption, and self-conceitedness. With the same, he humbles, pacifies and exercises it, making it to know its own misery. By means thereof he purifies and strips the heart to the end all its operations may be pure, and inestimable value.

Many Souls when they suffer these painful torments, are troubled, afflicted, and disquieted, it seeming to them, that they begin already in this life to suffer eternal punishments; and if by misfortune they go to an inexperienced Confessor, instead of comforting them, he leaves them in greater confusion and perplexities.

That you may not lose internal peace, it is necessary you believe, that it is the goodness of divine mercy, when thus it humbles, afflicts and tries you; since by that means your Soul comes to have a deep knowledge of itself, reckoning it self the worst, most impious and abominable of all Souls living, and hence with humility and lowliness it abhors it self. O how happy would Souls be, if they would be quiet and believe, that all these temptations are caused by the Devil, and received from the hand of God, for their gain and spiritual profit.

But you will say, that it is not the work of the Devil, when he molests you by means of creatures, but the effect of your neighbors fault and malice, in having wronged and injured you. Know that that is another cunning and hidden temptation, because though God wills not the sin of another, yet he wills his own effect in you, and the trouble which accrues to you from another's fault, that he may see you improved by the benefit of patience.

Do you receive an injury from any man? there are two things in it, the sin of him that does it, and the punishment that you suffer; the sin is against the will of God, and displeases him, though he permit it; the punishment is conform to his will, and he wills it for your good, wherefore you should receive it, as from his hand. The Passion and Death of our Lord Christ, were the effects of the wickedness and sins of Pilate, and yet it is certain, that God willed the death of his own Son for our redemption.

Consider how the Lord makes use of another's fault for the good of your Soul. O the greatness of the Divine Wisdom, who can pry into the depth of the secret and extraordinary means, and the hidden paths whereby he guides the Soul, which he would have purged, transformed and deified.

Chapter Eight

That the Soul may be the habitation of the celestial King, it is necessary, that it should be pure and without any blemish; wherefore the Lord purifies it as gold in the furnace of terrible and grievous temptations. Certain it is, that the Soul never loves, nor believes more, than when it is afflicted and baited with such temptations; because those doubts and fears that beset it, whether it believe or not; whether it consent or not, are nothing else but the quaintness of love.

The effects that remain in the Soul make this very clear; and commonly these are a loathing of it self with a most profound acknowledgment of the greatness and omnipotence of God, a great confidence in the Lord, that he will deliver it from all risk and danger; believing and confessing with far greater vigor of faith, that it is God who gives it strength to bear the torments of these temptations, because it would naturally be impossible, considering the force and violence wherewith sometimes they attack, to resist one quarter of an hour.

You should know then, that temptation is your great happiness, so that the more it besets you, the more you should rejoice in Peace, instead of being sad, and thank God for the favor he does you. In all these temptations, and odious thoughts, the remedy that is to work, is to despise them with a stayed neglect, because nothing more afflicts the proud Devil, than to see that he is slighted and despised, as are all things else that he suggests to us. And therefore you must tarry with him, as one that perceives him not, and to possess yourself in your peace without repining, and without multiplying Reasons and Answers; seeing nothing is more dangerous, than to vie in reasons with him who is ready to deceive you.

The Saints in arriving at holiness, passed through this doleful valley of temptation, and the greater Saints they were the greater temptations they grappled with. Nay after the Saints have attained to holiness and perfection; the Lord suffers them to be tempted with brisk temptations, that their Crown may be the greater, and that the spirit of Vain-glory may be checked, or else hindered from entering in them, keeping them in that manner secure, humble, and solicitous of their condition.

Finally you should know, that the greatest Temptation is to be without Temptation; wherefore you should be glad when it assaults you, and with Resignation, Peace and Constancy resist it:

Because if you will serve God, and arrive at the sublime Region of Internal Peace; you must pass through that rugged Path of Temptation; put on that heavy Armor; fight in that fierce and cruel War, and in that burning Furnace, polish, purge, renew, and purify yourself.

Chapter Nine

Declaring the Nature of internal Recollection, and instructing the Soul how it ought to behave itself therein, and in the Spiritual Welfare, whereby the Devil endeavors to disturb it at that time.

Internal Recollection is Faith, and Silence in the Presence of God. Hence you should be accustomed to recollect yourself in his Presence, with an affectionate attention, as one that is given up to God, and united unto him, with Reverence, Humility and Submission, beholding him in the most inward recess of your own Soul, without Form, Likeness, Manner, or Figure; in the view and general nature of a loving and obscure Faith, without any distinction of Perfection or Attribute.

There you are to be with attention, and a sincere regard, with a sedate heedfulness, and full of Love towards the same Lord, resigning and delivering yourself up into his hands, to the end he may dispose of you, according to his good Will and Pleasure; without reflecting on yourself; nay, nor on Perfection it self. Here you are to shut up the Senses, trusting God with all the care of your Welfare, and minding nothing of the affairs this Life. Finally, your Faith ought to be pure, without Representations or Likeness: Simple without Reasoning, and Universal without Distinctions.

The Prayer of Internal Recollection may be well typified by that Wrestling, which the holy Scripture says, the Patriarch Jacob had all Night with God, until Day broke, and he Blessed him. Wherefore the Soul is to persevere, and wrestle with the difficulties that it will find in internal Recollection, without desisting, until the Son of internal Light begin to appear, and the Lord give it his Blessing.

No sooner will you have given yourself up to your Lord in this inward Way, but all Hell will conspire against you, seeing one single Soul inwardly retired to its own Presence, makes greater War against the Enemy, than a thousand others that walk externally; because the Devil makes an infinite advantage of an internal Soul.

In the time of the recollection, Peace and Resignation of your Soul, God will more esteem the various impertinent, troublesome and ugly thoughts that you have, than the good purposes, and high sentiments. Know that the effort, which you make to resist Thoughts, is an impediment, and will leave your Soul in greater anxiety. The best thing that is to be done, is sweetly to despise them, to know your own wretchedness, and peacefully make an Offering to God of the Trouble.

Though you can not get rid of the anguish of Thoughts, has no Light, Comfort, nor spiritual Sentiment: Yet be not afflicted, neither leave off recollection, because they are the Snares of the Enemy: Resign yourself at the time with Vigor, endure with Patience, and persevere in his Presence; for while you persevere after that manner, your Soul will be internally improved.

Do you believe that when you come away from Prayer dry, in the same manner as you began it; that that was because of want of Preparation, and that it has done you no good: That is a Fallacy: Because the fruit of true Prayer consists not in enjoying the Light, nor in having Knowledge of spiritual things, since these may be found in a speculative Intellect, without true Virtue and Perfection; it only consists in enduring with Patience, and persevering in Faith and Silence, believing that you are in the Lord's Presence, turning to him your Heart with tranquility, and purity of Mind. So while you persevere in this manner, you will have the only Preparation and disposition which at that time is necessary, and will reap infinite fruit.

War is very usual in this internal Recollection, which on the one hand will deprive you of sensibility, to try, humble, and purge you. On the other, invisible Enemies will assault you with continual Suggestions, to trouble and disquiet you. Nature herself, apparently, will torment you, she being always an Enemy to the Spirit, which in depriving her of sensible Pleasures, remains Weak, Melancholy, and full of Irksomeness, so that it feels a Hell in all Spiritual Exercises, particularly in that of Prayer, hence it grows extremely impatient to be at an end of it, through the uneasiness of Thoughts, the lassitude of Body, importunate Sleep, and the not being able to curb the Senses, every one of which would for it own share, follow its own Pleasure. Happy are you if you can persevere amidst this Martyrdom!

That great Doctoress, and Mystical Mistress, Santa Teresa, confirms all this by her heavenly Doctrine, in the Letter she wrote to the Bishop of Osmia, to instruct him, how he was to behave himself in Prayer, and in the variety of troublesome thoughts, which attack us at that time, where she says: There is a necessity of suffering the trouble of a Troop of Thoughts, importune Imaginations, and the impetuosities of natural Notions, not only, of the Soul through the dryness and disunion it has, but of the Body also, occasioned by the want of submission to the Spirit, which it ought to have.

These are called drynesses in Spirituals, but are very profitable, if they be embraced and suffered with Patience. Who so shall accustom himself to suffer them without repining, will from that labor draw vast advantage. It is certain, that in recollection the Devil frequently charges the Soul more fiercely with a Battalion of Thoughts, to discomfit the quiet of the Soul, and alienate it from that most sweet and secure internal Conversation, raising horrors, to the end it may leave it off, reducing it most commonly to such a state, as if it were lead forth to a most rigorous Torment.

The Birds, which are the Devils, knowing this (said the Saint in the above cited Letter) pricks and molest the Soul with Imaginations, troublesome Thoughts, and the Interruptions which the Devil at that time brings in, transporting the Thought, distracting it from one thing to another, and after he is done with them attacking the Heart, and it is no small fruit of Prayer, patiently to suffer these Troubles and Importunities. That is an offering up of oneself, in a whole burnt Sacrifice, that's to say, to be wholly consumed in the Fire of Temptation, and no part spared. See, how this heavenly Mistress encourages to suffer and endure Thoughts and Temptations; because, provided they be not consented to, they double the profit.

As many times as you exercise yourself, calmly to reject these vain Thoughts, so many Crowns will the Lord set upon your Head, and though it may seem to you that you do nothing, be undeceived, for a good desire with firmness and steadfastness in Prayer, is very pleasing to the Lord.

Wherefore to be there (concludes the Saint) without sensible profit, is not lost time; but of great gain, while one toils without Interest, and merely for the glory of God; and though it may seem to be toiling in vain, yet it is not so, but it is as with Children, who toil and labor under the power of their Father: though in the evening they receive not the wages for their day's work, yet at the year's end they enjoy all. In fine, you see how the Saint confirms our document with her precious Doctrine.

God loves not him who does most, who hears most, nor who shows greatest affection, but who suffers most, if he pray with faith and reverence, believing that he is in the divine presence. The truth is to take from the Soul the prayer of the Senses, and of Nature, is a rigorous martyrdom to it, but the Lord rejoices, and is glad in its peace, if it be thus quiet and resigned. Use not at that time vocal Prayer, because however it be good and holy in it self, yet to use it then, is a manifest temptation, whereby the enemy pretends, that God speaks not to your heart, under pretext that you had not sentiments, and that you lose time.

God has no regard to the multitude of words, but to the purity of the intent. His greatest content and glory at that time, is to see the Soul in silence, desirous, humble, quiet, and resigned. Proceed, persevere, pray, and hold your peace; for where you don't find a sentiment, you will find a door whereby you may enter into your own nothingness; knowing yourself to be nothing, that you can do nothing, nay, and that you have not so much as a good thought.

How many have begun this happy practice of Prayer, and Internal Recollection, and have left it off, pretending that they feel no pleasure, that they lose time, that their thoughts trouble them, and that that Prayer is not for them, while they find not any sentiment of God, nor any ability to reason or discourse; whereas they might have believed, been silent, and had patience. All this is no more, but with ingratitude to hunt after sensible pleasures, suffering themselves to be transported with self-love, seeking themselves, and not God, because they cannot suffer a little pain and dryness, without reflecting on the infinite loss they sustain, whereas by the least act of reverence towards God, amidst dryness and sterility, they receive an eternal reward.

The Lord told the venerable Mother Francesca Lopez of Valenza, and a religious of the third Order of St. Francis, three things of great light and consequence in order to internal recollection. In the first place, that a quarter of an hour of Prayer, with recollection of the senses and faculties, and with resignation and humility, does more good to the Soul than five days of penitential exercises, hair cloths, disciplines, fasting, and sleeping on bare boards, because these are only mortifications of the body, and with recollection the Soul is purified.

Secondly, That it is more pleasing to the Divine Majesty, to have the Soul in quiet and devote Prayer for the space of an hour, than to go in great Pilgrimages; because that in Prayer it does good to itself, and to those for whom it prays, gives delight to God, and merits a high degree of glory, but in pilgrimage, commonly, the Soul is distracted, and the Senses diverted, with a debilitation of virtue, besides many other dangers.

Thirdly, That constant Prayer was to keep the Heart always right towards God, and that a Soul to be internal, ought rather to act with the affection of the Will, than the toil of the Intellect. All this is to be read in her Life.

The more the Soul rejoices in sensible love, the less delight God has in it; on the contrary, the less the Soul rejoices in this sensible love, the more God delights in it. And know that to fix the Will on God, restraining thoughts and temptations, with the greatest tranquility possible, is the highest pitch of Praying.

I'll conclude this Chapter by undeceiving you of the vulgar error of those who say, that in this internal Recollection, or

Prayer of Rest, the faculties operate not, and that the Soul is idle and wholly inactive. This is a manifest fallacy of those who have little experience, because although it operate not by means of the memory, nor by the second operation of the Intellect, which is the judgment, nor by the third, which is discourse or ratiocination, yet it operates by the first and chief operation of the intellect, which is simple apprehension, enlightened by holy Faith, and aided by the divine gifts of the holy Spirit. And the Will is more apt to continue one act, than to multiply many; so that as well the act of the Intellect, as that of the Will are so simple, imperceptible, and spiritual, that hardly the Soul knows them, and far less reflects upon them.

Chapter Ten

What the Soul ought to do in Internal Recollection.

You should go to Prayer, that you may deliver yourself wholly up into the hands of God, with perfect resignation, exerting an act of Faith, believing that you are in the divine Presence, afterwards settling in that holy repose, with quietness, silence and tranquility; and endeavoring for a whole day, a whole year, and your whole life to continue that first act of Contemplation, by faith and love.

It is not your businesses to multiply these acts, nor to repeat sensible affections, because they hinder the Purity of the spiritual and perfect act of the Will, besides that these sweet sentiments are imperfect, (considering the reflection wherewith they are made, the self-content, and external consolation wherewith they are fought after, the Soul being drawn outwards to the external faculties) there is no necessity of renewing them, as the mystical Falcon has excellently expressed it by the following similitude.

If a Jewel given to a friend were once put into his hands, it is not necessary to repeat such a donation already made, by daily telling him, (Sir, I give you that Jewel, Sir, I give you that Jewel, but to let him keep it, and not take it from him, because provided he take it not, or design not to take it from him, he has surely given it to him.

In the same manner, having once dedicated, and lovingly resigned yourself to the will of God, there is nothing else for you to do, but to continue the same, without repeating new and sensible acts, provided you don't take back the Jewel you have once given, by committing some notable fault against his divine Will, however you should still to exercise yourself outwardly in the external works of your calling and state, for in so doing you do the Will of God, and walk in continual and virtual oration: He always prays (said Theophylact) who does good works, nor does he neglect Prayer, but when he leaves off to be just.

You should then slight all those sensibilities, to the end your Soul may be established, and acquire a habit of internal recollection which is so effectual, that the resolution only of going to Prayer, awakens a lively presence of God, which is the preparation to the Prayer that is about to be made; or to say better, is no other than a more efficacious continuation of continual Prayer, wherein the contemplative person ought to be settled.

O how well did the venerable Mother of Cantal, the spiritual daughter of St. Francis of Sales, practice this Lesson, in whole Life are the following words, written to her Master: Most dear Father, I cannot do any act, it seems to me always that this is the most firm and secure disposition: my spirit in the upper part, is in a most simple unity; it is not united, because when it would perform acts of union (which it often sets about) it finds difficulty, and clearly perceives that it cannot unite, but be united. The Soul would make use of this union, for the service of Mattins, the holy Mass, preparation for the Communion, and thanksgiving; and in a word, it would for all things be always in that most simple unity of spirit, without reflecting on anything else. To all this the holy Father answered with approbation, persuading her to persist, and putting her in mind, that the repose of God is in peace.

Another time she wrote to the same Saint these words: Endeavoring to do some more special acts of my simple intuition, total resignation and annihilation in God, his divine goodness rebuked me, and gave me to understand, that that proceeded only from the love of myself, and that thereby I offended my Soul.

By this you will be undeceived, and know what is the perfect and spiritual way of Praying, and be advised what is to be done in Internal recollection: You will know that to the end Love may be perfect and pure, it is expedient to retrench the multiplication of sensible and fervent Acts, the Soul continuing quiet and resting in that inward Silence. Because, tenderness, delight, and sweet sentiments, which the Soul experiences in the Will, are not pure Spirits, but Acts blended with the sensibility of Nature. Nor is it perfect Love, but sensible Pleasure, which distracts and hurts the Soul, as the Lord told the venerable Mother of Cantal.

How happy and how well applied will your Soul be, if retreating within itself, it there shrink into its own nothing, both in its Center and superior Part, without minding what it does; whether it recollect or not, whether it walk well or ill; if it operate or not, without heeding, thinking, or minding any sensible thing? At that time the Intellect believes with a pure Act, and the Will loves with perfect love, without any kind of impediment, imitating that pure and continued Act of Intuition and Love, which the Saints say the Blessed in Heaven have, with no other difference, than that they see one another there Fact to Face, and the Soul here, through the Veil of an obscure Faith.

O how few are the Souls, that attain to this perfect way of Praying, because they penetrate not enough into this internal recollection, and Mystical Silence, and because they strip not themselves of imperfect reflection, and sensible pleasure! O that your Soul, without thoughtful advertency, even of itself, might give itself in Prayer to that holy and spiritual Tranquility and do nothing, forget itself, and plunge into that obscure Faith: How secure and safe would it be, though it might seem to it that thus inactive and doing nothing it were undone.

I'll sum up this doctrine with a Letter that the Illuminated Mother of Cantal wrote to a Sister, and great Servant of God: Divine Bounty (said she) granted me this way of Prayer, that with a single View of God, I felt my self wholly dedicated to him, absorbed and reposed in him; he still continued to me that Grace, though I opposed it by my Infidelity, giving way to fear, and thinking myself unprofitable in that state; for which cause, being willing to do something on my part, I quite spoil all; and to this present I find my self sometimes assaulted by the same Fear, though not in Prayer, but in other Exercises wherein I am always willing to employ my self a little, though I know very well, that in doing such acts, I come out of my Center, and see particularly that that simple View of God, is my only remedy and help still, in all troubles, temptations, and the events of this Life.

And certainly, would I have followed my internal Impulse, I should have made use of no other means in any thing whatsoever, without exception; because when I think to fortify my Soul with Arts, Reasoning and Resignations, then do I expose myself to new temptations and straights: Besides that, I cannot do it without great violence; which leaves me exhausted and dry, so that it behooves me speedily to return to this simple Resignation, knowing that God, in this manner, lets me see, that it is his Will and Pleasure, that a total stop should be put to the operations of my Soul, because he would have all things done by his own divine Activity; and happily he expects no more of me, but this only View in all spiritual Exercises, and in all the pains, temptations and afflictions that may befall me in this life. And the truth is, the quieter I keep my Spirit by this means, the better all things succeed with me; and my crosses and afflictions suddenly vanish. Many times has my blessed Father St. Frances of Sales, assured me of this.

Our late Mother Superior, encouraged me firmly to persist in that way, and not to fear anything in this simple View of God: She told me, That that was enough, and that the greater the nakedness, and quietness in God are, the greater sweetness and strength the Soul receives, which should endeavor to become so pure and simple, that it should have no other support, but in God alone.

To this purpose I remember, that a few days since, God communicated to me an Illumination, which made such an impression upon me, as if I had clearly seen him; and this it is,

That I should never look upon my self, but walk with eyes shut, leaning on my Beloved, without striving to see nor know the way, by which he guides me, neither fix my thoughts on anything, nor yet beg Favors of him, but as undone in myself, rest wholly and sincerely on him. Hitherto that Illuminated and Mystical Mistress, whose Words do Credit and Authorize our Doctrine.

Chapter Eleven

Declaring how the Soul putting it self in the Presence of God, with perfect Resignation, by the pure act of Faith, walks always in virtual and acquired contemplation.

You will tell me (as many Souls have told me) that though by a perfect Resignation you have put yourself in the Presence of God, by means of pure Faith, as has been already hinted, yet you do not merit nor improve, because your thoughts are so distracted, that you can not be fixed upon God.

Be not disconsolate, for you do not lose time, nor merit, neither desist you from Prayer; because it is not necessary, that during the whole time of recollection, you should actually think on God; it is enough that you have been attentive in the beginning; provided you discontinue not your purpose, nor revoke the actual attention which you had. As he, who hears Mass, and says the Divine Office, performs his Duty very well, by virtue of that primary actual attention, though afterwards he persevere not, in keeping his thoughts actually fixed on God.

This the Angelical Doctor St. Thomas confirms, in the following words: That first intention only and thinking of God when one Prays, has force and value enough to make the Prayer, during all the rest of the time it continues, to be true, impetratory and meritorious, though all that while there be no actual contemplation on God. See now if the Saint could speak more clearly to our purpose!

So that (in the Judgment of that Saint) the Prayer still continues, though the Imagination may ramble upon infinite numbers of thoughts, provided one consent not to it, shift not Place, intermit not the Prayer, nor change the first Intention of being with God. And it is certain, that he changes it not, while he does not leave his Place. Hence it follows in sound Doctrine, that one may persevere in Prayer, though the Imagination be carried about with various and involuntary thoughts. He prays in Spirit and Truth (says the Saint in the fore-cited place) whoever goes to Prayer with the Spirit and Intention of Praying, though afterwards through Misery and Frailty his Thoughts may straggle.

But you will say, at least, am I not to remember when I am in the presence of God, and often say to him, Lord abide within me; and I will give myself wholly up to you? I answer that there is no necessity for that, seeing you have a design to Pray, and for that end went to that place. Faith and Intention are sufficient, and these always continue; nay, the more simple that remembrance be, without words, or thoughts, the more pure, spiritual, internal, and worthy of God it is.

Would it not be impertinent and disrespectful, if being in the Presence of a King, you should ever now and then say to him, Sir, I believe Your Majesty is here? It's the very same thing. By the eye of pure Faith the Soul sees God, believes in him, and is in his Presence, and so when the Soul believes, it has no need to say, My God you are here; but to believe as it does believe, seeing when Prayer-time is come, Faith and Intention guide and conduct it to contemplate God by means of pure Faith, and perfect Resignation.

So that, so long as you don't retract that Faith, and Intention of being resigned, you walk always in Faith and Resignation, and consequently in Prayer, and in virtual and acquired Contemplation, although you perceive it not, remember it not, neither exert new Acts and Reflections thereon; after the example of a Christian, a Wife, and a Monk; who, though they exert us new Acts and Remembrances, the one as to his Profession, saying, I am a Monk, the other as to her Matrimony, saying I am a Wife, and the third as to his Baptism, saying, I am a Christian, they cease not for all that from being, the one Baptized, the other Married, and the third Professed. The Christian shall only be obliged to do good Works in Confirmation of his Faith; and to believe more with the Heart, than with the Mouth: The Wife ought to give demonstrations of the Fidelity which she promised to her Husband: And the Monk of the Obedience which he made profession of to his Superior.

In the same manner, the inward Soul being once resolved to Believe, that God is in it, and that it will not desire nor act anything but through God, ought to rest satisfied in that Faith and intention, in all its Works and Exercises, without forming or repeating new Acts of the same Faith, nor of such a Resignation.

This true Doctrine serves not only for the time of Prayer, but also after it is over, by Night and by Day, at all Hours, and in all the daily Functions of your Calling, your duty and Condition. And if you tell me, that many times you forget during a whole day, to renew your resignation, I answer, that though it seem to you, that you are diverted from it, by attending the daily occupations of your Vocation, as Studying, Reading, Preaching, Eating, Drinking, doing Business, and the like; you are mistaken; for the one destroys not the other, nor by so doing do you neglect to do the Will of God, nor to proceed in virtual Prayer, as St. Thomas says.

Because these occupations are not contrary to his Will, nor contrary to your Resignation, it being certain, that God would have you to Eat, Study, take Pains, do Business, etc. So that to perform these Exercises, which are conformed to his Will and Pleasure, you do not depart out of his Presence, nor from your own Resignation.

But if in Prayer, or out of it you should willingly be diverted or distracted, suffering yourself deliberately to be transported into any Passion; then it will be good for you to revert to God, and return into his Divine Presence, renewing the purest of Faith and Resignation. However it is not necessary to exert those Acts, when you find yourself in dryness, because dryness is good and holy, and cannot, no matter how severe it be, take from your Soul the Divine Presence, which is established in Faith. You should never call dryness distraction, because in beginners it is want of sensibility, and in proficient abstractedness, by means whereof, if you bear it out with constancy, resting quiet in your own emptiness, your Soul will become more and more inward; and the Lord will work wonders in it.

Strive then when you come from Prayer, to the end you may return to it again, not to be distracted, nor diverted; but to carry yourself with a total resignation to the Divine Will, that God may do with you and all yours, according to his heavenly pleasure, relying on him as on a kind and loving Father. Never recall that Intention, and though you be taken up about the Affairs of the Condition wherein God has placed you, yet you will still be in Prayer in the Presence of God, and in perpetual Resignation. Therefore St. John Chrysostom said, A just man leaves not off to Pray, unless he leaves off to be Just. He always prays, who always does well; the good desire is Prayer, and if the desire be continued, so is also the Prayer.

You will understand all that has been said, by this clear Example, when a man begins a Journey to Rome, every step he makes in the Progress is voluntary, and nevertheless it is not necessary, that at every step he should express his desire, or exert a new act of the Will, saying, I am going to Rome, I go to Rome: Because, by virtue of that first intention he had of traveling to Rome, the same Will still remains in him; so that he goes on without saying so, though he does not without intending so; you'll clearly find, besides, that this Traveler, with one single and explicit of the Will and Intention, travel, speaks, hears, sees, reasons, eats, drinks, and does several other things, without any interruption to his first intention, not yet of his actual journeying to Rome.

It is just so in the contemplative Soul: A man having once made the resolution of doing the Will of God, and of being in his Presence, he still perseveres in that act, so long as he recalls not the same, although he be taken up in hearing, speaking, eating, or in any other external good work or function of his Calling and Quality.

You will say, that all Christians walk in this Exercise, because all have Faith, and may although they be not internal fulfill this Doctrine especially such as go in the external Way of Meditation and Retiocination. It is true, all Christians have Faith, and more particularly they who Meditate and Consider: But the Faith of those who advance by the inward Way, is much different, because it is a lively Faith, universal and indistinct, and by consequent, more practical, active, effectual, and illuminated; insomuch as the Holy Ghost enlightens the Soul that is best disposed, most, and that Soul is always best disposed, which holds the Mind recollected; so proportionally to the Recollection the Holy Ghost Illuminates. And albeit it is true, that God communicates some light in Meditation, yet it is so scanty and different from that which he communicates to the Mind, recollected in a pure and universal Faith, that the one to the other, is no more than like two or three Drops of Water in respect of an Ocean: since in Meditation two or three particular Truths are communicated to the Soul; but in the internal Recollection, and the Exercise of pure and universal Faith, the Wisdom of God is an abundant Ocean which is communicated in that obscure, simple, general and universal Knowledge.

In like manner Resignation is more perfect in these Souls, because it springs from the internal and infused Fortitude, which grows as the internal Exercise of pure Faith, with Silence and Resignation, is continued: In the manner that the Gifts of God's Spirit grow in contemplative Souls; for though these divine Gifts are to be found in all those that are in a State of Grace, nevertheless, they are, as it were, dead, without strength, and in a manner infinitely different from these which reign in contemplative Persons, by reason of their illustration, vivacity and efficacy.

From all which, be persuaded, that the inward Soul, accustomed to go daily at certain hours to Prayer, with the Faith and Resignation I have mentioned to you, walks continually in the Presence of God. All holy, expert and mystical Masters, teach this true and important Doctrine, because they have all had one and the same Master, who is the Holy Ghost.

Chapter Twelve

A Way by which one may enter into internal Recollection, through the most Holy Humanity of Lord Christ.

There are two sorts of Spiritual Men Diametrically contrary one to another: The one say, That the Mysteries of the Passion of Christ, are always to be considered and Meditated upon: The others running to the opposite extreme, teach, That the Meditation of the Mysteries of the Life, Passion, and Death of our Savior, is not Prayer, nor yet a Remembrance of them; but the exalted Elevation to God, whose Divinity Contemplates the Soul in quiet and silence, ought only to be called Prayer.

It is certain that our Lord Christ is the Guide, the Door, and the Way; as he himself has said in his own Words (John 14.): I am the way, the truth, and the life. And before the Soul can be fit to enter into the Presence of the Divinity, and be united with it, it is to be washed with the precious Blood of a Redeemer, and adorned with the rich robes of his Passion.

Our Lord Christ with his Doctrine and Example, is the Mirror, the Guide of the Soul, the Way and the only door by which we enter into those Pastures of Life Eternal, and into the vast Ocean of the Divinity. Hence it follows, that the Remembrance of the Passion and Death of our Savior ought not wholly to be blotted out: nay, it is also certain, that whatsoever high elevation of Mind the Soul may be raised to, it ought not in all things to separate from the most holy Humanity. But then it follows, not from hence neither, that the Soul accustomed to internal recollection, that can no longer ratiocinate, should always be meditating on, and considering (as the other Spiritualists say) the most holy Mysteries of our Savior. It is holy and good to Meditate; and would to God that all men of this World practiced it. And the Soul, besides that meditates, reasons and considers with facility; ought to be let alone in that state, and not pushed on to another higher, so long as in that of Meditation it finds nourishment and profit.

It belongs to God alone, and not to the spiritual Guide, to promote the Soul from Meditation to Contemplation; because, if God through his special Grace, call it not to this state of Prayer, the Guide can do nothing with all his Wisdom and Instructions.

To strike a secure means then, and to avoid those two so contrary extremes, of not wholly blotting out the remembrance of the Humanity; and of not having it continually before our eyes; we ought to suppose, that there are two ways of attending to the Holy Humanity; that one may enter at the Divine Port, which is Christ our well being, The first is by considering the Mysteries, and meditating the Actions of the Life, Passion, and Death of our Savior. The second by thinking on him, by the application of the Intellect, pure Faith, or Memory.

When the Soul proceeds in perfecting and interiorizing itself, by means of internal recollection, having for sometime meditated on the Mysteries whereof it has been already informed; then it retains Faith and Love to the Word Incarnate, being ready for his sake to do whatever he inspires into it, walking according to his Precepts, although they be not always before its Eyes. As if it

should be said to a Son, that he ought never to forsake his Father, they intend not thereby to oblige him, to have his Father always in sight, but only to have him always in his Memory, that in time and place, he may be ready to do his Duty.

The Soul then that is entered into internal recollection, with the opinion and approbation of an expert Guide, has no need to enter by the first door of Meditation on the Mysteries, being always taken up in meditating upon them; because that is not to be done without great fatigue to the Intellect, not does it stand in need of such ratiocinations; since these serve only as a means to attain to believing, that which it has already got the possession of.

The most noble, spiritual and proper way for Souls that are Proficients in internal recollection, to enter by the Humanity of Christ our Lord, and entertain a remembrance of him is the second way; eying that Humanity, and the Passion thereof by a simple Act of Faith, loving and reflecting on the same as the Tabernacle of the Divinity, the beginning and end of our Salvation, Jesus Christ having been Born, Suffered, and died a shameful Death for our sakes.

This is the way that makes internal Souls profit, and this holy, pious, swift, and instantaneous remembrance of the Humanity, can be no obstacle to them in the course of internal recollection, unless if when the Soul enters into Prayer, it finds itself drawn back; for then it will be better, to continue recollection and mental excess. But not finding it self drawn back, the simple and swift remembrance of the Humanity of the Divine Word, gives no impediment to the highest and most elevated, the most abstracted and transformed Soul.

This is the way that Santa Teresa recommends to the contemplative, rejecting the tumultuous Opinions of some School-men. This is the strait and safe way, free from Dangers, which the Lord has taught to many Souls, for attaining to repose, and the Holy Tranquility of Contemplation.

Let the Soul then, when it enters into recollection, place it self at the Gate of Divine Mercy, which is the amiable and sweet remembrance of the Cross and Passion of the Word that was made Man, and Died for Love; let it stand there with Humility, resigned to the Will of God, in whatsoever it pleases the Divine Majesty, to do with it; and if from that holy and sweet remembrance, it soon fall into forgetfulness, there is no necessity of making a new repetition, but to continue silent and quiet in the presence of the Lord.

Wonderfully does St. Paul favor this our Doctrine, in the Epistle which he wrote to the Colossians, wherein he exhorts them and us, that whether we Eat, Drink, or do anything else, we should do it in the Name, and for the Sake of Jesus Christ. God grant that we may all begin by Jesus Christ, and that in him, and by him alone, we may arrive at perfection.

Chapter Thirteen

Of Internal and Mystical Silence.

There are three kinds of silence; the first is of Words, the Second of Desires, and the third of Thoughts. The first is perfect; the second more perfect; and the third more perfect. In the first, that is, of words, Virtue is acquired; in the second, to wit, of

Desires, quietness is attained to; in the third of Thoughts, Internal Recollection is gained. By not speaking, not desiring, and not thinking, one arrives at the true and perfect Mystical Silence, wherein God speaks with the Soul, communicates himself to it, and in the Abyss of its own Depth, teaches it the most perfect and exalted Wisdom.

He calls and guides it to this inward Solitude, and mystical Silence, when he says, That he will speak to it alone, in the most secret and hidden part of the Heart. You are to keep yourself in this mystical Silence, if you would hear the sweet and divine Voice. It is not enough for gaining this Treasure, to forsake the World, nor to renounce your own Desires, and all things created; if you wean not yourself from all Desires and Thoughts. Rest in this mystical Silence, and open the Door, that so God may communicate himself unto you, unite with you, and transform you into himself.

The perfection of the Soul consists not in speaking nor in thinking much on God; but in loving him sufficiently: This love is attained to by means of perfect Resignation and internal Silence, all consists in Works: The love of God has but few Words. Thus St. John the Evangelist confirms and inculcates it. My little Children, let us not love in Word, neither in Tongue, but in Deed and in Truth.

You are clearly convinced now, that perfect Love consists not in amorous Acts, nor tender Ejaculations, nor yet in the internal Acts, wherein you tell God, that you have an infinite Love for him, and you love him more than yourself. It may be that at that time you seek more yourself, and the love of yourself, than the true Love of God, Because Love consists in Works, and not in fair Discourses.

That a rational Creature may understand the secret desire and intention of your Heart, there is a necessity that you should express it to him in Words. But God who searches the Hearts, stand not in need that you should make profession and assure him of it; nor does he rest satisfied, as the Evangelist says, with Love in Word nor in Tongue, but with that which is true and indeed. What avails it to tell them with great zeal and fervor, that you tenderly and perfectly love him above all things, if at one bitter word, or slight injury, you do not resign yourself, nor are mortified for the love of him? A manifest proof that your love was a love in Tongue and not in Deed.

Strive to be resigned in all things with Silence, and in so doing, without saying that you love him, you will attain to the most perfect quiet, effectual and true love. St. Peter most affectionately told the Lord, that for his sake he was ready, willingly to lay down his Life; but at the word of a young Damsel, he denied him, and there was an end of his Zeal. Mary Magdalene said not a word,

and yet the Lord himself taken with her perfect Love, became her Panegyrist, saying that she had loved much. It is internally, then, that with dumb Silence, the most perfect Virtues of Faith, Hope, and Charity are practiced, without any necessity of telling God, that you love him, hope and believe in him; because the Lord knows better than you do, what the internal Motions of your Heart are.

How well was that pure act of Love understood and practiced by that profound and great Mystic, the Venerable Gregory Lopez, whose whole Life was a continual Prayer, and a continued Act of Contemplation; and of so pure and spiritual Love of God, that it never gave way to Affections and sensible Sentiments.

Having for the space of three Years continued that Ejaculation, Your will be done in Time, and in Eternity; repeating is as often as he breathed; God Almighty discovered to him, that infinite Treasure of the pure and continued Act of Faith and Love, with Silence and Resignation: so that he came to say, That during the thirty six Years he lived after, he always continued in his inward Man; that pure Act of Love, without ever uttering the least Petition, Ejaculation, or any thing that was Sensible, or sprung from Nature. O Incarnate Seraphim, and Deified Man! How well did you know how to dive into that internal and mystical Silence, and to distinguish betwixt the outward and inward Man?

The Second Book

Chapter One

The best way to baffle the Craft of the Enemy, is to be Subjected to a Ghostly Father.

It is every way convenient, to choose a Master experienced in the inward way, because God will not do all, what he did to St. Catharine of Siena, whom he took by the Hand, and immediately taught the mystical Way. If in the Progress of Nature there is a necessity of a Guide; how must it be in the Progress of Grace? If in the outward and visible ways there is need of a Master; how must it be for the internal and secret? If it must be so for the Moral, Scholastic and Explosive, Theology, which are plainly taught; how must it be for that which is mystical, secret, reserved and obscure? If in external and political Actions and Practices it is so; how must it be in the internal Transactions with God.

A Guide is in like manner necessary for resisting and overcoming the Craft and Wiles of Satan. St. Austin gave many Reasons why God appointed that in his Church, Doctors and Teachers, men of the same nature with others, should, for Light and Doctrine, have the Precedence: The chief is, to free us from the craft and cunning of the Enemy; for should we be left to our own Dictates and Natural Impulse, for the conduct of our Actions, we would trip and stumble every foot, and at length fall head-long into the Pit; as it happens to Heretics and proud People: Now if we had had Angels given to us for Masters, then would the Devils have dazzled our Eyes by transforming themselves into Angels of Light: therefore it was convenient that for Guides and Counselors, God should given us men like our selves. And if such a Guide be expert, he'll soon know the tricks and subtleties of the Devil; which being once known, as wanting substance, they soon evanish.

A Ghostly Father ought to come from the Hand of God, and therefore without previous Circumspection and Prayer; he is not to be chosen but being once chosen, he is not to be left, but for most urgent reasons; such as are for not knowing the Ways and States, through which God guides the Soul; because no man can teach what he does not know, according to that true Maxim of Philosophy.

And if he conceive not (as St. Paul says) the things of the Spirit, that will be Ignorance in him; because they are to be examined Spiritually, and he wants experience: but the spiritual and expert Man sees every thing clearly, and judges of it as it is. If a Guide then wants experience, it is a chief reason why one should leave him, and choose another more expert; because without such a one, the Soul will not profit.

To pass from a bad into a good state, there is no necessity of Counsel; but to change what is good into better, there is need of time, prayer and advice; because every thing which is best in itself, is not best for every one in particular; nor is every thing that is good for one, good for all: Some are called for the outward and ordinary Way; others for the internal and extraordinary, and all are not in the same state; so that there being so many and various persons who are engaged in the mystical way, it is impossible for one to make a step in those secret and internal Paths without an experienced Guide, because instead of going right, he'll tumble into a Precipice.

When a Soul walks with Fear; doubting if it walk safely, and desires to be clearly rid of these fears and doubts, the securest way is to submit to a Ghostly Father; because by the internal Light he clearly discovers what is Temptation, and what Inspiration, and distinguishes the motions that spring from Nature, from the Devil, and from the Soul it self, which ought totally to be subjected to him who has experience, and he can discover the engagements, the Idols and bad habits that hinder the Souls flight; which by this means will not only be delivered from the Snares of the Devil, but will proceed more in one Year, than it could have proceeded in a thousand, with other Guides of no Experience.

In the Life of the Illuminated Father, Friar John Tauler, it is related what that Layman who went before him in the State of Perfection, says of himself, How that being taken off from the World, and desirous to be Holy, he gave himself to great abstinence, till at length being extenuated and weak, he fell into a Dream, and heard a voice from Heaven which said to him, Man, if you voluntary kill yourself, before the time, you shall pay dear to yourself for it. Being full of terror, he went into a Desait, and there imparted the way he had taken, and his Abstinence to a holy Anchorite, who, by the favor of Heaven, freed him from that Diabolical Delusion. He told him, That he followed that course of Abstinence that he might please God. But the Anchorite having asked him, By what Advice he did it? And he having made answer By none. The Anchorite replied, That it was a manifest Temptation of the Devil. From that time forward, he opened his Eyes, and knowing his own Perdition, lived always by the Direction of a Spiritual Father; and he himself affirmed, That in seven years space he gave him greater Light, than all printed Books whatsoever could do.

There is far greater advantage to be had from having a Master in the mystical way, then from the use of Spiritual books; because a practical Master tells us in the nick of time, what ought to be done; but in a Book one may fall upon a thing that is less proper, and by that means the necessary Instruction is wanting: Besides, by mystical Books men raise to themselves many false Notions, the Soul thinking to have that, which in reality it has not, and to be farther on in the mystical State, than as yet it is; whence spring many prejudices and dangers.

It is certain that the frequent Reading of mystical Books, which are not founded in practical, but mere speculative Light, does rather hurt than good, because it confounds, instead of, enlightening Souls, and fills them with discursive Notions that might hinder them; since although they be Notices of Light, yet they enter from without, render the Faculties dull, and fill them with Ideas instead of emptying them, that God may replenish them with Himself. Many do continually Read in these speculative Books, because they will not submit to him who may tell them, that such Reading is not convenient for them; whereas there is no doubt but if they do submit, and the Guide be a man of Experience, he will not allow it them: And then they would profit, and not mind such Studies as the Souls do who are submitted, have Light, and make improvement. Hence it follows, that it contributes much to inward Quiet and Security, to have an experienced Guide, who may govern and instruct with actual Light, that the Soul may not be deluded by the Devil, nor by its own Judgment and Opinion: However, we do not condemn the Reading of spiritual Books in general, seeing here we speak in particular of Souls purely Internal and Mystical, for whom this Book is written.

All holy and mystical Masters confess that the security of a mystical Soul, consists in a cordial Submission to its Ghostly Father, communicating to him, whatever passes within it. And therefore he, who lives after his own Opinion, without applying himself to a Spiritual Director (although he take himself to be, and is reputed spiritual) opposes himself to the Doctrine of the Saints, and of enlightened Souls; because the more a Soul is illuminated and united with God, the more humble, submissive, subjected and obedient to the spiritual Guide it ought to be. For proof of this truth, I'll relate what the Lord said to Donna Marina d'Escobar: It is reported in her Life, that being Sick, she asked the Lord, If she should be Silent, and omit the acquainting her spiritual Father with the extraordinary things that happened in her Soul, that she might not tire herself, nor trouble the same Father. To whom the Lord answered, That not to give an Account of them to her Ghostly Father, would not be well done for three Reasons: First, Because as Gold is tried in the Furnace, and the value of Stones known by touching them with the Touch-stone; so the Soul is purified, and the worth of it known, when the Minister of God tries it by the Touch-stone. Secondly, Because to avoid Error, it was convenient that matters should be governed, according to the Order instituted by God in his Church, in the Scriptures and in the Doctrine of the Saints. Thirdly, That the Mercies which his Divine Majesty shows to his Servants and pure Souls, may not be concealed, but made manifest, that so Believers may be encouraged to serve their God, and he be glorified in them.

In the same place she has the following words, conform to the aforesaid truth: My Confessor being Sick, and having enjoined me that I should not make a full Discovery of all things that happened to me, to him, to whom, in the meantime, I Confessed my self, but only of some with prudence; I bewailed my condition to the Lord, that I had not one to whom I might communicate my affairs; and his Majesty made me answer, You have one already who supplies the want of your Confessor; tell him all that happens to you. I presently replied, Not so Lord, Not so Lord. (Why?) said the Lord. Because my Confessor commanded me that I should not give him Account of all; and I ought to obey him. His Majesty said to me, You have pleased me by that answer, and that I might hear you say so, I said what you have heard; do so, yet still you may acquaint him with some things, as he himself had you.

What Santa Teresa said of herself, comes in very pat in this place: Whenever (says she) the Lord commanded me anything, if my Confessor told me another, I turned to the Lord and told him, that I must obey my Confessor. Afterward his Majesty returned to him, to the end he might enjoin it me of new. This is sound and true doctrine, which secures Souls, and dissipates the illusions of the Devil.

Chapter Two

The Indiscreet Zeal of Souls, and the inordinate Love of our Neighbor, disturb internal Peace.

There is not a more acceptable Sacrifice to God (says St. Gregory) than the ardent Zeal of Soul: For that Ministry, the Eternal God sent his own Jesus Christ into the World, and ever since it has been the most noble and sublime of Offices. But if the Zeal be indiscreet, it brings a notable obstacle to the progress of the Spirit.

No sooner do you find in yourself any new and fervent light, but you would lay yourself wholly out for the good of Souls;

and in the mean time, its odds, but that that is self-love, which you take to be pure zeal. This uses sometime to put on a garb of a inordinate Desire, of a vain complacency, of an industrious affection and proper esteem; all Enemies to the peace of the Soul.

It is never good to love your Neighbor to the detriment of your own spiritual good. To please God in purity, ought to be the only scope of your Works; this ought to be your only desire and thought; endeavoring to moderate your inordinate fervor; that tranquility and internal peace may reign in your Soul. The true zeal of Souls, which you should strive for, should be the true love of your God. That is the fruitful, efficacious, and true zeal, which does wonders in Souls, though with dumb Voices.

St. Paul recommended to us first the care of our own Souls, before that of our Neighbor. Take heed unto yourself, and unto your Doctrine, said he in his Canonical Epistle. Struggle not to over do, for when it is time convenient, and you can be any way useful to your Neighbor; God will call you forth, and put you in the employment that will best suit with you: That thought belongs only to him, and to you, to continue in your rest, disengaged, and wholly resigned up to the Divine will and pleasure. Don't think that in that condition you are idle: He is busied enough, who is always ready waiting to perform the Will of God. Who takes heed to himself for God's sake, does every thing; because, one pure Act of internal Resignation, is more worth than a hundred thousand Exercises for ones own Will.

Though the Cistern is capable of containing much Water, yet it must still be without it, till Heaven favor it with Rain. Be at rest, blessed Soul be quiet, humble and resigned, to every thing that God shall be pleased to do with you, leave the care to God, for he as a Loving Father, knows best what is convenient for you; conform yourself totally to his Will, perfection being founded in that, inasmuch as he who does the will of the Lord, is his Mothers Son, and Brother of the Son of God himself.

Think not that God esteems him most, that does most. He is most beloved who is most humble, most faithful and resigned, and most correspondent to his own Internal Inspiration, and to the Divine will and pleasure.

Let all your desires conform to the Will of that God, who can bring streams of Water out of the dry Rock, who is much displeased with those Souls, which in helping others before the time, defraud themselves, suffering themselves to be transported by indiscreet zeal, and vain complacency.

As it was with the Servant of Elisha, who being sent by the Prophet, that with his Staff he might raise a dead Child; because of the complacency he had, it had not the effect, and he was reproved by Elisha. In like manner the Sacrifice of Cain was rejected, being the first that was offered to God in the World, through the vain-glory he had of being the first, and more than his own Father Adam, in offering Sacrifice to God.

In like manner the Disciples of our Lord Christ, were infected with that evil, feeling a vain joy, when they cast out Devils, and therefore were sharply reproved by their Heavenly Master. Before Paul Preached to the Gentiles the Gospel of the Kingdom of Heaven, being already a chosen Vessel, a Citizen of Heaven, and chosen of God for that Ministry, it was necessary to try and humble him, shutting him up in close Prison; and would you become a Preacher without passing through the Trial of Men and Devils? And could you thrust yourself into so great a Ministry, and produce Fruit, without passing through the fiery trial of temptation, tribulation, and passive purgation?

It concerns you more to be quiet and resigned in a holy case, than to do many and great things, by your own judgment and opinion; think not that the heroic Actions which great Saints have done, and do in the Church, are Works of their own Industry; for all things as well spiritual as temporal, to the shaking of the last Leaf, are by Divine Providence Decreed from all Eternity. He that does the Will of God, does all things; this your Soul should endeavor, resting in a perfect Resignation to whatever the Lord is pleased to dispose of you; acknowledge yourself unworthy of so high a Ministry, as the guiding of Souls to Heaven, and then you will put no obstacle to the rest, internal peace, and heavenly flight of your Soul.

Chapter Three

Light, Experience, and a Divine Call, are necessary for guiding Souls in the inward Way.

You will think and with great confidence too, that you are in a condition, to guide Souls in the way of the Spirit, and perhaps, that may be secret Vanity, spiritual Pride, and plain Blindness; seeing besides, that this high employment requires supernatural Light, total abstraction, and other qualities which I shall mention to you in the following Chapters; the Grace of a Call is also necessary, without which all is but vanity, confidence and self-conceit; because, although it be a holy and good thing to guide Souls, and conduct them to Contemplation; yet how do you know that God would have you so employed? And though you know (which yet is not easy) that you have great Light and Experience, yet what evidence have you that the Lord would have you be of that Profession?

This Ministry is of such importance that it is not our parts to take it upon us, until it please God, by means of our Superiors and spiritual Guides, to place us therein; otherwise it would be a heavy prejudice to us, though it might be profitable to our Neighbor. What advantage is it to gain the whole World to God, if our own Soul thereby suffer detriment?

Howsoever evident it may be to you, that your Soul is endowed with internal light and experience; the best thing still that you can do, is to keep quiet and resigned in your own nothingness, until God call you for the Good of Souls: That belongs only to him, who knows your sufficiency and abstraction: It is not your part to make that judgment, neither to press into that Ministry; because, if you are governed by your own opinion and judgment, in an affair of so high concern, self-love will blind, undo, and deceive you.

If then experience, light, and sufficiency are not sufficient, without the grace of a Call to qualify one for that employment, how must it be without sufficiency? how must it be without internal light? without due experience, which are gifts not communicated to all Souls; but to abstracted and resigned Souls, and to such as have advanced to perfect annihilation, by the way of terrible tribulation, and passive purgation. Be persuaded, O blessed Soul, that all works, which in this profession are not governed by a true zeal, springing from pure love, and a purged Soul, cloth the Soul with vanity, self-love, and spiritual pride.

O how many self confident men by their own judgment and opinion, undertake this Ministry; and instead of pleasing God, emptying and abstracting their own Souls, (though they may do some good to their Neighbor) are filled with Earth, Straw, and Self-conceit! Be quiet and Resigned, renounce your own Judgment and Desire, sink down into the Abyss of your own Insufficiency and Nothingness; for there only you will find God, the true Light, your Happiness, and greatest Perfection.

Chapter Four

Instructions and Counsels to Confessors and Spiritual Directors.

The highest and most profitable Ministry, is that of a Confessor, and Spiritual Director; and irreparable are the damages, if it be not well performed. It would be prudently done, to choose a Patron for so great a Ministry; and that should be the Saints to whom one has greatest Devotion.

The chief and most secure Document is, to endeavor the internal and continual retirement; and so he'll walk well in all the exercises and employments of his own State and Calling, particularly in that of the Confession seat; for when the Soul inwardly Recollected, sallies out to be employed in those external and necessary Exercises, it is God who Illuminates and Works in them. In the Conduct of Souls that are Internal, Documents are not to be given to them, but with mildness and prudence: The Obstacles which hinder the Influences of God, are only to be taken out of the way.

Many Souls think, that all Confessors are capable of internal Matters; but besides, that is a mistake, it is found by experience to be a great prejudice to communicate them to those who are not so: Because, although God has placed them in the inward Way, yet they'll not know these matters, nor advise them to Souls, for want of experience; so that they'll hinder the

Progress to Contemplation, enjoying them to Meditate by force, although they cannot; and by that means, they stun and ruin instead of helping them in their Flight: for God will have them to advance to Contemplation, and they draw them to Meditation, because they know no other way.

If a Confessor would reap Fruit, he is not to look out for any Soul that he may Guide it; it concerns them to come of themselves, and all are not to be admitted, especially if they be Women, because they are not wont to come with sufficient disposition: Not to make ones self a Master, nor be willing to appear so, is an excellent means of doing good. The Confessor is to make use of the name of Daughter, as little as he can; because it is most dangerous, God being so Jealous, and the Epithet so Amorous. The Employments which a confessor accepts of, out of his Confession seat, ought to be but few; because God will not have him to be an Agent in Business; and if it were possible, he should not be seen, but in his Confession chair. A God-father, or Executor to a Man's last Will and Testament, he ought not, so much as once, to be, all his life long, because it brings many disturbances to the Soul, all of 'um contrary to the Perfection of so high a Ministry.

The Confessor or spiritual Director never ought to Visit his spiritual Daughters, not so much as in case of Sickness, unless he should indeed be then sent for, on the part of her that is ill.

If the Confessor procures an inward and outward Recollection, his words will be (although he knows it not) like Coals kindled, setting their Souls afire.

In the Confessionary, his Reproofs must be ordinarily gentle and sweet, although in the Pulpit they are severe and rigorous; because in this he ought to be raging as a Lyon, and in that, he ought to put on the meekness of a Lamb: O how powerful is sweet Reproof for Penitents! In the Confessionary they are already moved; but in the Pulpit their blindness and hardness, makes it necessary to frighten 'um: yet these ought to be persuaded and reproved rigorously, who come indisposed, and would have Absolution by force.

When all that is possible, is done for the benefit of Souls, the Fruit of it is not to be looked after; because the Devil does subtly make that seem his own, which is God's; and assaults with self Conceit and vain Complacency, the capital Enemies of Annihilation; which the Confessor always ought to bring about for such a spiritual Dying. Although he often see that Souls are not advantaged, and that those which are edified, loose the Spirit, let him not be disquieted at this, but possess himself in peace, like the Guardian Angles; then let him take courage inwardly, with the sense of his own Sincerity, because sometimes God suffers such a thing among other ends, to humble him.

The Confessor ought to avoid himself, and persuade the Souls under his conduct, also, to avoid all sort of outwardness, because it is much abhorred by the Lord. Although he ought not to order Souls to be Communicated, nor take any Communion from them, whether for Trial or Mortification (since there are infinite ways of Trying them and Mortifying them, without so great a prejudice) yet he ought not to be niggardly with those Souls which are moved by a true Desire, because Jesus Christ endured not to be shut up.

Experience shows us that it's a difficult thing to fulfill a Penance, when it is great and immoderate: it's always best to have it, of some profitable and moderate matter. If the Spiritual Father shows, with any singularity, a greater affection to a Daughter, and such as gives very great disturbance to others of her Sex: here he must use privacy and prudence, and must not speak to any with particularity; because the Devil loves to make strife with the Guide of Souls, and makes use of those very words to disturb others.

The continual and principle Exercise of Souls, purely Mystical, must be in the interior Man, producing with privacy, the destruction of Self-love, and the encouraging of them to the enduring of inward Mortifications; by which the Lord Cleanses, Annihilates and perfects them.

The Desire of Revelations, uses to be a great hindrance to the interior Soul, especially to Women; and there is not an ordinary Dream, but they will Christen it with the name of a

Vision. It's necessary to show abhorrence to all these hindrances. Although Silence be a difficult thing to Women, in the things which the Director orders them, yet must he procure it: since it is not good that the things inspired into him from the Lord, should become the Mark for Censures to shoot at.

Chapter Five

Wherein the same thing is treated of; Discoursing the Interests which some Confessors and Spiritual Directors use to have; in which are declared the Qualities which they ought to have for the Exercise of Confession, and also for the Guiding of Souls through the Mystical Way.

The Confessor ought to get Penitents encouraged to Prayer; especially when they often present themselves at his Feet, and make known to him their Desire that they have of their Spiritual Good.

The Maxim which the Confessor ought mostly to observe, that he may never come into Perdition, is, Not to accept any Present, though the whole World were offered him.

Though there are abundance of Confessors, yet they are not all good ones, because some of them know but little; others are very Ignorant; others betake themselves to the Applauses of the Gentry; some seek the Favors of their Penitents; some their Presents; some are full of Spiritual Ambition, and seek Credit and Fame, getting a multitude of Spiritual Children to themselves; others affect their Mastership and Command; other, affect the Visions and Revelations of their Spiritual Children, and instead of despising them, the only way of securing them to Humility, they commend them, that they may not leave them off and make them write them that they may show them abroad for Ostentation: All this is Self-love and Vanity in these Guides, and great prejudice to the Spiritual Profit of Souls: since it is certain, that all these respects and interests serve only to hinder the use and exercise of their Office, with advantage and profit; which requires a universal freedom from such things, and whose end and aim ought only to be the glory of God.

Other Confessors there are, which with ease and lightness of A heart, do believe, and approve, and commend all Spirits: Others falling into the vicious extreme, do condemn without any reserve, all Visions and Revelations; such things are neither to be believed all, nor condemned all: Others also there are who are so enamored of the Spirit of their Spiritual Daughters, that whatever they Dream, let them be never so much Deceit, they reverence them as sacred Mysteries! O what a world of Miseries are known in the Church by these means! Others Confessors there are also, having on the Garb of worldly Courtesy and Civility, having little regard to the holy Place of the Confessionary, discoursing with their Penitents concerning things vain, superfluous distractive, and far from that decency which the Sacrament requires, and from that disposition which should be fit to receive divine Grace; making particularly like discourses, and about the Household Affairs of their Penitents, before they come to accuse themselves of their sins: whereupon that little Devotion which they brought along with them to the Sacrament, becomes cooled and good for nothing: Sometimes it happens that many Penitents are fain to wait to be Confessed, who are full of business of their own, and when they see such a long demur, they grow weary and sad, and fall into impatience, losing the actual disposition of Mind wherewith they were before prepared to receive so healthful a Sacrament: whereupon the medley of these distractive, superfluous and vain matters, not only make them lose their precious time, but also prejudice the holy Place, the Sacrament; the disposition of the Penitent who is confessed, and that of others who wait to be confessed; all of them considerable mischiefs, and worthy to be redressed.

For Confession, there are some good; but for the Government of Spirits by the mystical Way, there are so few (says Father John Davila) that in a thousand, you shall possibly find one: St. Francis of Sales says, One among ten thousand: And the illuminated Thauler says, That in a hundred thousand, it was a hard thing to find one expert Master of Spirit. The reason is, because there are so few who dispose themselves to receive the mystical Science. Would to God it were not so true as it is. For then there would not be so many Cheats in the World, and there would be more Saints and fewer Sinners.

When the spiritual Guide desires effectually, that all should be in love with Virtue, and the love which they have of God, is pure and perfect, with few Words, and few Reasons, he will reap a very great deal of Benefit.

If the interior Soul, when it is cleansing itself of Passions, and in the time of abstraction, has not a sure Guide to curb in the retirement and solitude, to which its Inclination and great Propensity draws it, it will be unable and unfit for exercises of Confession, Preaching and Study, and also for those of its own Obligation, State and Calling.

The skilful Director therefore, ought to mind carefully when the Powers of it begin to be employed in God, that there may not be given too free access to solitude, commanding the Soul not to omit the outward exercises of its state, as of Study, and other Employments, although' they should seem distractive, so that they be not contrary to his Calling; because the Soul is so much Abstracted in Solitude, is so turned inward in its retirement, and is removed to such a degree from Exteriority, that if it afterwards apply it self again, it does it with toil and resistance, and with prejudice to its powers, and the strength and soundness of Head: which is considerable hurt, and worthy the weighting of spiritual Directors.

But if these have no Experience, they will not know when the abstraction is formed, and at the same time, thinking it Holy Counsel, will encourage them to Retirement, and find destruction in it: O how necessary it is that the Guide be expert in the spiritual and mystical way! Those that govern Souls without Experience go in the dark, and arrive not at the Understanding of the states of the Soul in their internal and supernatural Operations, they only know that sometimes the Soul is well, and that it has Light; other times that it is in Darkness; but what the state of all these is, and what is the Root from whence these Changes grow, they neither know nor understand, nor can verify it by means of Books, till they come to find it experimentally in themselves, in whose Furnace the true and actual Light is made.

If the Guide has not passed himself through the secret and painful ways of the interior walk, how can he comprehend or approve it? It will be no small favor to the Soul, to find one only experienced Guide to strengthen it in insuperable Difficulties, and assure it in the continual doubts of this Voyage: otherwise he will never get to the holy and precious Mount of Perfection, without an extraordinary and singular Grace.

The spiritual Director, which lives disinterested, longs more for the internal Solitude than the Employment of Souls: and if any spiritual Master is displeased when a Soul goes from him, and leaves him for another Guide, it's a clear sign, that he did not live disinterested, nor sought purely the Glory of God, but his own proper Esteem.

The same loss and evil comes, when the Director is secretly diligent to draw some Soul to his direction, which goes under the government of another Guide; this is a notable mischief; for if he holds himself for a better Director than the other, he is proud; and if he knows himself to be a worse, he is a Traitor to God, to that Soul, and to himself, during the prejudice he does to the advantage and good of his Neighbors.

In like manner there is another considerable hurt that discovers itself in spiritual Masters, which is, that they do not suffer the Souls Guided by them, to communicate with others, though they are more Holy, Learned, and Expert than themselves: all this is Interest, Self-love, and Esteem of themselves. They do not permit Souls thus to unburden and vent themselves, for fear they should loose them, and that it may not be said, that their Spiritual Children seek that Satisfaction in others, which they cannot find in them; and for the most part, by these imperfect ends, they hinder Souls from being advantaged.

From all these, and infinite other imputations, the Director is free that is once arrived at hearing the inward Voice of God, by having passed through Tribulation, Temptation, and passive Purgation; because that interior Voice of God works innumerable and marvelous Effects in the Soul, which gives place to it, hearkens to it, and relishes it.

It is of so great Efficacy, that it rejects worldly Honor, Self-conceit, Spiritual Ambition, the desire of Fame, a wish to be Great, a presumption of being the only Man, and thinking that he knows all things; it bids adieu to Friends, Friendship, Visits, Letters of Complement, Commerce of the Creature, Interest with Spiritual Children, Mastership, and Business; it turns away too much inclination to Confessor-ship, the Affection that is disordered in the Government of Souls, that makes a man think he is fitting for it; it moves Self-love, Authority, Presumption, treating of Profit, making a show of the Letters which a man writes, showing those writ by his Spiritual children, to make known what a great Workman he is; it turns away the Envy of other Masters and Teachers, and the procuring more Customers to his chair of Confession.

Lastly, this interiors Voice of God in the Soul of Director, begets a mean Value, and Solitariness, and Silence, and Forgetfulness of Friends, Relations and Spiritual Children; because it makes him never remember them, but when they are speaking to him. This is the only sign to know the Disinterestedness of a Master; and therefore such a one doth more good by silent, than thousands of others that make never so great a noise with their infinite Documents.

Chapter Six

Showing how a simple and ready Obedience is the only means of for walking, safely in the inward Way, and of procuring internal Peace.

If you do in good earnest resolve to deny your Will, and do God's Obedience is the necessary means; whether it be by the indissoluble knot of your Vow, made in the hands of your Superior in your Religion, or the free tying of yourself by the Dedication of your Will, to a Spiritual and expert Guide, that has the Qualities sewn before in the precedent Chapters.

You will never get up the Mountain of Perfection, nor to any high Throne of Peace Internal, if you are only governed by your own Will: This cruel and fierce Enemy of God, and of your Soul, must be conquered; your own Direction, your own

Judgment, must be subdued and deposed as Rebels, and reduced to Ashes by the Fire of Obedience: there it will be found, as in a Touch-stone, whether the Love you follow be your own, or Divine; there in that Holocaust must your own Judgment, and your own Will be Annihilated and brought to its last Substance.

An ordinary Life under Obedience, is worth more than that which of its own will does great Penance; because obedience and subjection, besides that they are free from the deceits of Satan, are the truest Holocaust which can be sacrificed to God on the Altar of our Heart. Which made a great Servant of God say, That he had rather gather Dung by Obedience, than be caught up to the third Heaven of his own will.

You will know that Obedience is a ready way to arrive quickly at Perfection: its impossible for a Soul to purchase itself true peace of Heart, if it does not deny and overcome its own judgment and rebellion: And the means of denying and overcoming ones Judgment, is to be willing in everything to obey with resolution, him that stands in God's place; because the Heart remains free, secure, and unburdened by all that which goes from the Mouth, with true Submission, to the Ears of the Spiritual Father. The most effectual means therefore to advance in the way of the Spirit, is to imprint this in the Heart, that a man's spiritual Director stands in God's place, and whatever he orders and says, is said and ordered from the Divine Mouth.

The Lord often-times manifested to that venerable Mother Ann Mary of S. Joseph a Fransciscan Nun; That she should rather obey her spiritual Father, then Himself, To the venerable Sister Catherine Paulucci, the Lord also one day said, You ought to go to your spiritual Father, with pure and sincere Truth, as if you came to Me, and not inquire whether he be or be not Observant, but you should think that he is Governed by the Holy Ghost, and that he is in My stead, adding, When Souls will observe this, I will not permit that any be Deceived by him. O Divine Words worthy to be imprinted in the Hearts of those Souls which desire to advance in Perfection!

God revealed to Lady Marina of Escobar, that if our Lord Christ would have her communicate after his mind, and her spiritual Father should say nay; she was obliged to follow the mind of her spiritual Father: And a Saint was lowered down from Heaven to tell her the reason of it; which was, That in the first there might be Cheat, but in the second none.

The Holy Ghost advises us all in the Proverbs that we take Counsel, and trust not in our own Wisdom. And says by Tobit, That, to do well, you never should govern yourself with your own proper judgment; but always must ask others mind and judgment. Although the spiritual Father Err in giving counsel, you can never Err in taking it, and following it; because you act wisely. And God does not suffer Directors to Err, that he may preserve, although it should be with Miracles, the visible Tribunal of the spiritual Father; from whence is known with all Safety, what is the Divine Will.

Besides, that this is the common Doctrine of all the Saints, of all the Doctors and Masters of Spirit, Christ our Lord gave credit and security to it, when he said, That the spiritual Father should be understood and obeyed just like Himself. And this even when their Works do not correspond with their Words and Counsels; as is manifest by St. Matthew.

The Soul which is observant of holy Obedience, is, as St. Gregory says It is rewarded by God for its Humility and Obedience, illustrating and teaching its own Guide, to whose direction it should (as being in God's place) be every way subject, discovering freely, clearly, faithfully and simply all the thoughts, all the works, inclinations, inspirations, and temptations that it knows of it self: In this manner the Devil cannot deceive it; and it becomes secure of giving an account of its actions to God without fear, as well those actions which it does commit, as those it does omit. Insomuch, that whoever would walk without a Guide, if he is not deceived, he is very near it, because, Temptation will seem Inspiration to him.

You should know, that to be perfect, it is not enough to obey and honor Superiors, but it is also necessary to obey and honor Inferiors.

Obedience therefore, to make it perfect, must be voluntary, pure, ready, cheerful, internal, blind and persevering:

Voluntary, without force and fear: Pure, without worldly interest and respect, or self love, but purely for God: Ready, without reply, excuse or delay: Cheerful, without inward affliction, and with diligence: Internal, because it must not only be exterior and apparent, but from the mind and heart: Blind, without ones own judgment, but submitting that judgment with the will: to his that Commands it, without searching into the Intention, End, or Reason of the Obedience Persevering, with firmness and constancy unto Death.

Obedience (according to St. Bonaventure must be ready, without a delay; Devout with trying, Voluntary without contradiction, Simple, without examination, Persevering without resting; Orderly without breaking off; Pleasant without trouble; Valiant without Faint-heartedness, and Universal without exception. Remember, O blessed Soul! That although you have a mind to do the divine Will, with all diligence, you will never find the way, but by the means of Obedience. When a man is resolved to be governed by himself, he is lost and deceived: Although the Soul have very profound signs, that it is a good Spirit that speaks to it; yet unless it submit to the judgment of the Spiritual Director, let it be esteemed an evil Spirit.

This Doctrine will be confirmed by that case of St. Teresa. The holy Mother, seeing that Lady Catherine of Cordona, led a life of great and rigid Penance in the Wilderness, resolved to imitate her, contrary to the judgment of her spiritual Father, who forbid her; Then the Lord told her You must by no means do this, Daughter; the good way you must secure; you see all the Penance that Catherine does, but I value more your Obedience. She from that time forward, vowed to obey her spiritual Father: and in the 26th. Chapter of her Life, we read, that God often told her, that she must not omit to acquaint her spiritual Father with her whole Soul, and the graces that she had done her, and that she should always take care to obey him in everything.

You see how God has been willing to secure that heavenly and important Doctrine by the holy Scripture, the Saints, the Doctors, by Reasons, and by Examples, a purpose to root out altogether the deceits of the Enemy.

Chapter Seven

When, and in what things this Obedience does most concern the interior Soul.

That you may know when Obedience is most necessary, I will advise you, that when you shall find the horrible and importunate suggestions of the Enemy, greatest upon you, when you shall suffer most darkness, anguish, drought, forsaking, when you shall see yourself most beset with temptations, wrath, rage, blasphemy, lust, cursing, tediousness, despair, impatience, and desolation; then its most necessary for you to believe, and obey an expert Director, resting yourself on his holy Counsel, that you may not suffer yourself to be carried away by the strong persuasion of the Enemy, who would make you believe in affliction, and heavy desertion, that you are lost and abhorred by God, that you are out of his favor, and that Obedience is past doing you any good.

You will find yourself encompassed with troublesome scruples, grief, anguish, distress, martyrdom, distrust, forsaking of the Creatures, and troubles so bitter, that your afflictions shall seem past comfort, and your torments unconquerable. O blessed Soul! how happy will you be, if you do believe your Guide, and subject yourself to him and obey him? Then you will walk safe by the secret and interior way of the dark night, although you may seem to yourself to live in Error, and that you are worse then ever; that you see nothing in your Soul, but abomination and signs of condemnation.

You will think verily, that you are possessed by an evil Spirit; because the signs of this interior exercise, and horrible tribulation, seem as bad as the invasions of infernal Furies and Devils. Then take care to believe your Guide firmly, for your true Happiness consists in your obedience.

You must consider that when the Devil sees a Soul totally denying itself, and submitting to the obedience of its Director, he makes a strange uproar all Hell over to hinder this infinite Good, and this holy Sacrifice: Full of envy and fury as he is, he uses to make strife between the two, inspiring the Soul with weariness, anger, aversion, resistance, distrust, and hatred against the Guide, and sometimes he makes use of his Tongue to bespatter him with many Reproaches; But if this Director be an expert one, he laughs at theses subtle Snares and diabolical Craftiness. And however the Devil may persuade the Souls of such a state, with divers suggestions, not to believe their Director, that they may not obey him, nor profit under him; yet nevertheless they may believe, and they do believe enough to obey, although it be without their own satisfaction.

You will ask of your Guide some Liberty, or will communicate to him some Grace received. If in denying you that Liberty, or rejecting that Grace, that you may not grow proud, you withdraw yourself from his Counsel, and leave him, it is a sign that the Favor was false, and that your spirit walks in danger: But if you do believe and obey, although he do soundly displease you, its a sign that you are alive and un-mortified; nevertheless, you will profit with that violent and working Medicine: because although the inferior part be troubled and do resent, yet the superior part of the Soul does embrace him, and will be humbled and mortified; because it knows that this is the divine Will. And although you do not know it, yet satisction goes on improving in your Soul, and so does the confidence that you have in your Guide.

The means of denying self love, and of laying down ones own judgment, you must know, is subjecting it altogether with true submission to the Counsel of the spiritual Physician. If he hinders you your pleasure, or demands what you desire not, thousands of false and idle reasons do presently get about his holy Counsel; where it is presently known that the Spirit is not altogether mortified, nor his own judgment blinded, which are irreconcilable Enemies to a ready and blind obedience, and the peace of the Soul.

Then its necessary to overcome yourself and your quick sentiments, to despise those false and lying reasons, by obeying, holding your tongue, and executing his holy Counsel, because that is the way to root up your appetite and your own judgment.

For this reason the ancient Fathers, as expert and skilful Masters of Spirit, did exercise their Disciples in divers and extraordinary Ways: To some they gave order to plant lettuce with the leaves downward; to others, to Water dry and withered Trees; to others, to sew and un-sew again, many times, their Cloths; all marvelous and effectual stratagems to make trial of simple obedience and to cut by their roots the weeds of their own Will and Judgment.

Know that you can not fetch one step in the way of the Spirit, till you endeavor to conquer this fierce Enemy, your own judgment: And the Soul that will not know this hurt, can never be cured. A sick man that knows his Disease, knows for certain, that although he is dry, yet it is not good for him to drink, and that the medicine prescribed him, although it be bitter, yet is profitable for him: Therefore he believes not his Appetite, nor trusts in his own Judgment, but yields himself up to a skilful Physician, obeying him in every thing, as the means of his Recovery and Cure: The knowledge that he is sick, helps him not to trust to himself, but to follow the wise judgment of his Doctor.

We are all sick of the Disease of self love, and our own judgment; we are all full of our selves; we are always desiring things hurtful to us; and that which does us good, is unpleasant and irksome to us: Its necessary therefore for him that is Sick, to use the means of Recovery; which is, not to believe our own judgments and distempered sentiments, but the wise Judgment, of the spiritual and skilful Physician, without reply or excuse, despising the seeming reasons of self-love; and so, if we obey, we shall certainly recover, and this love of ours, which is the Enemy of our ease, and peace, and perfection, and the spirit, will be overcome.

How often will your own judgment deceive you? And how much will you change your judgment with shame, when you have trusted to your own self? If any man should deceive you twice or thrice, would you ever trust him more? Why therefore, do you repose confidence in your own judgment, which has so often cozened you? O blessed Soul, believe no more, believe not; subject yourself with true submission and follow blindfold this Obedience.

You will be much satisfied to have an experienced Guide, and will esteem him a great Happiness; but will little avail you, if you value your own judgment more than his Counsel, and do not submit to it in all truth and simplicity.

Suppose a great man be sick of a dangerous Disease: He has in his House a famous and skilful Physician; and he quickly knows the Disease, the causes, the conditions, and the state of it, and knowing for certain that the Distemper is to be treated with severe Cauteries he orders Lenitives for it: Now, is not this a great disorder? If his sure that Lenitives will do little good, and that Cauterizing is the proper way, why does he not apply it to him? Because, although the sick person would have his health, yet the Physician knows best, and that he is not disposed to take those strong Medicines, and therefore like a wise man, orders him gentle Lenitives; because although he may not presently get up again by them , yet he keeps the Disease from being mortal.

What matter is it, if you have the best Director in the World, if yet not withstanding you want true submission? although he be a man of skill and knows the grievance and the remedy, he does not apply the proper treatment, which concerns you most to deny your Will; because he knows your very Heart and Spirit, that it is not disposed to let the infirmities of your own judgment be removed. So you will never be cured, and it will be a Miracle, if he can keep you in Grace, with so fierce an Enemy of your Soul about you.

Your Director will scorn all manner of Favors, if he be a wise man; as if your Spirit may not be well grounded, believe him, obey him, embrace his Counsel, because with this contempt, if the Spirit be feigned and of the Evil One, the secret Pride formed by him that counterfeits these Spirits, will soon be known; but if the Spirit be real: though you find displeasure in this humiliation: it will serve you for an extraordinary good.

If the Soul take delight in esteem, and in having the favors which it receives from God, made open and public; if it does not obey and believes not its Director, which thinks meanly of them, its all a lie and cheat, and the Devil is that Angel that transforms himself. The Soul seeing that the skilful Director despises these cheats, if the Spirit be evil, withdraws the feigned affection, which it showed him, and endeavors by little and little to get from him, seeking some other that its cheats may take with: for the proud can never keep company with those that humble them: but on the other side, if the Spirit be true and of God, by these means the love and constancy increases by enduring them, desiring much more its own contempt, from whence the soundness and sincerity of the Spirit becomes qualified without deceit.

Chapter Eight

Frequent Communion is an effectual means of getting all Virtues, and in particular, Internal Peace.

There are four things the most necessary to get Perfection and internal Peace: The first is Prayer, the second Obedience; the third frequent Communion; the fourth internal Mortification. And now since we have treated of Prayer and Obedience, it will be fitting to treat also of Communion.

You ought to know that many Souls there are that deprive themselves of the infinite benefit of this precious Food, by judging that they are not sufficiently prepared, and that no less than an Angelical Purity is necessary for it. if you have a pure end, a true desire of doing the Will of God, without looking at sensible Devotion, or your own Satisfaction, come with confidence, because you are well disposed.

On this Rock of Desiring to do the Divine will, all difficulties must be broken, all scruples overcome, all temptations, doubts, fears, resistances and contradictions: And although the best Preparation for the Soul, be often Communicating, because one Communion disposes it for another; yet I will show the two ways of Preparation: The first for the exterior Souls which have good Desire and Will. And the second, for Spiritual Ones which live Internally, and have a greater Light and Knowledge of God, of his Mysteries, of his Operations and Sacraments.

The Preparation for the exterior Souls, is to be Confessed and retire from the Creatures, before the Communion to stand still and consider what is to be received, and who is it that receives it, and that he goes to do the greatest business in the World, which is to receive the great God. What a singular favor is that Purity itself condescends to be received by Faith! Majesty by Vileness! The Creator by the Creature!

The second Preparation in order to the interior and spiritual Souls, must be to endeavor to live with greater Purity and Self-denial, with an universal taking ones self off from the World, with an inward Mortification and continual Retirement: and when they walk in this Way, they have no need of any actual preparation, because their Life is a continual and perfect Preparation.

If you do not know these Virtues in your Soul, for the same reason you must often draw near to this Sovereign Table to get them. Never let it hinder you, to see yourself dry, defective and cold; because frequent Communion is the treatment that cures those diseases, and increases Virtue: for the same reason that you are Sick, you must go to the Physician; and that you are Cold to the Fire. If you draw near with humility, with a desire of doing the Divine Will, and with the leave of your Confessor, you may receive it every day, and every day you will grow better and better. Never be afraid for seeing yourself without that affectionate and sensible love, which some men say is necessary: because this sensible affection is not perfect, and ordinarily it is given to weak and nice Souls.

You will say that you feel yourself indisposed, without devotion, without fervor, without the desire of this Divine food, so as to ask how you must frequent it? believe for certain, that none of these things hinder or hurt you, while you preserve this purpose firm, not to sin, and your Will determined to avoid every offence: and if you have confessed all those that you could remember, doubt not but that you are well prepared to come to this Heavenly and Divine Table.

You must know that in this unspeakable Sacrament, Christ is united with the Soul, is made one thing with it, whose fineness and purity is the most profound and admirable, and the most worthy of consideration and thanks. Great was the pureness of him in being made Man; greater that of dying ignominiously on the Cross for our sake, but the giving of himself whole and entire to man in this admirable Sacrament, admits no comparison: This is singular favor, and infinite pureness: because there is no more to give; no more to receive. O that we could but comprehend him! O that we could but know him.

That God being what he is, should be communicated to my Soul! that God should be willing to make a reciprocally of union with it, which of itself is mere misery! O Souls, if we could but feed our selves at this Heavenly Table! O that we could scorch our selves at this burning fire! O that we could become one and the same spirit with this Sovereign Lord! who withholds us? Who deceives us? who takes us off from burning like Salamanders, in the Divine fire of this holy Table?

Its true, O Lord, that you enter into me a miserable creature, but true also it is, that you at the same time remain in your glory and brightness, and in yourself. Receive me therefore O my Jesus, in yourself, in your beauty and Majesty. I am infinitely glad that the vileness of my Soul cannot prejudice your beauty: you enter therefore into me, without going out of yourself; you live in

the midst of your brightness and magnificence, although you are in my darkness and misery.

O my Soul, how great is your vileness! how great your poverty! what is man, Lord, that you are so mindful of him? that you visit him and make him great? What is man, that you putt such an esteem upon him, being willing to have your delights with him and dwell personally with your greatnesses in him? how, O Lord, can a miserable creature receive an infinite Majesty? humble yourself, O my soul, to the very depth of nothing, confess your unworthiness, look upon your misery, and acknowledge the wonders of the Divine Love, which suffers itself to be mean in this incomprehensible Mystery, that it may be communicated and united with you.

O the greatness of love, which the amiable Jesus is, in a small host? who is there subject in some manner to man, giving himself whole and sacrificing himself for him to the Eternal Father! O Sovereign Lord, keep back my heart strongly, that it may never more return to its imperfect liberty, but all annihilated may die to the world, and remain united with you. If you would get all Virtues in the highest degree, come blessed Soul, come with frequency to this most holy Table; for there they do all dwell. Eat, O my Soul, of this Heavenly Food, eat and continue, come with humility, come with Faith to feed of this White and Divine Bread: for this is the Mark of Souls, and from hence Love draws its Arrows, saying, Come, O Soul, and eat this savory Food, if you would get Purity, Charity, Chastity, Light, Strength, Perfection and Peace.

Chapter Nine

Declaring when Spiritual and Corporal Penances ought to be used, and how hurtful they are, when they are done indiscreetly according to ones own Judgment and Opinion.

It is to be known, that there are some Souls who, to make too great advances in Holiness, become much behindhand in it, by doing indiscreet Penances; like those who would sing more than their strength allows them, who strain themselves till they are tired, and instead of doing better, do worse.

Many have fallen into this Precipice, for want of subjecting their judgment to their spiritual Fathers; while they have imagined, that unless they give themselves up to rigid Penances, they never can be Saints, as if sanctity did only consist in them. They say, that he that sows little, reaps little; but they sow no other seed, with their indiscreet Penances, than Self-love, instead of rooting it up.

But the worst of these indiscreet Penances, is, that by the use of these dry and barren Severities, is begotten and naturalized a certain bitterness of heart towards themselves and their neighbors, which is a great stranger to the true Spirit: towards themselves, because they do not feel the sweetness of Christ's

Yoke, the sweetness of Charity, but only the asperity of Penances; whereby their nature becomes embittered; and hence it follows, that such men become exasperated with their Neighbors, to the marking and reproving much their faults, and holding of them for very defective, for the same reason that they see them go a less rigorous way than themselves: hence they grow proud with their exercises of Penance, seeing few that do after them, and thinking themselves better than other folks, whereupon they much fall in the account of their Virtues. Hence comes the envy of others, to see them less penitent and greater favorites of God; a clear proof, that they fixed their confidence in their own proper diligences.

Prayer is the nourishment of the Soul; and the Soul of Prayer is internal mortification: for however bodily Penance, and all other exercises chastening the flesh, be good and holy and praiseworthy, (so as they be moderated by discretion, according to the state and quality of every one, and by the help of the spiritual Director's judgment) yet you will never gain any virtue by these means, but only vanity and the wind of vain-glory, if they do not grow from within. Wherefore now you will know when you are to use most chiefly External Penances.

When the Soul begins to retire from the World and Vice, it ought to tame the body with rigor, that it may be subject to the Spirit and follow the Law of God with ease; then it concerns you to manage the Weapons of Haircloth, Fasting and Discipline, to take from the flesh the roots of sin; but when the Soul enters into the way of the Spirit, embracing internal mortification, corporal chastisements ought to be relaxed, because there is trouble enough in the Spirit: the heart is weakened, the breast suffers, the brain is weary, the whole Body grieved and disabled for the functions of the Soul.

The wise and skillful Director therefore must consider, not to give way to these Souls to perform such excesses of Corporal and External Penance, to whom he moves the great love of God, which they do conceive in the internal, darksome and cleansing retirement of them; because its not good to spend the Body and the Sprit all at once, nor break their strength by rigorous and excessive Penances, seeing they are weakened by internal mortification. For which reason St. Ignatius Loyola said very well in his Exercises, That in the cleansing way, Corporal Penances were necessary, which in the illuminating way ought to be moderated, and much more in the unitive.

But you will say, That the Saints always used grievous Penances. I answer, that they did them not with indiscretion, nor after their own proper judgment, but with the opinion of their Superiors and Spiritual Directors which permitted them to use them, because they knew them to be moved inwardly by the Lord to those rigors, to confound the misery of sinners by their examples, or for many other reasons. Other times they gave them leave to use them to humble the fervor of their Spirit and counterpoise their Raptures; which are all particular Motives and make not any general Rule for all.

Chapter Ten

The great difference between External and Internal Penances.

Know that the Mortifications and Penances which someone undertakes of himself, are light (although they may be the most rigorous, which hitherto have been done) in comparison to those he takes from another's hands: because in the first, he himself enters at his own will, which abate the grief, the more voluntary it is, while at last he does but that which he is willing: But in the second, all that is endured, is painful: and the way also painful, in which it is endured, that is to say, by the will of another.

This is that which Christ our Lord told St. Peter, (St. John 21. 18.) When you were young and a beginner in virtue, you girded and mortified yourself; but when you go to greater Schools, and shall be a proficient in virtue, an other shall gird and mortify you: and then if you will follow me perfectly, altogether denying yourself, you must leave that cross of yours, and take up mine, that is, be contented that another crucify you.

There must be no difference made between these and those, between your Father and your Son, your Friend and your Brother; these must be the first to mortify you, or to rise up against you, whether with reason or without reason, thinking the virtue of your Soul, cheat, hypocrisy or imprudence, and putting stumbling-blocks in the way of your holy Exercises. This, and much more will befall you if you will heartily serve the Lord, and make yourself pure from his hand.

Hold it for certain, that however good those Mortification and External Penances be, which you shall undertake of your own self, you will never by those only purchase perfection: for although they tame the Body, yet they purify not the Soul, nor purge the internal Passions, which do really hinder perfect Contemplation and the Divine Union.

Its very easy to mortify the Body by means of the Spirit; but not the Sprit by means of the Body. True it is, that in Internal Mortification, and that of the Spirit, it much concerns you, for conquering your Passions and rooting up your own Judgment and self-love, to labor even to death, without any manner of sparing your self, although the Soul be in the highest state: and therefore the principal diligence ought to be in Internal Mortification: because Corporal and External Mortification is not enough, though it be good and holy.

Though a man should receive the punishments of all men together, and do the roughest Penances that ever have been done in God's Church, yet if he do not deny himself and mortify himself with interior mortification, he will be far from arriving at perfection.

A good proof of this truth is that which befell Saint Henry Suson, to whom after twenty years of rigorous Hair-cloth, Discipline, and Abstinence so great, that even to read them is enough to make ones hair stand on end, God communicated light by means of an Ecstasy, by which he arrived at the knowledge that he had not yet begun, and it was in such a manner, as that, till the Lord mortified him with temptations and great persecutions, he never could arrive at perfection. Hence you will clearly know the great difference that there is between External and Internal Penances, and Internal and External Mortification.

Chapter Eleven

How the Soul is to carry it self in the Faults it commits, that it may not be disquieted thereby, but reap good out of it.

When you fall into a fault, in what matter so ever it be, do not trouble nor afflict yourself for it: for they are effects of our frail nature, stained by Original Sin; so prone to Evil, that it has a necessity of a most special Grace and Privilege, as the most holy Virgin had, to be free and exempt from Venial Sins.

If when you fall into a fault or a piece of neglect, you do disturb and chide yourself, its a manifest sign, that secret pride does still reign in your soul: did you believe, that you could not more fall into faults and frailties? if God permits some failings even in the most holy and perfect men, it is to leave them some remnant of themselves of the time that they were beginners, to keep them more secure and humble, it is that they may think always, that they are never departed from that state, whilst they still keep upon the faults of their beginnings.

What do you marvel at, if you fall into some light fault or frailty? humble yourself; know your misery and thank God that he has preserved you from infinite sins, into which you might have infallibly fallen, and would have fallen according to your inclination and appetite: What can be expected from the slippery ground of our nature, but stumps, briers and thorns? Its a Miracle of Divine Grace, not to fall every moment into faults innumerable. We should offend all the World, if God should not hold his hand continually over us.

The common enemy will make you believe, that, as soon as you fall into any fault, you do not go well grounded in the way of the Spirit, that you walk in Error, that you have not in earnest reformed yourself, that thou did not make well the general confession, that you have not true grief, and therefore are out of God and of his favor: and if you shall sometimes commit again, by misfortune, a venial fault, how many fears, frights, confusions, discouragements and various discourses will the Devil put into your heart? he will represent to you, that you employ your time in vain; that you do just as much as comes to nothing; that your Prayer does you no good; that you dispose not the self, as you should, to receive the holy Sacrament; that you do not mortify yourself, as you promise to God daily; that Prayer and Communion without Mortification is mere vanity: herewith would he make you distrust of the Divine Grace, telling you of your misery and making a Giant of it, and putting into your head, that every day your Soul grows worse instead of better, while it so often repeats those failings.

O blessed Soul, open your eyes, suffer not yourself to be carried away by the deceitful and gilded tricks of Satan, who seeks your ruin and cowardice with these lying and seeming reasons: Cut off these discourses and considerations, and shut the gate against these vain Thoughts and diabolical Suggestions; lay aside these vain fears, and remove this faint-heartedness, knowing your misery, and trusting in the Mercy Divine: and if tomorrow you fall again, as you did today, trust again the more in that supreme, and more than infinite Goodness, so ready to forget our faults, and receive us into his Arms as dear Children.

At all times therefore you should, when you see yourself in fault, without losing time, or making discourses upon the failing, to drive away vain Fear and Cowardice, without disturbing or chiding yourself, but knowing your fault with Humility, looking on your misery, rolling yourself with a loving confidence on the Lord, going into his presence, asking him Pardon heartily, and without noise of words; keep yourself reposed in doing this, without discoursing whether he has or has not forgiven you, returning to your Exercises and Retirements, as if you have not Sinned.

Would not he be a mere Fool, which running at Tournament with others, and falling in the best of the Career, should lie weeping on the ground, and afflicting himself with discourses upon his fall? Man (they would tell him) loose no time, get up and take the Course again; for he that rises again quickly, and continues his Race, is as if he had never fallen.

If you have a desire to get to a high degree of Perfection and inward Peace, you must use the Weapon of Confidence in the Divine Goodness, night and day, and always when you fall. This humble and loving Conversation, and total Confidence in the Mercy Divine, you must exercise in all faults, imperfections, and failings that you shall commit, either by advertence or inadvertency.

And although you often fall, and see your Pusillanimity, and endeavor to get courage, and afflict not yourself; because what God does not do in forty Years, he sometimes does in an instant, with a particular Mystery, that we may live low and humble, and know that its the Work of his powerful Hand, to free us from Sins.

God also is willing, of ineffable Wisdom, that, not only by Virtues, but also by Vices and the Passions wherewith the Devil seeks and pretends to strike us down to the bottomless Pit, we make a Ladder to scale Heaven with. That we may not make Poison of Medicine, and Vices of Virtues, by becoming vain by them; God would have us make Virtues of Vices, healing us by that very thing which would hurt us.

By means of small failings, the Lord makes us know that his Majesty is that which frees us from great ones; and herewith he keeps us humbled and vigilant; of which our proud Nature has most need: And therefore though you should walk with great care, not to fall into any fault or imperfection, if you see yourself fallen once and a thousand times, you should make use of the Remedy which I have given you, that is, a loving Confidence in the Divine Mercy: These are the Weapons with which you must fight and conquer Cowardice and vain Thoughts: This is the means you should use, not to lose time, not to disturb yourself, and reap good: This is the Treasure wherewith you must enrich your Soul: and lastly, hereby must you get up the high Mountain of Perfection, Tranquility and Internal Peace.

The Third Book

Chapter One

The Difference between the Outward and Inward Man.

There are two sorts of Spiritual Persons, Internal and External: these seek God by without, by Discourse, by Imagination and Consideration: they endeavor mainly to get Virtues, many Abstinences, Maceration of Body, and Mortification of the Senses: they give themselves to rigorous Penance; they put on Sack-cloth, chastise the flesh by Discipline, endeavor silence, bear the presence of God, forming him present to themselves in their Idea of him, or their Imagination, sometimes as a Pastor, sometimes as a Physician, and sometimes as a Father and Lord: they delight to be continually speaking of God, very often making fervent Acts of Love; and all this is Art and Meditation: by this way they desire to be great, and by the power of voluntary and exterior Mortifications, they go in quest of sensible Affections and warm Sentiments, thinking that God resides only in them, when they have them. This is the External Way, and the Way of Beginners, and though it be good, yet there is no arriving at Perfection by it; nay, there is not so much as one step towards it, as Experience shows in many, that after fifty years of this external exercise, are void of God, and full of themselves, having nothing of spiritual Men, but just the name of such.

There are others truly Spiritual, which have passed by the beginnings of the Interior Way which leads to Perfection and Union with God; and to which the Lord called them by his infinite Mercy, from that outward Way, in which before they exercised themselves. These men retired in the inward part of their Souls, with true Resignation into the Hands of God, with a total putting off and forgetting even of themselves; do always go with a raised Spirit to the Presence of the Lord, by the means of pure Faith, without Image, Form or Figure, but with great assurance founded in tranquility and rest Internal: in whose infused meeting and entertainment, the spirit draws with so much force, that it makes the Soul contract inwardly, the Heart, the Body and all the Powers of it.

These Souls, as they are already passed by the interior Mortification, and have been cleansed by God with the Fire of Tribulation, with infinite and horrible Torments, all of them ordained by his hand, and after his way, are Masters of themselves, because they are entirely subdued and denied; which makes them live with great Repose and internal Peace: and although in many occasions they feel Resistance and Temptations, yet they become presently Victorious, because being already Souls of Proof, and endued with Divine Strength, the motions of Passions cannot last long upon them; and although vehement Temptations and troublesome Suggestions of the Enemy may persevere a long time about them, yet they are all conquered with infinite gain; God being he that Fights within them.

These Souls have already procured themselves a great Light, and a true Knowledge of Christ our Lord, both of his Divinity and his Humanity: They exercise this infused Knowledge with a quiet Silence in the inward entertainment, and the superior part of their Souls, with a Spirit free from Images and external Representations, with a love that is pure and stripped of all Creatures; they are raised also from outward Actions to the love of Humanity and Divinity; so much as they enjoy, they forget, and in all of it they find that they love their God with all their Heart and Spirit.

These blessed and sublimated Souls take no pleasure in any thing of the World, but contempt and in being alone, and in being forsaken and forgotten by every body: They live so disinterested and taken off, that though they continually receive many supernatural Graces, yet they are not changed, no not at those inclinations, being just as if they had not received them, keeping always in the in-most of their Hearts a great lowliness and contempt of themselves; always humbled in the depth of their own unworthiness and vileness: In the same manner they are always quiet, serene, and possessed with evenness of mind in Graces and Favors extraordinary, as also in the most rigorous and bitter Torments. There is no News that cheers them; no Success that makes them sad; Tribulation never disturb them; nor the interior, continual and divine Communication make them vain and conceited; they remain always full of holy and filial Fear, in a wonderful Peace, Constancy and Serenity.

In the external Way they take care to do continual Acts of all the Virtues, one after another, to get to the attainment of them: They pretend to purge Imperfections with Industries, proportional to Destruction; they take care to root up Interests, one after another, with a different and contrary Exercise. But though they endeavor never so much, they arrive at nothing: because we cannot do anything which is not Imperfection and Misery.

But in the inward Way and loving Entertainment in the Presence Divine, as the Lord is he that works, Virtue is established, Interests are rooted up, Imperfections are destroyed and Passions removed; which makes the Soul free unexpectedly, and taken off, when occasions are represented, without so much as thinking of the good which God of his infinite Mercy prepared for them.

It must be known that these Souls, though thus Perfect, as they have the true Light of God, yet by it they know profoundly, their own miseries, weakness and imperfections, and what they yet want to arrive at Perfection, towards which they are walking; they are afflicted and abhor themselves; they exercise themselves in a loving fear of God, and contempt of themselves, but with a true Hope in God, and Dis-confidence in themselves. The more they are humbled with true contempt and knowledge of themselves, the more they please God, and arrive at a singular respect and veneration in his Presence. Of all the good Works that they do, and of all that they continually suffer, as well within as without, they make no manner of account before that Divine Presence.

Their continual Exercise is, to enter into themselves, in God, with quiet and silence; because there is his Center, Habitation and Delight. They make a greater account of this interior Retirement, than of speaking of God; they retire into that interior and secret Center of the Soul, to know God and receive his Divine Influence, with fear and loving reverence; if they go out, they go out only to know and despise themselves.

But know that few are the Souls which arrive at this happy State; because few there are that are willing to embrace contempt, and suffer themselves to be Refined and Purified; upon which account, although there are many that enter into this interior Way, yet its a rare thing for a Soul to go on, and not stick upon the entrance. The Lord said to a Soul, "This inward Way is tread by few; its so high a Grace, that none deserves it; few walk in it, because its no other than a Death of the senses; and few there be that are willing so to Die and be Annihilated; in which disposition this so sovereign a Gift is founded."

Herewith you will undeceive yourself, and perfectly know the great difference which there is between the external and internal Way, and how different that Presence of God is which arise from Meditation, from that which is Infused and Supernatural, arising from the interior and infused Entertainment, and from passive Contemplation; and lastly, you will know the great difference which is between the outward and inward Man.

Chapter Two

The means of obtaining Peace Internal, is not the Delight of Sense nor Spiritual Consolation, but the denying of Self-love.

It is the saying of S. Bernard, That to serve God, is nothing else but to do Good and suffer Evil. He that would go to Perfection by the means of sweetness and consolation, is mistaken: You must desire no other Consolation from God, than to end your Life for his sake, in the state of true Obedience and Subjection. Christ our Lord's way was not that of Sweetness and Softness, nor did he invite us to any such, either by his words or Example, when he said, --He that will come after me, let him deny himself, and let him take up his Cross and follow me, The Soul that would be United to Christ, must be conformable to him, following him in the way of suffering.

You will scarce begin to relish the sweetness of Divine Love in Prayer, but the Enemy with his deceitful Craftiness will be kindling in your Heart desires of the Desert and Solitude, that you may without any bodies hindrance spread the sails to continual & delightful Prayer. Open your eyes and consider that this counsel and desire is not conformable to the true counsel of Christ our Lord, who has not invited us to follow the sweetness and comfort of our own Will, but the denying of ourselves: As if he should say, He that will follow me, and come unto Perfection, let him part with his own Will wholly, and leaving all things, let him entirely submit to the Yoke of Obedience and Subjection, by means of Self-denial, which is the truest Cross.

There are many Souls dedicated to God, which receive from his Hand great Thoughts, Visions, and mental Elevations, and yet for all that, the Lord keeps from them, the Grace of working Miracles, understanding hidden Secrets, foretelling future Contingencies, as he communicates these things to other Souls which have constantly gone through Tribulations, Temptations, and the true Cross, in the state of perfect Humility, Obedience and Subjection.

O what a great Happiness is it for a Soul to be subdued and subject! what great Riches is it to be Poor! what a mighty honor to be despised! what a height is it to be beaten down! what a comfort is it to be afflicted! what a credit of knowledge is it to be reputed Ignorant! and finally, what a Happiness of Happiness's is it to be Crucified with Christ! This is that lot which the Apostle gloried, Let others boast in their Riches, Dignities, Delights and Honors; but to us there is no higher honor, than to be denied, despised and crucified with Christ.

But what a grief is this, that scarce is there one Soul which despises spiritual pleasures and is willing to be denied for Christ, embracing his Cross with love, many are they who are called to perfection, but few are they that arrive at it: because they are few who embrace the Cross with patience, constancy, peace and resignation.

To deny ones self in all things, to be subject to another's judgment, to mortify continually all inward passions, to annihilate ones self in all respects, to follow always that which is contrary to ones own will, appetite and judgment, are things that few can do: many are those that teach them, but few are they that practice them.

Many Souls have undertaken, and daily do undertake, this Way; and they persevere all the while they keep the sweet relish of their primitive Fervor; but this sweetness and sensible delight is scarce done, but presently, upon the overtaking of a Storm of Trouble, Temptation and Dryness (which are necessary things to help a man up the high Mountain of Perfection) they falter and turn back: a clear sign that they sought themselves, and not God or Perfection.

May it please God, that the Souls which have had light, and been called to an inward peace, and by not being constant in dryness and tribulation and temptation, have started back may not be cast into outer darkness, with him that had not on him a wedding garment; although he was a servant, for not being disposed, giving himself up to self-love.

This Monster must be vanquished, this seven-headed beast of self-love must be beheaded, in order to get up to the top of the high mountain of peace. This Monster put his head everywhere; sometimes it gets amongst Relations, which strangely hinder with their conversation; to which nature easily let's itself be lead; sometimes it gets with a good look of gratitude, into passionate affection, and without restraint, towards the Confessor; sometimes into affection to most subtle Spiritual vain-glories and temporal ones, and niceties of honor; which things stick very close; sometimes it cleaves to spiritual pleasures, staying even in the gifts of God, and in his graces freely bestowed; sometimes it desires exceedingly the preservation of health, and with disguise, to be used well, and its own proper profit, and conveniences; sometimes it would seem well, with very curious subtitles: and lastly, it cleaves with a notable propensity, to its own proper judgment and opinion in all things; the roots of which are closely fixed in its own will: All these are effects of Self-love, and if they be not denied, impossible it is that a man should ever get up to the height of perfect Contemplation, to the highest, happiness of the loving Union, and the lofty Throne of Peace Internal.

Chapter Three

Of two Spiritual Martyrdoms, wherewith God cleanses the Soul that he unites with Himself.

Now you shall know that God uses two ways for the Cleansing the Souls which he would perfect and enlighten, to unite them closely to himself: The first (of which we will treat in this and the following Chapter) is with the bitter Waters of Afflictions, Anguish, Distress, and inward Torments. The second is, with the burning Fire of an inflamed Love, a Love impatient and hungry: Sometimes he makes use of both in those Souls which he would fill with Perfection; sometimes he puts them into the strong steeping of Tribulations, and inward and outward Bitterness, scorching them with the Fire of rigorous Temptation; sometimes he puts them into the Crucible of anxious and distrustful Love, making them fast there with a mighty force; because so much the greater as the Lord would have the Illumination and Union of a Soul to be, so much the more strong is the Torment and the Purgation; because all the Knowledge and Union with God, arises from suffering, which is the truest proof of Love.

O that you would understand the great Good of Tribulation! This is that which blots out Sins, cleanses the Soul, and produces Patience: this in Prayer inflames it, enlarges it, and puts it upon the exercise of the most sublime act of Charity: this rejoices the Soul, brings it near to God, calls it to, and gives it entrance into Heaven: The same is that which tries the true Servants of God, and renders them sweet, valiant and constant: that is it which makes God hear them with speed. It's that which Annihilates, Refines and Perfects them: and finally, this is that which of Earthly, makes Souls Heavenly, of Humane, Divine, transforming them and uniting them in an admirable manner with the Lord's Humanity and Divinity. It was well said by St. Augustine, That the Life of the Soul, upon Earth is Temptation. Blessed is the Soul which is always opposed, if it does constantly resist Temptation. This is the means which the Lord makes use of to Humble it, to Annihilate it, to Spend it, to Mortify it, to Deny it, to Perfect it, and fill it with this Divine Gifts: By this means of Tribulation and Temptation he comes to Crown and Transform it. Persuade yourself that Temptations and Fightings are necessary for the Soul, to make it Perfect.

O blessed Soul, if you know how to be constant and quiet in the Fire of Tribulation, and would but let yourself be washed with the bitter Waters of Affliction, how quickly would you find yourself rich in heavenly Gifts; how soon would the Divine Bounty make a rich Throne in your Soul, and a goodly Habitation for you to refresh and solace yourself in it!

Know that this Lord has his repose no where but in quiet Souls, and in those in which the Fire of Tribulation and Temptation has burnt up the dregs of Passion, and the bitter Water of Afflictions have washed off the filthy spots of inordinate Appetites; in a word, this Lord reposes not himself any where, but where Quietness reigns, and Self-love is banished.

But you will never arrive at this happy State, nor find in your Soul the precious Pledge of Peace Internal, although you have gotten the better of the External Senses by the Grace of God, till it become purified from the disordered Passions of Concupiscence, Self-esteem Desire and Thoughts, how spiritual so ever, and many other Interests and secret Vices, which lye within the very Soul of you, miserably hindering the peaceable entrance of that great Lord into it, who would be united and transformed with you.

The very Virtues acquired, and not purified, are a hindrance to this great Gift of the Peace of the Soul: and more, the Soul is clogged by an inordinate desire of sublime Gifts, by the Appetite of feeling spiritual Consolation, by sticking to Infused and Divine Graces, entertaining itself in them, and desiring more of them, to enjoy them, and finally, by a desire of begin great.

O how much is there to be purified in a Soul that must arrive at the holy Mountain of Perfection, and of Transformation with God! O how disposed, naked, denied, annihilated ought the Soul to be, which would not hinder the entrance of this Divine Lord into it, nor his continual Communication.

This disposition of preparing the Soul, in its bottom, for Divine Entrance, must of necessity be made by the Divine Wisdom. If a Seraphim is not sufficient to purify the Soul, how shall a Soul that is frail miserable and without experience, ever be able to purify it self?

Therefore the Lord himself will dispose you and prepare you passively by a way you understand not, with the Fire of Tribulation and inward Torment, without any other disposition on your side, than a consent to the internal and external Cross.

You will find within yourself a passive dryness, darkness, anguish, contradictions, continual resistance, inward desertions, horrible desolations, continual and strong suggestions, and vehement temptations of the Enemy; finally, you will see yourself so afflicted, that you will not be able to lift up your Heart, being full of sorrow and heaviness, nor do the least act of Faith, Hope or Charity.

Here you will see yourself forlorn and subject to Passions of impatience, anger, rage, swearing, and disordered appetites, seeming to yourself the most miserable Creature, the greatest Sinner in the World, the most abhorred of God, deprived and stripped of all Virtue, with a pain like that of Hell, seeing yourself afflicted and desolate, to think that you have altogether lost God; this will be your cruel cutting and most bitter torment.

But though you shall see yourself so oppressed, seeming to yourself to be proud, impatient and wrathful; yet these temptations shall lose their force and power upon you, they shall have no place in your Soul, by a secret Virtue, the sovereign Gift of inward Strength, which rules in the in-most part of it, conquering the most frightening punishment and pain, and the strongest temptation.

Keep constant, O blessed Soul, keep constant; for it will not be as you imagine, nor are you at any time nearer to God, than in such cases of desertion; for although the Sun is hid in the Clouds, yet it changes not its place, nor a jot the more loses its brightness. The Lord permits this painful desertion in your Soul, to purge and polish you, to cleanse you and disrobe you of yourself; and that you may in this manner be all his, and give yourself wholly up to him, as his infinite Bounty is entirely given to you, that you may be his delight; for although you groan, and lament, and weep, yet he is joyful and glad in the most secret and hidden place of your Soul.

Chapter Four

How important and necessary it is, to the interior Soul, to suffer blindfold this first and Spiritual Martyrdom.

To the end that the Soul of Earthly may become Heavenly, and may come to that greatest good of Union with God, it is necessary for it to be purified in the Fire of Tribulation and Temptation: And although it be true, and a known and approved Maxim, That all those that Serve the Lord, must suffer troubles, persecutions and tribulations: yet the happy Souls which are Guided by God, by the secret way of the interior Walk, and of purgative Contemplation, must suffer above all, strong and horrible Temptations and Torments, more bitter than those wherewith the Martyrs were crowned in the Primitive Church.

The Martyrs, besides the shortness of their Torment, which hardly endured days, were comforted, with a clear light and special help, in hope of the near and sure Rewards. But the desolate Soul that must dye in it self, and put off, and make clean its Heart, seeing it self abandoned by God, surrounded by temptations, darkness, anguish, affliction, sorrows and rigid droughts, does taste of Death every moment in its painful Torment and tremendous Desolation, without feeling the least comfort, with an affliction so great, that the pain of it seems nothing else but a Death prolonged, and a continual Martyrdom: wherein with great reason it may be said, that although there be many Martyrs, yet there are few Souls which follow Christ our Lord with Peace and Resignation in such Torments.

Then it was men that Martyred them; and God comforted their Souls: but now it is God that afflicts and hides himself; and the Devils, like cruel Executioners, have a thousand ways to torment the Soul and Body, the whole Man being Crucified within and without.

Your sorrows will seem to you insuperable, and your afflictions past the power of comfort, and that Heaven rains no more upon you: you will feel yourself begirt with grief, and besieged with sorrows Internal, from the darkness of your powers, from the weakness of discourses: strong Temptations will afflict you, painful distrusts and troublesome scruples; nay Light and Judgment will forsake you.

All the Creatures will give you trouble; spiritual Counsels will bring you pain; the reading of Books, how holy so ever, will not comfort you, as it used to do: If they speak to you of Patience, they will exceedingly trouble you: the fear of losing God through your unthankful ness and want of returns, will torment you to the Soul; if you groan and beg help of God, you will find, instead of comfort, inward reproof and disfavor; like another Canaanitish Woman, to whom he made no answer at first, and then treated her as the Creature he was speaking of [* here Molinos is beside his Text.]

And although at this time the Lord will not abandon you, because it would be impossible to live one moment without his help, yet the succor will be so secret that your Soul will not know it, nor be capable of hope and consolation; nay, it will seem to be without remedy; suffering, like condemned persons, the pains of Hell, and it would change them, as such, with a violent Death, which would be a great comfort; but (like those) the end of those afflictions and bitter nesses will seem impossible.

But if you, O blessed Soul, should know how much you are beloved and defended by that Divine Lord, in the midst of your living torments, you would find them so sweet, that it would be necessary that God should work a Miracle, to let you live. Be constant, O happy Soul, be constant and of good courage; for however intolerable you are to yourself, yet you will be protected, enriched, and beloved by that greatest Good, as if he had nothing else to do, than to lead you to Perfection, by the highest steps of love: and if you do not turn away but persevere constantly, without leaving off your undertaking, know, that you offer to God the most accepted Sacrifice; so, that if this Lord were capable of pain, he would find no ease till he has completed this loving Union with your Soul.

If from the Chaos of Nothing, his Omnipotence has produced so many wonders, what will he do in your Soul, created after his own Image and Likeness, if you keep constant quiet, and resigned, with a true knowledge of your Nothing? Happy Soul, which, even when its disturbed, afflicted and disconsolated, keeps steady there within, without going forth to declare exterior Comfort.

Afflict not yourself too much, and with inquietude, because these sharp Martyrdoms may continue; persevere in Humility, and go not out of yourself to seek aid; for all the good consists in being silent, suffering, and holding patience with rest and resignation: there will you find the Divine strength to overcome so hard a warfare: he is within you that fights for you: and he is strength itself.

When you shall come to this painful state of fearful desolation, weeping and lamentation are not forbidden your Soul, while in the upper part of it, it keeps resigned. Who can bear the Lord's heavy hand without tears and Lamentation? That great Champion Job, even he lamented; so did Christ our Lord, in his forsaking: but their weeping was accompanied with resignation.

Afflict not yourself, though God do crucify you and make trial of your fidelity; imitate the Woman of Canaan, who being rejected and injured, did importune and persevere, humbling herself and following him, though she were treated as she was. It is necessary to drink the cup and not go back: if the scales were taken from your eyes, as they were from St. Paul's, you would see the necessity of suffering and glory, as he did; esteeming more the being Crucified, than being an Apostle.

Your good luck consists not in enjoying, but in suffering with quiet and resignation. St. Teresa appeared after her death to a certain Soul, and told it, that she had only been rewarded for her pain; but had not received one dram of reward for so many Ecstasies and Revelations and Comforts that she had here enjoyed in this World.

Although this painful martyrdom of horrible desolation and passive purgation be so tremendous, that with reason it has gotten the name of Hell amongst mystic Divines, (because it seems impossible to be able to live a moment with so grievous a torment; so that with great reason it may be said, that he that suffers it, lives dying, and dying lives a lingering death) yet know, that it is necessary to endure it, to arrive at the sweet, joyous and abundant riches of high contemplation and loving union: and there has been no holy Soul, which has not passed through this spiritual martyrdom and painful torment. St. Gregory the Pope, in the two last Months of his Life; St. Francis of Assize two years and a half; St. Mary Maudlin of Pazzi five years; St. Rose of Peru fifteen years; and after such miracles, as made the world amazed, St. Dominick suffered it even till half an hour of his happy exit.

Chapter Five

The other more profitable and meritorious martyrdom in Souls already advanced in perfection and deep contemplation, is a fire of divine love, which burns the soul and makes it painful with the same love: sometimes the absence of its beloved afflicts it; sometimes the sweet, ardent and welcome weight of the loving and divine Presence torments it: This sweet martyrdom always makes it sigh sometimes if it enjoys and has its beloved, for the pleasure of having him; so that it cannot contain itself; other times, if he does not manifest himself, through the ardent anxiety of seeking, finding and enjoying him: all this is panting, suffering and dying for love.

O that you could but come to conceive the contrariety of accidents that an enamored Soul suffers! the combat so terrible and strong on one side; so sweet and melting and amiable on the other! the martyrdom so piercing and sharp with which love torments it; and the cross so painful and sweet withal, without ever being in the mind of getting free from it while you live!

Just so much as light and love increases, just so much increases the grief in seeing that good absent, which it loves so well. To feel it near itself is enjoyment; and never to have done knowing and possessing, it, consumes its life: it has food and drink near its mouth, while it wants either, and cannot be satisfied: it sees itself swallowed up and drowned in a sea of love, while the powerful hand that is able to save it, is near it; and yet does not do it; nor does it know when he will come, who it so much does desire.

Sometimes it hears the inward voice of its beloved, which courts and calls it; and a soft and delicate whisper, which goes forth from the secret of the Soul, where it abides, which pierces it strongly, even like to melt and dissolve it, in seeing how near it has him within itself, and yet how far off from it, while it cannot come to possess him. This intoxicates it, brings it lower, scares it, and fills it with an unsatisfied feeling: and therefore love is said to be as strong as death, while it kills just as that does.

Chapter Six

Inward Mortification and Perfect Resignation are necessary for obtaining Internal Peace.

The most subtle Arrow that is shot at us from Nature, is, to induce us to that which is unlawful, with a pretence, that it may be necessary and useful. O how many Souls have suffered themselves to be lead away, and have lost the spirit by this Cheat! You will never taste the delicious Manna unless you perfectly overcome yourself even to die in yourself; because he who endeavors not to die to his Passions, is not well disposed to receive the Gift of Understanding, without the infusion whereof it is impossible for him to go into himself and be changed in his Spirit; and therefore those that keep without having nothing of it.

Never disquiet yourself for any accident: for inquietude is the door by which the Enemy gets into the Soul to rob it of its peace. Resign and deny yourself wholly; for though true self-denial is harsh at the beginning, its easy in the middle and becomes most sweet in the end. You will find yourself far from Perfection, if you do not find God in every thing. Know that pure, perfect and essential Love consists in the Cross, in self-denial and resignation, in perfect humility, in poverty of spirit, and in a mean opinion of yourself. In the time of strong temptation, desertion and desolation, its necessary for you to get close into your center, that you may only look at and contemplate God, who keeps his throne and his abode in the bottom of your Soul.

You will find impatience and bitterness of heart to grow from the depth of sensible, empty and mortified love. True love is known, with its effects, when the Soul is profoundly humbled, and desires to be truly mortified and despised. Many there be, who, however they have been dedicated to Prayer, yet have no relish of God; because in the end of their Prayers, they are neither mortified nor attend upon God any longer: for obtaining that peaceable and continual attending, its necessary to get a great purity of mind and heart, great peace of soul, and an universal resignation. To the simple and the mortified, the recreation of the senses is a sort of death: they never go to it, unless compelled by necessity and edification of their neighbors.

The bottom of our soul, you will know, is the place of our happiness. There the Lord shows us wonders: there we engulf and lose our selves in the immense ocean of his infinite goodness, in which we keep fixed and unmovable. There, there resides the incomparable fruition of our Soul and that eminent and sweet rest of it. A humble and resigned Soul, which is come to this bottom, seeks no more than merely to please God, and the holy and loving spirit teaches it every thing with his sweet and enlivening unction.

Amongst the Saints there are some gigantic ones, who continually suffer with patience indispositions of body, of which God takes great care. But high and sovereign is their gift, who by the strength of the Holy Ghost, suffer both internal and external crosses with content and resignation. This is that sort of holiness so much the more rare, as it is more precious in the sight of God. The spiritual ones, which walk this way, are rare: because there are few in the world, who do totally deny themselves, to follow Christ crucified, with simpleness and bareness of spirit, through the lonesome and thorny ways of the Cross, without making reflexions upon themselves.

A Life of Self denial is above all the Miracles of the Saints; and it does not know whether it be alive or dead; lost or gained; whether it agrees or resists: this is the true resigned Life. But although it should be a long time before you come to this state, and you should think not to have made one step towards it, yet affright not yourself at this, for God uses to bestow upon a Soul that Blessing in one moment, which was denied it for many years before.

He that desires to suffer blindfold, without the comfort of God or the creatures, is gotten too far onwards to be able to resist unjust accusations which his enemies make against him, even in the most dreadful and interior desolation. The spiritual man that lives by God, and in him, is inwardly contented in the midst of his adversities; because the Cross and Affliction are his Life and Delight.

Tribulation is a great treasure, wherewith God honors those that be his, in this life: therefore evil men are necessary for those that are good; and so are the Devils themselves, which by afflicting us do try to ruin us: but instead of doing us harm, they do us the greatest good imaginable. There must be tribulation to make a man's life acceptable to God; without it, it's like the Body without the Soul, the Soul without Grace, the Earth without the Sun. With the wind of tribulation God separates, in the floor of the Soul, the Chaff from the Corn.

When God crucifies in the inmost part of the Soul, no creature is able to comfort it; nay, comforts are but grievous and bitter crosses to it. And if it be well-instructed in the laws and discipline of the ways of pure love, in the time of great desolation and inward troubles, it ought not to seek abroad among the creatures for comfort, nor lament itself with them, nor will it be able to read Spiritual Books: because this is a secret way of getting at a distance from suffering. Those Souls are to be pitied, who cannot find in their hearts to believe, that Tribulation and Suffering is their greatest Blessing. They who are perfect ought always to be desirous of dying and suffering, being always in a state of death and suffering: vain is the man who does not suffer: because he is born to toil and suffering; but much more the Friends and Elect of God.

Undeceive yourself, and believe, that in order for your Soul's being totally transformed with God, it is necessary for it to be lost and be denied in its life, sense, knowledge, and power; and to die living, and not living; dying, and not dying; suffering, and not suffering; resigning up, and not resigning up itself, without reflecting upon any thing. Perfection, in its followers, receives not its glories but by Fire and Martyrdom, Grief, Torment, Punishment and Contempt, suffered and endured with gallantry and courage; and he that would have some place to set his feet on and rest himself, and does not go beyond the reason of reason and of sense, will never get into the secret cabinet of knowledge, though by reading he may chance to get a taste and relish the understanding of it.

You must know, that the Lord will not manifest himself in your Soul, till it be denied in itself, and dead in its senses and powers: nor will it ever come to this state, till being perfectly resigned, it resolves to be with God all alone; making an equal account of Gifts and Contempt, Light and Darkness, Peace and War. In summary, that the Soul may arrive at perfect quietness and supreme internal peace, it ought first to die in itself, and live only in God and for him: and the more dead it shall be in itself, the more shall it know God: but if it does not mind this continual denying of itself and internal mortification, it will never arrive at this state, nor preserve God within it; and then it will be continually subject to accidents and passions of the mind, such as are judging, murmuring, resenting, excusing, defending, to keep its honor and reputation, which are enemies to Perfection, Peace, and the Spirit.

Know that the diversity of states amongst those that be spiritual, consists only in dying all alike; but in the happy, which die continually, God has his honor, his blessing and delights here below. Great is the difference which is between doing, suffering, and dying; doing is delightful and belongs to beginners; suffering, with desire, belongs to those who are proficient; dying always in themselves, belongs to those who are accomplished and perfect; of which number there are very few in the world. How happy will you be, if you have no other thought, but to die in yourself! you will then become not only victorious over your enemies, but also over yourself: in which victory you will certainly find pure love, perfect peace, and divine wisdom. It is impossible for a man to be able to think and live mystically in a simple understanding of the divine and infused wisdom, if he does not first die in himself by the total denying of sense, and the reasonable appetite.

The true lesson of the spiritual man, and that which you should learn, is, to leave all things in their place, and not meddle with any, but what your office may bind you to: because the Soul which leaves every thing to find God, does then begin to have all in the eternity it seeks. Some Souls there are, who seek repose: others without seeking have the pleasure of it; others have a pleasure in pain; and others seek it. The first do as good as nothing; the second are in the way towards it; the third run, and the last fly. The disesteem of delights, and the counting of them torment, is the property of a truly mortified man.

Enjoyment and Internal Peace are the Fruits of the Spirit Divine; and no man gets them into his possession, if in the closet of his soul he is not a resigned man. You see that the displeasures of the good pass presently away; but for all that endeavor never to have them, nor to stop in them: for they damage your health, disturb your reason, and disquiet your spirit.

Amongst other holy Counsels which you must observe, remember well this that follows: Look not upon other men's faults, but your own: keep silence with a continued internal conversation: mortify yourself in all things and at all hours, and by this means you will get free from many imperfections, and make yourself Commander of great Virtues. Mortify yourself in not judging ill of any body at any time; because the suspicion of your neighbor disturbs the purity of heart, discomposes it, brings the Soul out and takes away its repose.

Never will you have perfect resignation, if you mind humane respects, and reflect upon the little idol of what people say. The Soul that goes by the inward way, will soon lose itself, if once it come to look at reason amongst the creatures, and in commerce and conversation with them. There is no other reason, than not to look at reason; but to imagine that God permits grievances to fall on us, to humble and annihilate us and make us live wholly resigned. Behold how God makes greater account of a Soul that lives internally resigned, than of another that does miracles, even to the raising of the dead. Many Souls there are, which, though they exercise Prayer, yet because they are not mortified, are always imperfect and full of self-love.

Hold it for a true maxim, that nobody can do a grievance or injury to a Soul despised by itself, and one that is nothing in its own account. Finally, be of hope, suffer, be silent, and patient: let nothing affright you: all of it will have a time to end: God only is he that is unchangeable: patience brings a man in every thing. He that has God, has all things; and he that has him not, has nothing.

Chapter Seven

For the obtaining of Internal Peace, it's necessary for the Soul to know its misery.

If the Soul should not fall into some faults, it would never come to understand its own misery, though it hears men speak and reads spiritual Books; nor can it ever obtain precious peace, if it do not first know its own miserable weakness: because there the remedy is difficult, where there is no clear knowledge of the defect. God will suffer in you sometimes one fault, sometimes another, that by this knowledge of yourself, seeing you so often fallen, you may believe that you are a mere nothing; in which knowledge and belief true peace and perfect humility is founded:

and that you may the better search into your mystery and see what you are, I will try to undeceive you in some of your manifold imperfections.

You are so quick and nice, that it may be if you do but trip as you walk or find your way molested, you feel even Hell itself: if you are denied your due or your pleasure opposed, you presently briskest up with a warm resentment of it. If though spy a fault in your neighbor, instead of pitying him, and thinking that you are liable to the same failing, you indiscreetly reprove him; if you see a thing convenient for you and can not compass it, you grow sad and full of sorrow; if you receive a slight injury from your neighbor, you chide at him and complain for it: insomuch that for any trifle you are inwardly and outwardly discomposed and lose yourself.

You would be penitent, but with another's patience; and if the impatience still continues, you lay the fault with much pains upon your companion, without considering, that you are intolerable to yourself: and when the rancor is over, you cunningly return to make yourself virtuous, giving documents and relating spiritual sayings with artifice of wit, without mending your past faults. Although you willingly condemn yourself, reproving your faults before others, yet this you do more to justify yourself with him that sees your faults, that you may return again afresh to the former esteem of yourself, than through any effect of perfect humility.

Other times you subtly allege, that is it not through fault but zeal of justice, that you complain of your neighbor. You believe for the most part that you are virtuous, constant and courageous, even to the giving up your life into the tyrant's hand, solely for the sake of divine love; yet you can't scarce hear the least word of anger but presently you afflict and trouble and disquiet yourself. These are all industrious engines of self-love and the secret pride of your soul. Know therefore that self-love reigns in you, and that from purchasing this precious peace, that is your greatest hindrance.

Chapter Eight

In which is showed and discovered what is the false humility, and what the true; with the effects of them.

94. You must know that there are two sorts of humility; one false and counterfeit, the other true. The false one is theirs, who, like water which must mount upward, receive an external fall and artificial submission, to rise up again immediately. These avoid esteem and honor, that so they may be took to be humble; they say of themselves, that they are very evil, that they may be thought good; and though they know their own misery, yet they are loath that other folks should know it. This is dissembled humility, and feigned, and nothing but secret pride.

Theirs is the true humility, which have gotten a perfect habit of it; these never think of it, but judge humbly of themselves; they do things with courage and patience; they live and dye in God; they mind not themselves nor the Creatures; they are constant and quiet in all things; they suffer molestation with joy, desiring more of it, that they may imitate their dear and despised Jesus; they covet to be reputed trifles and sport by the World; they are contented with what God allots them, and are convinced of their faults with a pleasing shame; they are not humbled by the counsel of Reason, but by the affection of the Will; there is no honor that they look after, nor injury to disturb them.; no trouble to vex them; no prosperity to make them proud; because they are always immovable in their Nothing, and in themselves with absolute peace.

And that you may be acquainted with interior and true Humility, know, that it does not consist in external Acts, in taking the lowest place, in going poor in clothes, in speaking submissively, in shutting the eyes, in affectionate sighing, nor in condemning your ways, calling yourself miserable, to give others to understand that you are humble: It consists only in the contempt of yourself, and the desire to be despised, with a low and profound knowledge, without concerning yourself, whether you are esteemed humble or no, though an Angel should reveal such a thing to you.

The torrent of Light wherewith the Lord with his Graces enlightens the soul, does two things: It discovers the Greatness of God, and at the same time the Soul knows its own stench and misery, insomuch, that no Tongue is able to express the depth in which it is overwhelmed, being desirous that every one should know its Humility, and its so far from vain-glory and Complacency, as it sees that Grace of God to be the mere Goodness of him, and nothing but his Mercy, which is pleased to take pity on it.

You shall never be hurt by Men or Devils, but by yourself, your own proper Pride, and the violence of your Passions; take heed of yourself, for you are the greatest Devil of all to yourself. Have no Mind to be esteemed, when God incarnate was called Fool, Drunkard, and said to have a Devil. O the Folly of Christians! that we should be willing to enjoy Happiness, without being willing to imitate him on the Cross, in Reproaches, Humility, Poverty, and in other Virtues! The truly humble Man is at rest and ease in his Heart; there he stands the Trial of God, and Men, and the Devil himself, above all reason and discretion possessing himself in Peace and Quietness, looking for, with all Humility, the pure pleasure of God, as well in Life as Death: Things without do no more disquiet him, than if they never were. The Cross to him, and even Death itself, are Delights, though he make no such show outwardly: But oh! who do we speak of? for few there are of these sort of humble Men in the whole World! Hope you, and desire, and suffer, and die without any Bodies knowing it; for herein consists the humbler and perfect Love. O how much Peace will you find in your Soul, if you profoundly humble yourself, and even hug Contempt! You will never be perfectly humble, though you know your own Misery, unless you desire that all Men should know it: then you will avoid Praises, embrace Injuries, despise every thing, that makes a fair show, even to your own self: and if any Tribulation come upon you, blame none for it; but Judge that it comes from God's Hand, as the Giver of every Good.

If you would bear your Neighbors faults, cast your Eyes upon your own: and if you think to yourself, that you have made any Progress in Perfection by yourself, know that you are not humble at all, nor have yet made one step in the way of the Spirit. The degrees of Humility, are the qualities of a Body in the Grave; that is, to be in the lowest place, buried like one that's dead, to stink, and be corrupted to itself, to be dust, and nothing in ones own account; finally, if you would be Blessed, learn to despise yourself, and to be despised by others.

Chapter Nine

Maxims to know a simple, humble, and true Heart.

Encourage yourself to be Humble, embracing Tribulations as Instruments of your Good; rejoice in Contempt, and desire that God may be your only Refuge, Comfort and Protector. None, let him be never so great in this World, can be greater than he that is in the eye and favor of God: and therefore the truly humble Man despises whatever there is in the World, even to himself, and puts his only trust and repose in God. The truly humble Man suffers quietly and patiently internal troubles, and he is the Man that makes great way in a little time, like one that sails before the Wind.

The truly humble Man finds God in all things; so that whatever contempt, injury or affront comes to him by means of the Creatures, he receives it with great peace and quiet Internal, as sent from the Divine Hand, and loves greatly the instrument with which the Lord tries him. He is not yet arrived at profound Humility that is taken with Praise, though he does not desire it, nor seek it, but rather avoids it: because to a humble Heart praises are bitter crosses although it be wholly quiet and immovable. He has no internal Humility who does not abhor himself, with a mortal, but withal a peaceable and quiet hatred: But he will never come to possess this treasure, that has not a low and profound knowledge of his own vileness, rottenness and misery.

He that is upon excuses and replies, has not a simple and humble heart, especially if he does this with his Superiors: because replies grow from a secret pride that reigns in the Soul; and from thence the total ruin of it. Perfidiousness supposes little submission, and this less humility; and both together they are the fuel of inquietude, discord and disturbance.

The humble heart is not disquieted by imperfections, though these do grieve it to the Soul; because they are against its loving Lord: nor is he concerned that he cannot do great things; for he always stands in his own Nothing and Misery; nay, he wonders at himself, that he can do anything of Virtue, and presently thanks the Lord for it, with a true knowledge that it is God that does all, and remains dissatisfied with what he does himself.

The truly humble man, though he see all, yet he looks upon nothing to judge it, because he judge ill only of himself. The truly humble man does always find an excuse to defend him that mortifies him, and least in a sound intention: Who therefore would be angry with a Man of good intention? So much (nay more) does false humility displease God, as true Pride does; because that is Hypocrisy besides. The truly humble Man, though every thing falls out contrary to him, is neither disquieted nor afflicted at it; because he is prepared, and thinks he deserves no less; he is not disquieted under troublesome Thoughts, wherewith the Devil seeks to torment him, nor under temptations, tribulations and desertions, but rather acknowledges his unworthiness, and is affected that the Lord chastises him by the Devil's means, though he be a vile instrument; all he suffers seems nothing to him, and he never does a thing that he thinks worth any great matter.

He that is arrived at perfect and inward Humility, although he be disturbed at nothing, as one that abhors himself, because he knows his imperfection in every thing, his ingratitude and his misery, yet he suffers a great Cross in enduring himself. This is the sign to know true humility of Heart by. But the happy Soul which is gotten to this holy hatred of itself, lives overwhelmed, drowned and swallowed up in the depth of its own Nothing; out of which the Lord raises him by communicating Divine Wisdom to him, and filling him with Light, Peace, Tranquility and Love.

Chapter Ten

Inward solitude is that which chiefly brings a Man to the purchase of Internal Peace.

Know that although exterior Solitude does much assist for the obtaining internal Peace, yet the Lord did not mean this, when he spoke by his Prophet, I will bring her into solitude, and speak privately to her: But he meant the interior Solitude, which jointly conduces to the obtaining the precious Jewel of Peace Internal. Internal Solitude consists in the forgetting all the Creatures, in disengaging ones self from them, in a perfect nakedness of all the affections, desires, thoughts, and ones own will. This is the true Solitude where the Soul reposes with a sweet and inward serenity in the arms of its greatest good.

O what infinite room is there in a Soul that is arrived at this divine Solitude! O what inward, what retired, what secret, what spacious, what vast distances are there within a happy Soul that is once come to be truly Solitary! There the Lord converses and communicates himself, inwardly with the Soul: there he fills it with himself, because it is empty; clothes it with Light, and with his Love, because it is naked; lifts it up, because its low; and unites it with himself, and transforms it, because it is alone.

O delightful Solitude, and Giver of eternal Blessings! O Mirror, in which the eternal Father is always beheld! There is great reason to call you Solitude; for you are so much alone, that there is scarce a Soul that looks after you, that loves and knows you. O Divine Lord! How is it that Souls do not go from Earth to this Glory! How come they to lose so great a good, through the only love and desire of created things! Blessed Soul, how happy will you be, if you but leave all for God! seek him only, breathe after none but him, let him only have your sighs. Desire nothing, and then nothing can trouble you; and if you desire any good, how spiritual so ever it be, let it be in such a manner, that you may not be disquieted, if you miss it.

If, with this liberty, you will give your Soul to God, taken off from the World, free and alone, you will be the happiest creature upon Earth; because the most High has his secret habitation in this holy Solitude; in this Desert and Paradise, is enjoyed the conversation of God, and it is only in this internal Retirement that that marvelous, powerful and divine Voice is heard. If you would enter into this Heaven of Earth, forget every care and every thought; get out of yourself, that the love of God may live in your Soul.

Live as much as ever you can, abstracted from the Creatures; dedicate yourself wholly to your Creator, and offer yourself in Sacrifice with Peace and quietness of Spirit: Know, that the more the Soul disrobes itself, the more way it makes into this interior Solitude, and becomes clothed with God, and the more lonesome and empty of itself the Soul gets to be, the more the divine Spirit fills it.

There is not a more blessed Life than a solitary one; because in this happy Life, God gives himself all to the Creature, and the Creature all to God by an intimate and sweet union of Love. O how few are there that come to relish this true Solitude! To make the Soul truly Solitary, it ought to forget all the Creatures, and even itself; otherwise it will never be able to make any near approach to God. Many men leave and forsake all things, but they do not leave their own liking, their own will, and themselves; and therefore these truly solitary ones are so few; wherefore if the Soul does not get off from its own Appetite and Desire, from its own will, from spiritual Gifts, and from repose even in the Spirit itself, it never can arrive at this high felicity of internal Solitude. Go on, blessed Soul! go on, without stop, towards this blessedness of internal Solitude: See how God calls you to enter into your inward Center, where he will renew you, change you, fill you, cloth you, and show you a new and Heavenly Kingdom, full of joy, peace, content and serenity.

Chapter Eleven

In which is showed what infused and passive Contemplation, is, and its wonderful Effects.

You must know, that when once the Soul is habituated to internal Recollection, and acquired Contemplation, that we have spoken of; when once its mortified, and desires wholly to be denied its Appetites; when once it efficaciously embraces internal and external Mortification, and is willing to die heartily to its passions and its own ways, then God uses to take it alone by itself, and raise it more then it knows, to a complete repose, where he sweetly and inwardly infuses in it his Light, his Love and his Strength, in kindling and inflaming it with a true disposition to all manner of Virtue.

There the Divine Spouse, suspending its Powers, puts it to sleep in a most sweet and pleasant rest: There it sleeps, and quietly receives and enjoys (without knowing it) what it enjoys, with a most lovely and charming Calm: There the Soul raised and lifted up to this passive State, becomes united to its greatest Good, without costing it any trouble or pains for this Union: There in that supreme Region, and sacred Temple of the Soul, that greatest Good takes its Complacency, manifests itself, and creates a relish from the Creature, in a way above Sense and all humane understanding: There also only the pure Spirit, who is God, (the purity of the Soul being incapable of sensible things) rules it, and gets the mastership of it, communicating to it its illustrations, and those Sentiments which are necessary for the most pure and perfect Union.

The Soul coming to itself again from these sweet and divine Embracings, becomes rich in light and love, and a mighty esteem of the divine Greatness, and the knowledge of its own Misery, finding itself all changed divinely, and disposed to embrace, to suffer, and to practice perfect Virtue.

A simple, pure, infused, and perfect Contemplation, therefore is a known and inward manifestation which God gives of himself, of his goodness, of his Peace, of his sweetness, whose object is God, pure, unspeakable, abstracted from all particular thoughts, within an inward silence: but it is God delights us, God that draws us, God that sweetly raises us in a spiritual and pure manner, an admirable gift, which the divine Majesty bestows to whom he will, as he will, and when he will, and for what time he will, though the state of this Life be rather a state of the cross of Patience, of humility, and of suffering, than of enjoying.

Never will you enjoy this divine Nectar, till you are advanced in Virtue and inward Mortification; till you heartily endeavor to fix in your Soul a great Peace, silence, forgetfulness and internal solitude: How is it possible to hear the sweet, inward and powerful Voice of God in the midst of the noise and tumults of the Creatures? And how can the pure spirit be heard in the midst of Considerations and discourses of Artifice? If the Soul will not continually die in itself, denying itself to all these Materiallities and satisfactions, the Contemplation can be no more but a mere vanity, a vain complacency and Presumption.

God does not always communicate himself with equal abundance in this sweetest and infused Contemplation: sometimes he grants this Grace more than he does at other times; and sometimes he expects not that the Soul should be so dead and denied, because this Gift being his mere Grace, he gives it when he pleases, and as he pleases; so that no general rule can be made of it, nor any rate set to his Divine greatness: nay, by means of this very Contemplation be comes to deny it to annihilate and die.

Sometimes the Lord gives greater light to the understanding; sometimes greater love to the will. There is no need here for the Soul to take any pains or trouble; it must receive what God gives it, and rest united, as he will have it; because His Majesty is Lord, and in the very time that he lays it asleep, he possesses and fills it, and works in it powerfully and sweetly, without any industry or knowledge of its own: insomuch, that before ever it is aware of this so great Mercy, it is gained, convinced, and changed already.

The Soul which is in this happy state, has two things to avoid, the activity of human Spirit, and interestedness: Our humane Spirit is unwilling to die in it self, but loves to be doing and discoursing after its way, being in Love with its own Actions. A Man had need to have a great fidelity, and divesting himself of selfishness, to get a perfect and passive Capacity of the Divine Influences; the continual habits of operating freely, which it has, are a hindrance to its annihilation.

The second is interestedness in contemplation itself: You must therefore procure in your Soul a perfect divesting of all which is not God, without seeking any other end or interest, within or without, but the Divine Will. In a word, the manner that you must use, on your part, to fit yourself for this pure, passive, and perfect Prayer, is, a total and absolute consignment of yourself into the hands of God, with a perfect submission to his most holy Will, to be busied according to his Pleasure and Disposition, with a perfect resignation.

You must know, that few be the Souls which arrive at this infused and passive Prayer; because few of them are capable of these divine influences with a total nakedness and death of their own activity and Powers, those only which feel it, know it so, that this perfect nakedness is acquired (by the help of God's Grace) by a continual and inward mortification, dying to all its own inclinations

and desires. At no time must you look at the effects which are wrought in your Soul, but especially herein; because it would be a hindrance to the divine operations, which enrich it, so to do: all that you have to do is to pant after indifference, resignation, forgetfulness, and, without your being sensible of it; the greatest good will leave in your Soul a fit disposition for the practice of virtue, a true love of the Cross of your own contempt, of your Annihilation, and greater and stronger desires still of your greater Perfection, and the most pure and affective Union.

Chapter Twelve

Of the two means, whereby the Soul ascends up to infused Contemplation, with the Explication of what and how many the steps of it are.

The means whereby the Soul ascends to the felicity of Contemplation and Affective Love, are two; the Pleasure, and the Desires of it. God uses at first to fill the Soul with sensible Pleasures; because its so frail and miserable, that, without this preventive Consolation, it cannot take wing towards the fruition of Heavenly things. In this first step it is disposed by Contrition, and is exercised in Repentance, meditating upon the Redeemer's Passion, rooting out diligently all worldly desires and vicious Courses of Life: because the Kingdom of Heaven suffers violence, and the faint-heart, the delicate never conquer it, but those that use violence and force with themselves.

The second is the Desires. The more the things of Heaven are delighted in, the more they are desired; and from thence there do ensue upon spiritual Pleasures, desires of enjoying heavenly and divine Blessings, and contempt of worldly ones. From these desires arises the inclination of following Christ our Lord, who said, I am the way, the steps of his imitation, by which a Man must go up, are Charity, Humility, Meekness, Patience, Poverty, Self-contempt, the Cross, Prayer, and Mortification.

The steps of infused Contemplation are three. The first is Satiety. When the soul is filled with God, it conceives a Hatred to all worldly things; then its quiet and satisfied only with Divine Love. The second is intoxication. And this step is an excess of Mind, and an Elevation of Soul, arising from Divine Love and satiety of it. The third is Security. This step turns out all fear: the soul is so drenched with love divine, and resigned up in such a manner to the divine good pleasure, that it would go willingly to Hell, if it did but know it so to be the will of the most high. In this step it feels such a certain Bond of the divine Union, that it seems to it an impossible thing, to be separated from its beloved, and his infinite Treasure. There are six other steps of Contemplation, which are these, Fire, Union, Elevation, Illumination, Pleasure, and Repose. With the first the Soul is enkindled, and being enkindled, is anointed; being anointed, is raised; being raised, Contemplates; Contemplating, it receives Pleasure; and receiving Pleasure, it finds repose. By these steps the soul rises higher, being abstracted and experienced in the Spiritual and Internal way.

In the first step, which is Fire, the Soul is illustrated, by the means of a divine and ardent ray, in kindling the affections divine, and drying up those which are but humane. The second is the Unction, which is a sweet and spiritual Liquor, which diffusing it self all the Soul over, teaches it, strengthens it, and disposes it to receive and contemplate the divine truth: and sometimes it extends even to nature itself, corroborating it by patience, with a sensible pleasure that seems celestial. The third is the Elevation of the Inner Man over itself, that it may get fittest to the clear fountain of pure love. The fourth step, which is Illumination, is an infused knowledge, whereby the Soul contemplates sweetly the divine truth, rising still from one clearness to another, from one light to another, from knowledge to knowledge, begin guided by the Spirit Divine. The fifth is a Savory Pleasure of the divine sweetness, issuing forth from the plentiful and precious fountain of the Holy Ghost. The sixth is a sweet and Admirable tranquility, arising from the conquest of Fighting within, and frequent Prayer; and this, very, very few have Experience of. Here the abundance of Joy, and Peace is so great, that the soul seems to be in a sweet sleep, solacing and reposing itself in the Divine breast of Love.

Many other steps of Contemplation there are, as Ecstasies, Raptures, Melting, Delinquium's, Glee, Kisses, Embraces, Exultation, Union, Transformation, Espousing, and Matrimony, which I omit to explain, to give no occasion to Speculation: And because there are whole Books which treat of these Points; though they are all for him who finds nothing of them, any more than a blind Man does of Color, or a deaf Man of Music. In a word, by these steps we get up to the Chamber and repose of the pacifick King and the true Solomon.

Chapter Thirteen

Signs to know the Inner Man, and the Mind that's Purged.

The Signs to know the Inner Man by, are four. The first, If the understanding produce not other Thoughts than those which stir up to the light of Faith; and the Will is so habituated, that it begets no other Acts of Love than of God, and in order to him. The second, If, when he ceases from an External Work, in which he was employed, the Understanding and the Will are presently and easily turned to God. The third, if in entering, upon Prayer, he forgets all outward things, as if he had not seen nor used them. The fourth, If he carries himself orderly towards outward things, as if he were entering into the World again, fearing to embroil himself in Business, and naturally abhorring it, unless when Charity requires it of him.

Such a Soul as this is free from the outward Man, and easily enters into the interior solitude, where it sees none but God and itself in him: loving him with quiet and peace and true Love. There in that secret Center God is kindly speaking to it, teaching it a new Kingdom, and true Peace and Joy.

This Spiritual, abstracted and retired Soul has its Peace no more broken, though outwardly it may meet with Combats; because through the infinite distance, tempests do never reach to that serenest Heaven within, where pure and perfect Love resides; and though sometimes it may be naked, forsaken, fought against and desolate, this is only the fury of the storm, which threatens and rages no where but without. This secret Love within, has four effects: The first is called Illumination, which is a savory and experimental Knowledge of the greatness of God, and of its own nothing. The second is Inflammation, which is an ardent desire of being burnt, like the Salamander, in this kind and divine fire. The third is Sweetness, which is a peaceable, joyful, sweet and intimate fruition. The fourth, is a swallowing up of the Powers in God; by which immersion the Soul is so much drenched and filled with God, that it can't any longer seek, or will any thing, but its greatest and infinite good. From this fullest satiety, two effects arise. The first is, a great Courage to suffer for God. The second is, a certain hope or assurance that it can never lose him, nor be separated from him.

Here in this internal retirement, the beloved Jesus has his Paradise, to whom we may go up, standing and conversing on the Earth. And if you desire to know who he is, who is altogether drawn to this inward retirement, with enlightened Exemplification in God, I tell you, it is he that in adversity, in discomfort of Spirit, and in the want of necessities stands firm and unshaken. These constant and inward Souls are outwardly naked and wholly diffused in God, whom they continually do Contemplate: they have no spot; they live in God and of himself; they shine brighter than a thousand Suns; they are beloved by the

Son of God; they are the darlings of God the Father, and elect Spouses of the Holy Ghost.

By three signs is a mind that is purged, to be known, as St. Thomas says in a Treatise of his. The first sign is diligence, which is a strength of Mind, which banishes all neglect and sloth, that it may be disposed with earnestness and confidence to the pursuit of virtue. The second is severity; which likewise is a strength of Mind against Concupiscence, accompanied with an ardent love of roughness, vileness and holy Poverty. The third is benignity and sweetness of Mind, which drives away all rancor, envy, aversion and hatred against ones neighbor. Till the mind be purged, the affection purified, the memory naked, the understanding brightened, the will denied and set a fire, the Soul can never arrive at the intimate and affective union with God, and therefore because the Spirit of God is purity itself, and light and rest, the Soul, where he intends to make his abode, must have great Purity, Peace, attention and quiet. Finally the precious Gift of a purged Mind, those only have, who with continual diligence do seek Love and retain it, and desire to be reputed the most vile in the World.

Chapter Fourteen

Of Divine Wisdom.

Divine Wisdom is an intellectual and infused knowledge of the divine perfections and things Eternal; which ought rather to be called Contemplation than Speculation. Science is acquired and begets the knowledge of Nature. Wisdom is infused and begets the Knowledge of the Divine Goodness. That desires to know what is not to be attained unto without pains and sweat: This desires not to know what it does know, although it understands it all. In a word, the Men who are scientific entertain themselves in the knowledge of the things of the World; and the wise live swallowed up in God himself.

Reason enlightened in the Wise is a high and simple elevation of Spirit, whereby he sees, with a clear and sharp sight all that is inferior to him, and what concerns his Life and Estate.

This is that which renders the Soul simple, illustrated, uniform, spiritual, and altogether introverted, and abstracted from every created thing. This moves and draws away with a sweet Violence, the hearts of the humble and teachable, filling them with abundance of sweetness, peace, and pleasantness. Finally, the wise Man says of it, that it brought him all good things at once.

You must know, that the greatest part of Men lives by Opinion, and judges according to the deceivableness of imagination and Sense: but the Man that's wise judges of everything according to the real verity, which is in it; whose business is to understand, conceive, penetrate into, and transcend every created being, even to himself. Its a great property of a wise Man to do much and say little. Wisdom is discovered in the works and words of the wise; because he being absolute master of all his passions, motions, and affections is know in all his doings, like a quiet and still water, in which wisdom shines with clearness. The understanding of mystical truths is secret and shut up from Men who are purely Scholastic, unless they be humble; because it is the Science of Saints, and none know it but those which heartily love and seek their own Contempt: Therefore the Souls, who by embracing this means, get to be purely mystical and truly humble, dive even to the profoundest apprehensions of the Divinity: and the more sensually men do live according to flesh and blood, the greater distance are they at from this mystical Science. Ordinarily it is seen that in the man which has much scholastic and speculative Knowledge, divine Wisdom does not predominate; yet they make an admirable composition, when they both meet together. The men of Learning, who by God's Mercy have attained to this mystic Science, are worthy of Veneration and Praise in Religion.

The external actions of the mystical and wise, which they do rather passively than actively, though, they are a great torment to them, yet are ordered prudently by them, by number, weight, and measure. The Sermons of Men of Learning, who want the Spirit, though they are made up of divers stories, elegant descriptions, acute discourses, and exquisite Proofs, yet are by no means the word of God; but the word of Men, plated over with false Gold: These Preachers spoil Christians, feeding them with wind and vanity, and so they are, both of them, void of God.

These Teachers feed their Hearers with the wind of hurtful subtleties, giving them stones instead of Bread, leaves instead of Fruit, and unsavory Earth mixed with poisoned Honey instead of true Food. These are they that hunt after honor, raising up an idol of reputation and applause, instead of seeking God's Glory, and the spiritual Edification of Men. Those that preach with Zeal and sincerity, preach for God. Those that preach without them, preach for themselves. Those that preach the word of God with spirit, makes it take impression in the Heart; but those that Preach it without spirit, carry it no farther than to the ear. Perfection does not consist in teaching it, but in doing it; because he is neither the greatest Saint, nor the wisest Man, that knows the Truth most, but he that practices it.

Its a constant Maxim, That Divine Wisdom begets Humility; and that which is acquired by the Learned, begets Pride. Holiness does not consist in forming deep and subtle conceits of the Knowledge and attributes of God, but in the Love of God, and in self-denial. Therefore its frequently observed, that Holiness is more amongst the simple, and humble, than among the learned. How many poor old Women are there in the World, which have little or nothing of humane science, but are rich in the love of God! How many Divines do we see that are over head and ears in their vain Wisdom, and yet very bare in things of true light and Charity!

Remember that its always good to speak like one that learns, and not like one that knows: Count it a greater Honor to be reputed a mere Ignoramus, than a man of Wisdom and Prudence. However, the Learned, who are purely speculative, have some little Sparks of Spirit, yet these do not fly out from the simple bottom of eminent and divine Wisdom, which has a mortal hatred to Forms and Species': the mixing of a little Science is always a hindrance to the eternal, profound, pure, simple, and true Wisdom.

Chapter Fifteen

Treating of the Same.

There are two ways which lead to the knowledge of God. The one remote, the other near: The first is called Speculation; the second, Contemplation. The Learned, who follow Scientific Speculation by the Sweetness of sensible Discourses, get up to God by this means, as well as they can, that by this help they may be able to love him: But none of those who follow that way which they call Scholastic, ever arrives by that only, to the Mystical Way, or to the Excellence of Union, Transformation, Simplicity, Light, Peace, Tranquility and Love, as he does, who is brought by the Divine Grace by the mystical way of Contemplation.

These men of Learning, who are merely scholastic, don't know what the Spirit is, nor what it is to be lost in God: nor are they come yet to the taste of the sweet Ambrosia which is in the inmost depth and bottom of the Soul, where it keeps its Throne, and communicates itself with incredible, intimate and delicious affluence: Nay, some there are which do and condemn this mystical Science, because they neither do understand nor relish it.

The Divine who does not taste the sweetness of Contemplation, has not other reason to give for it, but because he enters not by the Gate which St. Paul points to, when he says, If anyone among you seem to himself to be wise, let him become a fool that he may be wise; let him show his humility by reputing himself ignorant.

Its a general Rule; and also a Maxim in Mystic Theology, That the Practical ought to be gotten before the Theory. That there ought to be some experimental Exercise of supernatural Contemplation, before the search of the knowledge, and an enquiry after the full apprehension of it. Although the mystical Science does commonly belong to the humble and simple, yet notwithstanding that, men of Learning are not incapable of it, if they do not seek themselves nor set any great value upon their own artificial knowledge; but more, if they can forget it, as if they never had it, and only make use of it, in its own proper place and time, for preaching and disputing when their turn comes, and afterwards give their minds to the simple and naked Contemplation of God, without form, figure or consideration.

The Study, which is not ordered for God's glory only, is but a short way to Hell; not through the Study, but the Wind of Pride, which begets it. Miserable is the greatest part of Men at this time, whose only Study is to satisfy the un-satisfyable curiosity of Nature.

Many seek God and find him not; because they are more moved by curiosity than sincere, pure and upright intention: they rather desire Spiritual Comforts than God himself; and as they seek him not with truth, they neither find God nor Spiritual Pleasures. He that does not endeavor the total denying of himself, will not be truly abstracted; and so can never be capable of the truth and the light of the Spirit. To go towards the mystical Science, a man must never meddle with things which are without, but with prudence, and in that which his Office calls him to. Rare are men who set a higher price upon hearing than speaking? But the wise and purely mystical Man never speaks but when he cannot help it; nor does he concern himself in anything but what belongs to his Office, and then he carries himself with great Prudence.

The spirit of Divine Wisdom fills men with Sweetness, governs them with Courage, and enlightens those with excellence who are subject to its direction. Where the Divine Spirit dwells, there is always simplicity and a holy Liberty. But Craft and Double-mindedness, Fiction, Artifices, Policy and worldly Respects, are Hell itself to wise and sincere men.

Know that he who would attain to the Mystical Science, must be denied and taken off from five things: 1. From the Creatures. 2. From Temporal things. 3. From the very Gifts of the Holy Ghost. 4. From himself. 5. He must be lost in God. This last is the most complete of all; because that Soul only that knows how to be so taken off, is that which attains to being lost in God, and only knows where to be in safety.

God is more satisfied with the affection of the Heart, than that of Worldly Science. Its one thing to cleanse the Heart of all that which captivates and pollutes it, and another to do a thousand things, though good and holy, without minding that purity of Heart which is the main of all for attaining of Divine Wisdom.

Never will you get to this Sovereign and Divine Wisdom, if you have not strength, when God cleanses you in his own time, not only of your adherence to Temporal and Natural Blessings, but further, to Supernatural and Sublime ones, such as internal Communications, Ecstasies, Raptures, and other gratuitous Graces, whereon the Soul rests and entertains it self.

Many Souls come short of arriving to quiet Contemplation, to divine Wisdom and true Knowledge, notwithstanding that they spend many Hours in Prayer, and receive the Sacrament every day; because they do not subject and submit themselves wholly and entirely to him that has Light, nor deny and conquer themselves, nor give up themselves totally to God, with a perfect divesting and disinteresting of themselves: In a word, till the Soul be purified in the Fire of Inward Pain, it will never get to a State of Renovation, of Transformation, of perfect Contemplation, of divine Wisdom and affective Union.

Chapter Sixteen

Of true and perfect Annihilation.

You must know that all this Fabric of Annihilation has its foundation but in two Principles. The first is, to keep ones self and all worldly things in a low esteem and value; from whence the putting in practice of this Self-divesting, and of Self-renunciation and forsaking all created things, must have its rise, and that with the affection, and in deed.

The second Principle must be a great esteem of God, to love, adore and follow him without the least interest of ones own, let it be never so holy. From these two Principles will arise a full conformity to the Divine Will. This powerful and practical conformity to the Divine Will in all things, leads the Soul to Annihilation and Transformation with God, without the mixture of Raptures, or external Ecstasies, or vehement Affections: This way being liable to many illusions, with the danger of weakness and anguish of the understanding, by which path there is seldom any that gets up to the top of perfection, which is acquired by the other safe, firm and real way, though not without a weighty Cross; because therein the Highway of Annihilation and Perfection is founded; which is seconded by many gifts of Light and divine Effects, and infinite other Graces, yet the Soul that is annihilated must be unclothed of it all, if it would not have them be a hindrance to it in its way to Deification. As the Soul makes continual progress from its meanness, it ought to walk on to the practice of Annihilation, which consists in the abhorring of Honor, Dignity and Praise; there being no reason that Dignity and Honor should be given to Vileness and a mere Nothing. To the Soul that is sensible of its own Vileness, it appear an impossible thing to deserve anything; its rather confounded and knows itself unworthy of Virtue and Praise: it embraces with equal courage all occasions of Contempt, Persecution, Infamy, Shame and Affront; and as truly deserving of such reproaches, it renders the Lord thanks, when it lights upon such occasions, to be treated as it deserves; and knows itself also unworthy, that he should use his Justice upon it; but above all, its glad of contempt and affront, because its God gets great glory by it. Such a Soul as this always chooses the lowest, the vilest, and the most despised degree, as well of place, as of clothing, and of all other things, without the least affectation of singularity; being of the opinion, that the greatest Vileness is beyond its deserts, and acknowledging itself also unworthy even of this. This is the practice that brings the Soul to a true Annihilation of itself.

The Soul that would be perfect, begins to mortify its Passions; and when its advanced in that Exercise, it denies itself; then with the Divine Aid, it passes to the State of Nothing, where it despises, abhors and plunges itself upon the knowledge that it is nothing, that it can do nothing, and that it is worth nothing. From hence springs the dying in it self, and in its senses, in many ways, and at all hours; and finally, from this spiritual Death the true and perfect Annihilation derives its original; insomuch, that when the Soul is once dead to its will and understanding, its properly said to be arrived at the perfect and happy state of Annihilation, which is the last disposition for Transformation and

Union, which the Soul itself does not understand, because it would not be annihilated if it should come to know it. And although it does get to this happy state of Annihilation, yet it must know that it must walk still on, and must be further and further purified and annihilated. [Here is most delicious Nonsense, and a very curious Bull.]

You must know, that this Annihilation to make it perfect in the Soul, must be in a man's own Judgment, in his Will, in his Works, Inclinations, Desires, Thoughts, and in itself: so that the Soul must find itself dead to its Will, Desire, Endeavour, Understanding and Thought; willing, as if it did not will; desiring, as if it did not desire; understanding, as if it did not understand; thinking, as if it did not think, without inclining to anything, embracing equally Contempt and Honors, Benefits and Corrections. O what a happy Soul is that which is thus dead and annihilated! It lives no longer in itself, because God lives in it: And now it may most truly be said of it, that it is a renewed Phoenix; because its changed, spiritualized, transformed and deified.

Chapter Seventeen

In which is showed how this Nothing is the ready way to obtain Purity of Soul, perfect Contemplation, and the rich Treasure of Peace internal.

The way to attain that high state of a Mind reformed, whereby a man immediately gets to the greatest Good, to our first Original, and to the highest Peace, is his Nothingness: Endeavour, O Soul, to be always buried in that misery. This Nothing, and this acknowledged Misery, is the means by which the Lord works wonders in your Soul. Cloth yourself with this Nothing, and with this Misery, and see that this Misery and this Nothing be your continual Food and Habitation, even to the casting down yourself low therein; and then I assure you, that you being in that manner, the Nothing, the Lord will be the Whole in your Soul.

Why, think you, do infinite Souls hinder the abundant Current of the divine gifts? Its only because they would be doing something, and have a desire to be great: all this is to come away from internal Humility, and from their own Nothing; and therefore they prevent those wonders which that infinite goodness would work in them. They betake themselves to the very gifts of the Spirit, and there they stick, that they may come out from the Center of Nothing, and so the whole Work is spoiled. They seek not God with truth, and therefore they find him not: For know you must, that there is no finding of Him, but in the undervaluing of our own selves, and in nothing. We seek ourselves every time we get out of our Nothing; and therefore we never get to quiet and perfect Contemplation. Creep in as far as you can into the truth of your Nothing, and then nothing will disquiet you: Nay, you will be humble and ashamed, losing openly your own reputation and esteem.

O what a strong Bulwark will you find of that Nothing! Who can ever afflict you, if once you retire into that Fortress? Because the Soul which is despised by itself, and in its own knowledge is Nothing, is not capable of receiving Grievance or Injury from anybody. The Soul which keeps within its Nothing, is internally silent, lives resigned in any torment whatsoever, by thinking it less than what it does deserve: It shuns the suspicion of a Neighbor, never looks at other folks faults, but its own is free from abundance of Imperfections, and becomes Commander of great Virtue. While the Soul keeps still and quiet in its nothing, it perfects it, it enriches it, the Lord draws his own Image and Likeness in it, without anything to hinder it.

By the way of Nothing you must come to lose yourself in God (which is the last degree of perfection) and happy will you be, if you can so lose yourself; then you will get yourself again, and find yourself most certainly. In this same Shop of Nothing, Simplicity is made; interior and infused recollection is possessed, quiet is obtained, and the heart is cleansed from all manner of imperfections. O what a Treasure will you find, if you shall once fix your habitation in Nothing and if you once get but snug into the Center of Nothing, you will never concern yourself with anything that is without (the great ugly large step that so many thousand Souls do stumble at) unless it be as your Office may call you to it.

If you get shut up in Nothing, (where the blows of adversity can never come) nothing will vex you or break your peace. This is the way of getting to the command of yourself, because perfect and true dominion does only govern in Nothing: with the Helmet of Nothing you will be too hard for strong temptations and the terrible suggestions of the envious enemy. [I defy all the Quakers in England to match this incomparable piece of Nonsense and Enthusiastic Cant.] Knowing that you are nothing, that you can do nothing, and are worth just nothing, you will quietly embrace passive dryness, you will endure horrible desolations; you will undergo spiritual martyrdoms and inward torments. By means of this Nothing you must die in yourself, many ways, at all times, and all hours.

Who must awaken the Soul out of that sweet and pleasant Sleep, if once it comes to take a Nap in Nothing? This is the way that David got a perfect annihilation, without so much as knowing it. Keeping yourself in Nothing, you will bar the door against every thing that is not God; you will retire also from your own self, and walk toward that internal solitude, where the Divine Spouse speaks in the Heart of his Bride, teaching her high and divine Wisdom. Drown yourself in this Nothing, and there you will find a holy Sanctuary against any Tempest whatsoever.

By this way must you return to the happy state of Innocence forfeited by our first Parents. By this Gate you must enter into the happy land of the living, where you will find the greatest Good, the breath of Charity, the beauty of Righteousness, the straight Line of Equity and Justice, and, in sum, every jot and tittle of Perfection. Lastly, do not look at nothing, desire nothing, will nothing, nor endeavor nothing, and then in every thing your Soul will live reposed, with quiet and enjoyment. This is the way to get purity of Soul, perfect contemplation and peace internal; walk therefore in this safe path, and endeavor to overwhelm yourself in this Nothing, endeavor to lose yourself, to sink deep into it, if you have a mind to be annihilated, united and transformed.

Chapter Eighteen

Of the high Felicity of internal Peace, and the wonderful Effects of it.

The Soul being once annihilated and renewed with perfect nakedness, finds in its superior part a profound peace, and a sweet rest, which brings it to such a perfect Union of love, that it is joyful all over. And such a Soul as this is already arrived to such a happiness, that it neither wills nor desires any thing but what its Beloved wills; it conforms itself to this Will in all emergencies, as well of comfort as anguish, and rejoices also in every thing to do the Divine Good Pleasure.

There is nothing but what comforts it; nor does it want anything, but what it can well want: To die, is enjoyment to it; and to live, is its joy. It is as contented here upon Earth, as it can be in Paradise; it is as glad under privation, as it can be in possession; in sickness as it can be in health; because it know that this is the will of its Lord. This is its life, this is its glory, its paradise, its peace, its repose, its rest, its consolation and highest happiness.

If it were necessary to such a Soul as this, which is gotten up by the steps of annihilation to the region of peace, to make its choice, it would choose desolation before comfort, contempt before honor; because the loving Jesus made great esteem of reproach and pain: if it first endured the hunger of the blessings of Heaven, if it thirsted for God, if it had the fear of losing him, the lamentation of heart, and the fighting of the Devil; now things are altered, and hunger is turned into satisfying, the thirst into satiety, the fear into assurance, the sadness into joy, the weeping into merriment, and the fierce fighting into the greatest peace. O happy Soul, that enjoys here on earth so great a felicity! You must know, that these kind of Souls (though few they are) be the strong Pillars which support the Church, and such as abate the divine indignation.

And now this Soul that is entered into the heaven of peace, acknowledges itself full of God and his supernatural gifts, because it lives grounded in a pure love, receiving equal Pleasure in light and darkness, in night and day, in affliction and consolation. Through this holy and heavenly indifference, it never loses its peace in adversity, nor its tranquility in tribulations, but sees itself full of unspeakable enjoyments. And although the Prince of Darkness makes all the assaults of Hell against it, with horrible temptations, yet it makes head against them, and stands like a strong Pillar; no more happening to it by them, than happens to a high mountain and a deep valley in the time of storm and tempest. The valley is darkened with thick clouds, fierce tempests of hail, thunder, lightning and hail-stones, which looks like the picture of Hell: at the same time the lofty Mountain glitters by the bright beams of the Sun, in quietness and serenity, continuing clear, like heaven, immovable and full of light.

The same happens to this blessed soul; the valley of the part below is suffering tribulations, combats, darkness, desolations, torments, martyrdoms and suggestions; and at the same time, on the lofty mountain of the higher part of the Soul, the true Sun casts its beams; it enflames and enlightens it; and so it becomes clear, peaceable, resplendent, quiet, serene, being a mere ocean of joy. So great therefore is the quiet of this pure Soul, which is gotten up the mountain of tranquility, so great is the peace of its spirit, so great the serenity and cheerfulness that is within, that a remnant and glimmering of God do rebound even to the outside of it.

Because in the throne of quiet are manifest the perfections of spiritual beauty; here the true light of the secret and divine Mysteries of our holy faith, here perfect humility, even to the annihilation of itself, the amplest resignation, chastity, poverty of spirit, the sincerity and innocence of the Dove, external modesty, silence and internal fortitude, liberty and purity of heart; here the forgetfulness of every created thing, even of itself, joyful simplicity, heavenly indifference, continual Prayer, a total nakedness, perfect disinterestedness, a most wise contemplation, a conversation of heaven; and lastly, the most perfect and serene peace within, of which this happy soul may say what the wise man said of wisdom, that all other graces came along in the company with her.

This is the rich and hidden treasure, this is the lost groat of the Gospel; this is the blessed life, the happy life, the true life, and the blessedness here below. O you lovely greatness that surpasses the knowledge of the sons of men! O excellent supernatural life, how admirable and unspeakable are you, for you are the very draught of blessedness! O how much do you raise a soul from earth, which loses in its view all things of the vileness of earth! you are poor to look upon; but inwardly you are full of wealth: you seem low, but are exceedingly high; in a word, you are that which makes men live a life divine here below. Give me, O Lord, your greatest goodness, give me a good portion of this heavenly happiness and true peace, that the World, sensual as it is, is neither capable of understanding nor receiving.

Chapter Nineteen

A mournful Exclamation and lamentable Moan to God for the Small Company of Souls that arrive at Perfection, the Loving Union and the Divine Transformation.

O Divine Majesty, in whose presence the Pillars of Heaven do quake and tremble! O you Goodness, more than infinite, in whose love the Seraphim's burn! give me leave, O Lord, to lament our blindness and ingratitude. We all live in Mistakes, seeking the foolish world, and forsaking you, who are our God. We all forsake you, the Fountain of Living Waters, for the stinking Dirt of the World.

O we children of men, how long shall we follow after lying and vanity? Who is it that has thus deceived us, that we should forsake God our greatest good? Who is it that speaks the most truth to us? Who is it that loves us most? Who defends us most? Who is it that does more to show himself a Friend, who more tender to show himself a Spouse, and more good to be a Father? That our blindness should be so great, that we should all forsake this greatest and infinite goodness?

O Divine Lord! what a few Souls are there in the World, which do serve you with perfection! how small is the number of those, who are willing to suffer, that they may follow Christ crucified, that they may embrace the Cross, that they may deny and contemn themselves! O what a scarcity of Souls is there, which are disinterested and totally naked! how few are those Souls which are dead to themselves and alive to God, which are totally resigned to his divine good pleasure! How few those, who are adorned with simple obedience, profound knowledge of themselves; and true humility! how few those, which with an entire indifference give up themselves into the hands of God, to do what he pleases with them! how few are there of those pure Souls which be of a simple and disinterested heart, and which, putting off their own understanding, knowledge, desire and will, do long for self-denial and spiritual death! O what a scarcity of Souls is there which are willing to let the Divine Creator work in them a mind to suffer, that they may not suffer, and to die, that they may not die! How few are the Souls which are willing to forget themselves, to free their hearts from their own affections, their own desires, their own satisfactions, their own love and judgments! that are willing to be led by the highway of self-denial and the internal way! that are willing to be annihilated, dying to themselves and their senses! that are willing to let themselves be emptied, purified and unclothed, that God may fill and cloth and perfect them! In a word, how small, O Lord, is the number of those Souls which are blind, deaf and dumb and perfectly contemplative!

O the shame of us the Children of Adam! who, for a thing of mere vileness, do despise true felicity, and hinder our greatest good, the rich treasure and infinite goodness! Great reason has Heaven to lament, that there are so few Souls to follow its precious path-way. I submit everything, with humble prostration, to the Correction of the Holy Roman Catholic Church.

DAILY COMMUNION

ଔଓ

The Preface

The following Treatise was approved of at Rome by Fryer Pater Damian, a Discalceate Carmelite, Visitor General and Reader of Theology in the Convent of S. Mary della Scala, in the Year 1675, when the foregoing Book was so highly applauded and set out with so many Formalities: And after him, Nicholas Martinez, a Jesuite, Chief Reader of Theology in the Roman Colledg, (which is one of the most eminent Offices in one of the most eminent Houses of Education in the whole City) comes to set his Approbation to it: And then, after these two, our old Friend, that we were beholden to before, Fryer Dominick of the most Holy Trinity, Qualifier of the Holy Office in Rome, &c. he tells us, that forasmuch as he found nothing in it contrary to Faith or good Manners, or repugnant to the Reverence due to the Sacrament, etc. he takes it to be worthy to be Printed for divers and sundry reasons. So that though it met not with those Acclamations which the former Book did, (the reason whereof you will presently smell out, when you read it) yet these three Testimonies (besides the pains that the devout Priest (as he calls himself) took to get it out of Spanish into Italian) were enough to give it Credit and Authority in the World: And as it came tacked to the other Book so it was pity to make it part Company. But whilst these Reverend Gentlemen have been so kind to help it into the World, and speak such good things of it, its plain that they either winked at, or did not know one gross Contradiction that it makes to the foregoing Book; and that is this: That this, Mich. Molinos does lay it down as a Principle, in his Spiritual Guide, That the Penitent ought to resign up his Will, his Judgment, his Knowledge, his Choice to the determination of his Spiritual Director. And produces Examples for it, and tells him, that he must be led blindfold by his Confessor, though he should put him upon never so useless and nonsensical Penance and Mortification, as planting Lettuce with the Roots upwards, etc. (a specimen of which sort of asinine and undisputing Obedience is to be seen pressed by the Founder of the Jesuitical Order, in his Epistle to the Brethren of his Society, wherein he instances in Abbot John, that watered a withered Tree for a whole Year together; (Which did him as much good as if he had tied a Whiting to his Girdle.) And, at his Superior's command, tried to move a vast Stone which was beyond the strength of many men together to do; which he had no more reason to do, than to knock his Head against it). And the reason that is given for this sort of affected and foolish Humility, forsooth, must be because the Father Confessor is in God's place, and whatever he tells his Penitent, must be done by an absolute and unlimited Obedience, without asking, why or wherefore, or entering into any thoughts of the reasonableness or unreasonableness, convenience or inconvenience, good or hurt of such a ranting sort of Discipline: And what fine work may there be sometimes done, when a silly Priest meets with a Penitent that is as wise as himself? But if the business be really, thus, then what's the reason that this Author does so often in this Treatise, flies in the face of the Ministers, (who in his sense, are these Confessors) and tax them with I know not what, and make most lamentable out-cries against them for hindering their Penitents from Daily Communion? This is going backward and forward, saying and unsaying again: For if the Confessor have a power of disposing of his Penitent's (I was going to say Client's) Will, etc. as he pleases, and an unaccountable Empire and Government over him; I would fain see how he can advise him amiss? And why should all this noise be made against these Ministers who are made Judges of the disposition of their People, whom they Shrine, and therefore are presumed to do no more than what there is reason for, in hindering them from Daily Communion? If the foregoing Book were first Penned by the Author, then he either retracted his judgment, in this Treatise, or else forgot himself, (which he presses often as a Duty of Religion.) If this Treatise was Penned first, then the Author was willing to give Confessors more scope and power in [his Spiritual Guide] than he though fit to allow them in his [Daily Communion.] However the matter was, there is a filthy Mistake some where or other; to press blind Obedience to Confessors in one Book, and yet bawl at them for requiring it in another. The least that can be said of it, is, that its an argument of an inconstant or forgetful Head, And I leave it to him to make it out, or to anybody else that has a mind to clear the point. The Treatise itself is like other Popish Treatises upon that Subject; only its a question, whether the Author be so far Annihilated yet (as his word is) as to believe Transubstantiation so stoutly as others of that Communion would make us believe they do. He has been mightily conversant in Modern Casuists and Schoolmen, and that makes him so ill a Divine, as to tell us of receiving good by the Sacrament, Never minding what is done, but only the doing the bare action of it. I could not forbear showing a mark of dislike, when I found him quoting two such bouncing Authorities out of St. Austine and St. Jerome for delivering Souls out of Purgatory by the efficacy of Mass. I confess they are very pregnant for his purpose, if he can but show us those Words in the true Writings of those two Fathers: but to send us to the Man in the Moon to know further, this is not fair nor Scholar-like. If any man else will undertake to show us those Words in the undoubted and un-forged Works of St. Austine and St. Jerome, he will make me (for my part) in that point.

A Quietist.

The Author's Advertisement

Its none of my intention to Discourse in this subject by the way of Humane Respect or Passion, nor to defend hard Controversies, nor promote my own Opinions; and though I have Written this short Treatise at the continual engagements and instances of Zealous Persons, yet God's greater Glory, and the Spiritual advantage of Souls, have been my only desire: Nor is it any less my design, that by this Treatise and these Reasons, the Faithful should govern themselves in the business of frequent Communion, without the Prudent and Holy Counsel of their Spiritual Fathers; because I always look upon it more fitting to obey their Orders, though it should hinder the Communion, than to communicate every day according to their own Sense and Judgment. This Compendium of the Reasons and Authorities of Councils, Saints, and Doctors, is only drawn up a-purpose, that Confessors may see the small reason there is to hinder those Souls from taking the Communion, which desire it, receive good by it, and are obedient to their Directions.

Chapter One

No Minister ought to keep a faithful Person from the Communion, that does desire and ask it, while he does not know his Conscience defiled with mortal Sin. The Custom of the Church makes it clear, that Examination and Proof is necessary in order for the Communion; that no man, knowing himself guilty of mortal Sin, though he may seem Contrite to himself, come to the Sacrament, unless he have before been at Sacramental Confession. Which comprehends all Christians, and even Priests, who are bound by their Office to Celebrate it: from whence its clearly to be inferred, that the Council makes no other disposition necessary for the Communicating of Laymen, and the Priest's saying Mass, than not to have any mortal Sin. Why then should the Ministers be a hindrance to those which have that disposition? The Ministers will not say that their Authority is greater than that of the Council; nor that they are more Learned than all those Fathers of the Church that came to it; nor will they say, less, that they have a greater light from God, than that which he then communicated to his Spouse, the Church: Therefore the Ministers ought not to require a greater disposition, than being without mortal Sin, while the Council requires no more. Either the Ministers and Priests, which say Mass daily, have this Holiness and Perfection themselves, which they require in Laymen, or else they have it not: they will not say they have it, because it would then be pride in them: If they have it not, and yet Celebrate Mass every day, why do they require it from Laymen, in order for the granting them the Communion daily? Its good to advise them to this Perfection, but if they should not have it, it will not be reasonable to deprive them of so great a good, because they may have reason to fear that Christ our Lord may say to them as he did to the Pharisees, That they bind heavy burdens upon men, and they themselves will not touch them with one of their fingers. And that also is verified which David said, That men are deceitful in the weight. Since they have one weight for themselves and another for Laymen. If the Council judges that not being in mortal Sin, is a worthy disposition towards saying Mass daily, consecrating and offering Sacrifice, which is the holiest Service, how much more worthy will such a disposition be for only the receiving the Communion? If Councils, the Church, Popes, Saints, and Doctors require no greater disposition to receive fruit from this Sacrament, than not being in mortal Sin, why must the Ministers require a greater? The Council of Trent has the following words: the holy Council would look upon it as a very good thing that in every days Mass, the Faithful who assist at it, would be Communicated, not only Spiritually and in their desires, but also Sacramentally by receiving the Holy Eucharist, that they might thus obtain the more abundant benefit by this most Holy Sacrament. The Council therefore desires that the Faithful would communicate every day that they hear Mass, with the disposition of having no mortal Sin. Will any Ministers say, that this is not well, and so openly set themselves in opposition to the desires of the Church? The Congregation of the Council declared it an Error that any Bishops in a Capriccio should limit and hinder Daily Communion from being taken by Merchants and House-keepers: The holy Rota reports it in the year 1587 and after it had Decreed that all Laymen might be communicated, even every day, though they should be Merchants and House-keepers, it adds the following words: —wherefore the Faithful are to be exhorted, that as they Sin daily, so they daily receive this Medicine of the Sacrament of the Eucharist. And the same Council of Trent says. ---- The Communion is as an Antidote to free us from daily Sins, and preserve us from mortal Sins. If the Council and its Decree speaks here, not of the Basils and Antonies, nor of the Catharines and Clares, as some say it is required for them to be, but of those that Sin daily; why should they be kept from the Medicine, that they may not Sin? The Council of Milan and that of Cabilon are of the same mind. The blessed Pius Quintus says, The Curates are bound to exhort the Faithful often, that as they hold it necessary to feed the Body daily, so they hold it also necessary to feed the Soul as often with this Sacrament: because the Children of Israel did eat Manna in the wilderness daily; and that Manna was the Figure of this sacred Food; And that sentence [You sin every day, be communicated also every day.] is not only St. Augustine's, but the saying of all the Saints. St. Ignatius, Bishop and Martyr, exhorts that we often come and receive the Eucharist; because the frequency of it weakens the power of Satan. The Council of Alexandria says, That without this frequency, it will be a hard matter to preserve Grace. St. John Chrisostome says, It is no rashness for a Christian to come often to the Sacrament: he that remembers not a great fault of himself, may come to it every day. Theophylact says, To know whether you may Communicate, be your own Judge, and having examined yourself, you may do it, without staying for a Festival, unless you find yourself burdened with a great fault. St. Cyprian says, Let us ask this daily Bread, being in no great fault let us receive this Bread every day, which gives us Life Eternal; and let us beg that our Bread, which is Christ our Lord, may be daily given us, to keep us in his Grace: No small loss it is, to forbear Communicating every day. St. Hilary says, If your Sins are not so grievous as to deserve Excommunication, not being mortal, if they should be mortal, after Confession, as Suarez expounds it, never keep off from the daily Medicine, which is the Body and Blood of the Lord. St. Ambrose says, Receive daily, that which is to help you daily: he that does not deserve to receive it every day, does not deserve to receive it in a whole year: Sins are daily committed, and therefore this Divine Bread is for every day. You offend every day, wash yourself therefore of your Sin every day in the Fountain of Repentance; and if you come every day to this Divine Sacrament, you will find wholesome Medicine, and not the Poison of Judgment. St. Jerom says, We should always receive the Holy Eucharist, that we may be without mortal Sin: And in his time, which was the Year 470, he says, the holy Custom of Communicating every day, continued in Rome and in Spain. St. Augustine says, If you come without Sin, come and welcome; its Bread and not Poison; Again, Its better to Communicate for Devotion, than let it alone for Reverence. And in another place, This is the daily Bread, receive it daily, because it will daily do you good, and you may receive it every day. With which a Bishop reproved S. Catharine of Siena, because she took the Sacrament every day: and the Saint replied to him, how he does reprove in her, that which St. Austine does not reprove? Bellarmine therefore (in the Year 420.) says that this sentence is not S. Austine's, but Gennadius's of Marseilles; and so many other Authors assure us. S. Gregory says, The Lord gave us this Salutary Sacrament to pardon our daily sins; let us receive it every day. St. Bernard says, The wounded man seeks Medicine: we are all of us wounded, when we have Sinned; our Medicine is the Divine Sacrament: receive it daily and you will recover daily. St. Apollonius advised his Monks to be communicated every day, that they might be preserved in Grace. St. Bonaventure, Although you should find yourself lukewarm, with little Fervor in you, yet trusting in the Mercy of God, you may safely come to the Communion: if you think yourself unworthy, (so that you remember no mortal Sin of your own) come; because the weaker you are, the greater need have you of the Physician. You do not receive Christ to sanctify Him, but that he may sanctify you. The Council of Alexandria says, Without this frequency, its hard to keep in Grace. S. Antony of Florence says, Those that live well must be sure to be advised to receive this most holy Sacrament frequently; because as long abstinence from bodily Food, weakens the Body, and disposes it for Death, so the much abstaining from this spiritual Food, weakens the Soul, spends the fervor, and by degrees inclines it to mortal Sin. Pope Adrian says, When once the preparation is made according to Humane frailty, its safer to receive than keep from the most Holy Sacrament. St. Thomas Aquinas asks, If it be lawful to Communicate every day? And answers with St. Austine, This is daily Bread: receive it every day, that you may every day be profited by it. St. Isidore has this, Some say, that if there be no Sin, the Communion ought to be taken daily; and they say well, if they receive it with Veneration and Humility. St. Anaclete, Pope, perceiving Daily Communion grow into disuse, brought it up again, ordering, that after Consecration all those that were present should be communicated, because this Custom (as he says in a Decree of his) was established by the Apostles and kept by the Roman Church: and those that did not communicate, were turned out of the Church. Innocent the Third says, He may communicate who has his conscience free from mortal sin, and is grieved for that which is venial. St. Athanasius, having examined your Conscience, always come to the Communion, without staying for a holy day. Henriquez relates it, that St. Austin, St. Ambrose, and St. Jerome, do commend those who communicate daily, without fail. Those that the Confessor shall judge worthy of absolution, may be advised by him to receive the Communion, though they fear an easy relapse. Its not necessary to make an experiment of frequent Communion from a man's good and profit by it: because spiritual profit (which is insensible) is much less found than corporal profit. Thomas a Kempis says, If I am lukewarm when I do communicate, what should I be, if I should not communicate? I would add, if I am naughty when I do communicate, by not communicating I should offend the whole world and damn myself. The following Doctors defend Daily Communion with very strong reasons, which for brevity sake are omitted. Innocent the Third, St. Athanasius, Heneriquez, Thomas a Kempis, Alexander of Hales, Gerson, The Patriach of Jerusalem, John Colaya, Ranier of Pisa, Martin of Ledesma, Nider, Astensis, Father Salmeron, Father Francis Suarez, Durandin 4, Victoria, John of Friburg, John Altestaing, Gabriel Mayor, Raimond, Peter de Soto, Lewis Blois, Stephen Boluser, Rosela, Father Christopher of Madrid, Reynalds, Francis de Lavata, Dionysius Carthusianus, John Mayor, Venantius Fortunatus, Cardinal Hosias, Bishop Perez, Vivaldus, Christopher Morenus, James Baius, The illumniate Father John Thaulerus, Alphonse Rodriguez, Antony Molina, Lewis Fandone, Father Joseph of St. Mary, Mauras Antonius, Peter Marsilia, Father Antony de Alvarado, Alphonse of Chinchilla, Father Lewis of Granada, Villalobos, Almai, John Sanchez, Palao, Basil, Veracruz, Sa. de verb, Henry Henriquez, Ferrer, Escobar, Mendoza, Cassian, Medini, Jerom Perez, Adrian, Finally, the illuminate Thauler says, that to receive the most holy Sacrament without mortal sin, as has been said, does more good than to hear a hundred Masses, or a hundred Sermons: and so say many Authors, as Jerom Perez relates that he does but once receive the most holy Sacrament without mortal sin, gets more grace by it, than if he should go thrice in Pilgrimage to the holy Sepulcher at Jerusalem; and that never did any body communicate, without obtaining particular Grace thereby, and a singular degree of Charity which he had not before, though he were never so lukewarm and dry. A grave religious man adds this consideration, That if all the Charity should be put together, which all man have had or shall have, which have been, are, or shall be, and the merits of them all, and the praises that have been given and shall be given, and all the good works which have been done and shall be done, and the torments of Martyrs, the Fasting, Disciplines, and Hair-clothes of all the Saints, Confessors, Patriarchs, Virgins and Prophets, with whatever else that shall be done as long as the World endures; put it all together, and it does not please God so much, as the receiving of this Divine Sacrament. Others say, as the above said Author relates, that if all the Quires of Angels, all the Courtiers of Heaven, and the most holy Virgin (Mistress of them all, who incomparably exceed them all) should meet together, it is not in their power to do a more pleasing Sacrifice to God, nor a more acceptable Offering, than Saying of Mass, or, when men communicate, to offer to his Majesty that Divine Sacrament. St. Cyril affirms, that the only delaying of it never creates a better disposition to it; and it commonly happens, that those who are slowest to come to the Communion, come less prepared: and further, these following Reasons do make it evident. To communicate worthily without mortal sin is good of it self; to forbear it, is not so: To go often to the Sacrament is a product of Charity: to delay it, comes from negligence or fear: better is the work of Charity than that of Fear. He that communicates gets the better of him that lets it alone in the good he receives by the Sacrament Ex opere operato: and at the most may easily be equal to him, since the desire of communicating worthily, is no less good, than keeping from it out of reverence. If it be sometimes good to abstain, it ought to be for the obtaining or preserving the reverence and devotion of it: and for this reason the frequency of the most holy Sacrament is not of less advantage, since thereby the Soul gets cleansed of those evil habits and affections and natural imperfections that we have. If the Scripture therefore in many places, if the Apostles, Councils, Popes, and the Saints and Doctors do advise us to daily communion, without limitation or laxing, and if there be no Law divine or humane to forbid it to him that has no mortal sin to hinder him, what is the reason that the Ministers should forbid or limit that which neither Christ nor the Church nor any Law does limit? It will be prudence therefore not to oppose the Sayings of Doctors, Saints, Popes and Councils, to get free from the punishment given to many Ministers for forbidding of it. Father Bernadino of Villagas, in the Life of St. Lutgard, says, that among other persons that thought ill of the frequent communion of that Saint, the Abbess was one, who being led by an indiscreet zeal, ordered her not to communicate so often: to whom the humble Virgin returned this Answer, with great reverence, That she was ready and prepared to obey her order with content, but she knew for certain, that this disfavor she did her, would displease Jesus Christ, and that in the punishment which would follow, she would quickly understand how ill she did, in depriving her of the Communion. The Saint obeyed, and in recompense of her obedience, it seems, the Lord making good the Voice of her Prophecy, sent the Abbess a great fit of sickness, which afflicted her much with continual and sharp pains, till acknowledging her fault, and that this chastisement befell her for her indiscreet zeal used to the Saint, she sent for her and gave her leave to follow her holy custom, and so the fault ending, the punishment ended also, and the disease which had brought her to a very sad condition. Other persons also who in like manner used to keep a pother with the Saint about her often Communions, repenting of what they had done, asked her pardon. And other of their complices in their prate and gossiping, because they never laid to heart what they had said of her, were punished of God with a sudden death. In the third Book of St. Gertrudes Life chap. 23. its told, that a certain Preacher or Confessor, being a little warmed with the zeal of God's Honor, took a pet at some religious Women, thinking that they were often communicated: At this the Saint made a Prayer, and asked the Lord, Whether this were acceptable to him, or no? The Lord make her this answer; it being my delight to be with the children of men, and I having, of infinite love, left this Sacrament to be often received in remembrance of me, and being in it to the faithful to the World's end, whosoever shall, with words or other ways of persuasion, to go about to hinder any from taking it, who are free from mortal sin, does in a certain manner hinder me, and rob me of my pleasure and delight, which I might have with them. Some Ministers there are who have had a mind to restrain this matter too much: as if the Sacrament were not instituted for Laymen, or as if they had no right to ask it as often as they are disposed to receive it. O, as if Christ our Lord had instituted it with a limitation or precept, that it should not be taken but by such and such men, and on such and such days. Expert Teachers do strangely wonder to see the scruple and cautiousness, with which some Confessors speak about this matter, as if the Communion were a very dangerous thing for Souls, or through the too much frequenting of it, the Honor of God or the Virtue of the Sacraments must need be lost or lessened: whereas the frequency of it is the very remedy and health of Souls and the work in which there is the greatest honor done to God and which they ought most to endeavor, who desire his glory. And if the Minister should at any time find himself dissatisfied at this, let him peruse that holy Appointment of the Church, And if the dispenser himself cannot hinder this, much less can they hinder it, who have nothing to do to dispense it: and if this which has been said is not enough, let him be afraid of those infinite Punishments which God has raised upon those Ministers which have forbid it. But for all this, the Communion should always be used at the spiritual Father's order, who neither ought to hinder nor delay it, when he knows the Soul, that desires it and reaps good of it, to be so disposed as the Council requires. And if another Confessor should order him the quite contrary, let him follow the judgment of that ghostly Father, who knows better than any other, how his Conscience is, and by whose Counsel he goes and acts safely.

Chapter Two

Answering the Reasons which those Ministers give, which hinder the Faithful from Communicating, and the Priest from Celebrating, having their Consciences free from Mortal Sin.

Either the Communion must be forbidden to those that ask it and desire it without the guilt of Mortal Sin, because they are not worthy of it, or for the greater reverence of it, or, because much Familiarity breeds Contempt, or else for Mortification and

Penance: The first reason, of not being worthy, is not sufficient; because if they make a Christian forbear, till he be worthy of the Communion, then he must never receive it: because no man is worthy to receive Christ, no not Heaven itself. Whereupon many holy men say, that the Communion taken to day is a disposition for that tomorrow. Besides, that Councils, the Saints and Doctors do assure us, that not being in Mortal sin, is that necessary worthiness and disposition which is required for the Communion; we are not to go to it, as worthy, but as having need of it: we do not go to sanctify Jesus Christ, but to be sanctified and healed by him, by the means of the Sacrament, as St. Ambrose tells us, -- I who do continually sin, ought continually to receive the Medicine of this Sacrament against the pestilent Disease of Sin. Nor may a Christian be debarred the Communion for the second reason of greater reverence, because its contrary to St. Austin's Doctrine, who says, that its better to communicate through Devotion, than let it alone through Reverence. Dionysius Carthusianus says the same thing, Its better to communicate through Love, than abstain from it through Humility and Fear, There is not more devotion, love and respect showed to God by less frequent coming to the Sacrament: but rather he loves and fears God most, who without mortal sin, and with a desire of his own spiritual advantage, comes every day to it: and the delaying of it is not a greater disposedness nor veneration, but a manifest temptation. By keeping away, they think to find better devotion and fervor, and in the mean time they are dry, lukewarm and cold, as we see by experience. These people that will not communicate unless they be sensibly and actually devout, are like those who are cold, who will not come near the fire, till they are warm; or like those sick men that will not ask the Physicians counsel, till they are grown well. Christ's Body is like a spiritual fire, let us approach towards it, and it will warm us. The flesh of Christ, says Damascene, is a live coal, which heats and burns. The third reason which some give for the hindering Christians the Communion, that desire and ask it, is a certain whimsy or capricio, which they imprint in their minds, telling them, that to go frequently to the Sacrament is too much familiarity, and that this breeds contempt. O hurtful Deceit! O pernicious Doctrine! Although, taught by the Ministers with no bad zeal. Is it possible, that among so many Saints and Doctors of the Church which have written professedly upon this Point, as is manifest by the former Chapter, none of them should light upon the reason, that these Ministers talk of? Its well inferred therefore, that its of small consideration and account. True it is, that to much familiarity is sometimes the occasion of contempt, but of what, and to whom? The too much familiarity with a vile thing, occasions contempt, but how can familiar conversation with a thing that is grave, good, and amiable, how can this cause contempt? In earthly things familiarity begets contempt; because the more one man gets acquainted and intimate with another, he discovers his defects by degrees, and so values him less then he did at first. But with God the thing is quite otherwise: because as the creature proceeds in the knowledge of that fountain of true perfection, by the same measure the love and esteem of that great Lord grows more. If by communicating daily there could be any defect discovered in Jesus Christ, certain it is, that this frequency and familiarity would breed contempt of him; but the more that boundless ocean of perfection is received, the more is his goodness known, and the greater does the love, the respect and the reverence to him grow. And if it were true, that to much frequency occasioned contempt, it would be necessary to give laws to God himself, and take care not to render himself so easy and familiar to the Saints and Angels of Heaven, with whom he has so great and continual an intimacy. Who is more familiar with God than the Angels who continually behold his divine countenance? and what, does this make them leave off honoring, reverencing and loving him? But they will say, it is not good to abuse this familiarity and intimacy with God. What a blindness is this! what should the meaning of this be, unless they would not have us so united with God, and have a mind that we should serve him at a distance, and not near and more by name than affection. These words arise rather from the little will they have that we should receive this divine Lord, than from the respect of not displeasing him: if they had true charity, and did but heartily love Jesus Christ, they would despise all fear, and not remove us from the frequency of this divine Sacrament; nay, they would desire and prompt us on to receive him daily, that we might be united unto God. If they know, that Christ desires to be united with us, why should they be unwilling that we should be united with him our great Lord, fearing where no fear is? if they see that an infinite God desires our familiarity and friendship, what is it that they build upon, to hinder us from being his friends? do they think that by this continual frequency that will be tedious to us, without which everything else is tedious? do they believe that that will make our life uneasy, which gives us life? that that good will be a trouble to us, from which all goodness proceeds? and in a word, that he who is the pleasure and delight of all Creatures, of all the Seraphim, of all the Saints, and of the whole Court of Heaven, will be a tediousness to us? true it is, that he satiates, but never becomes tedious. Nor any less ought a Christian to be denied the Communion, to mortify him, which is the fourth reason: because in Mortification, to be without the Communion, he only exercises one Virtue, and in the Communion he exercises them all. Would it therefore be well that a Christian, for obtaining one Virtue, should be deprived of all the rest? Its great pity to deprive him of the great good he receives in the Communion, only for mortification-sake: which being well thought of, will prove rather a privation of good than the virtue of mortification. Besides, to be able to say Mass and communicate perfectly, it is not the best way to leave off communicating and celebrating: but rather its the best that can be, to say Mass and communicate every day, though it be with some imperfections. To enable a man to pray perfectly, or to obtain some virtue in perfection, its not a good way to leave off doing acts of that virtue. Who will say, that to make a perfect Prayer, its a good way to let it alone some days? and that to have patience, its a good way not to do any acts of it? rather the best means to obtain patience and to make a perfect Prayer, is to exercise those things day by day, though there should be some imperfection in them. If the divine Majesty vouchsafes to be with sinners, to lodge in their houses, to eat with them at the same Table, (for which he bears for his Arms and commands to be fixed on the doors of his house an Inscription, that says, This Lord receives sinners and eats at one Table with them) why is the Minister and Servant of this same Lord so loath to receive a Christian, if he be changed and mended by repentance? is it therefore reason that the Ministers of this Lord should limit a thing not limited by their Master? The

Lord invites, and calls us to his banquet: and will the servant pretend to give leave to those who are invited, when they are introduced to God in his own house? Let them come in, if they have no mortal sin about them: and if they have, its washed away in the fountain of repentance. Put this on the account of their Lord, that will have it so, and commands it, though it seem inconvenient to the Minister, wherefore the Lord may answer him with great reason, "Its well known, that the sinner costs the nothing, and that having so narrow a breast as you have, you admit him not to the Communion, though he desires it and I invite him to it: but I came down from Heaven for him, and was made man, suffering 33 years incredible torments, even to death itself. I will have him, thus penitent as he is, and because I am God, I have a heart of infinite extend, where all, how wicked so ever they may have been, do come, if they turn to me and become reformed by means of repentance." Christ our Lord moves the tongue of Angels to exhort men to frequent Communion, and the Prince of darkness moves the tongues of men to persuade them the contrary. The Angel said to Elijah, Arise and eat, for you have a long journey to go. So the Angel persuades him to the Communion; and not only once, but twice he awaked the Prophet that was asleep, to eat Bread, the figure of the Eucharist. Its the propriety of Angels to invite to frequent Communion. Well did St. Jerom say, ---He is an Angel to you who puts you upon the Communion, and a Devil that hinders you from it. Its plain, that the Devil shows himself against this Sacrament more than any other, in that he seeks by so many disturbances and ways to hinder it, amongst which its not the least powerful and effectual which he makes use of by Preachers and Confessors, and Ministers themselves, because many of them with a cloak of zeal disturb it. Those who reckon themselves Ministers of Jesus Christ, ought to make it their proper work and business to set themselves against the Devil's intentions; not depriving people of their Daily Communion, but advising them to it, and procuring it for them. Fryer Joseph of St. Mary, after he had told us the words of the holy Council of Trent, where he says --- that he desires that all men would communicate daily (in his Apology for frequent Communion) has these following words --- Is it therefore possible, O my Christian Fathers and Brethren, that the Church should have any such children who do so openly contradict her; and that, understanding from their Mother, that it would be a good thing for Christians to communicate every day, they should say it is not convenient, and so oppose themselves to her and contradict her? Certainly this looks like the Devil's temptation, to hinder the growth of Souls, though it be done with good zeal, and to such as be zealous of God's honor, and of the Church their Mother, this will not look well. Now let any Summist and Learned Man, that has a great opinion of himself, see whether it be lawful to oppose the Authority of so great a Tribunal and the laudable Custom of the Church and her Declarations, against the Practice and Doctrine of the Apostles, and against the Preaching of the holy Doctors of the Church. Let not man mutter or deny the holy Communion, says Lewis Fundone, as if there were no occasion for it, and let him have a care that God do not deny him Heaven; since to condemn this, is to condemn the commendable Customs and most ancient Practice of the Church and the greatest Servants of God. Father Peter of Marselles, a Benedictine, says, "That as often as a man communicates without the guilt of mortal sin, either by not having committed it, or by being pardoned it, he receives grace by it. This disposition is not of so small moment, as some think, since the holy Counsel of Trent thinks it enough for reverence and holiness. They are mightily to be commended, that do their best to persuade the faithful to communicate daily; and consequently, what a great error and prejudice of Soul are they that hinder Lay-men the Sacramental Communion every day. Nothing but Mortal sin (says St. Thomas) can keep a Christian from the Communion. How therefore does it come to pass, that the Ministers keep men from it, when they have no Mortal sin to indispose them. It would be well considered that Christ is in this Sacrament for salve for our wounds, for comfort to our troubles, and for strength in our adversities, and lastly for a pledge and memorial of the love that he bears to Souls, and that this great Lord stands crying out whether there be any that would have him, and the Souls answer that they will have him, but asking the Ministers of the Church to give them their Lord, and divide to them their daily bread, the Ministers turn the deaf ear to it, being stewards for Gods house, and are very pinching and niggardly in distributing that which the Lord commands, and so freely gives. Such a stinginess as this is to be lamented with Tears of Blood. Who would not weep to see that when Gods hand is so open in giving, his servants should be so close-fisted and covetous in distributing: and that God being so bountiful of his own blessings which cost him his blood, they should be so greedy in a thing that cost them nothing? and in a word, this Sacrament being that open fountain of David, free to all the Sons of Jacob, who go to it for the precious water without giving anything for it, the Ministers sell it so dear that it costs many even tears of blood to obtain it: which gives them the lamentation of Jeremy, that they are fain to buy the water which is their own, as dear as if it did belong to somebody else. Master John d' Avila, a Man known sufficiently for his exemplar Goodness and Learning and Preaching, being asked whether a Superior or one that had the cure of Souls, might deny the Communion to him that should ask it of him every day, not having lawful impediment, made answer thus, My opinion is, that no lawful impediment appearing, the Prelate (and he that in his room has the business of Administrating the Eucharist) is obliged to give it to him that is under him, every time that he asks it. He that denies the most holy Sacrament, is unjust, and deprives him of his right and due that asks it. A Christian (as S. Thomas says) has so much a right to ask it, that the Prelate cannot deny it him, except if be for a public sin. Asking it in public he ought to give it him, though he knows that he has Sin in secret: and then how much more ought he to one that asks it devoutly? he is cruel, he takes away the Spiritual Bread from his Child, and I must condemn him for a sinner in it. All this says the above mentioned Author, Will they say, if it be a good and holy thing to Communicate every day, why doesn't the Church then command it? and why did not the Founders of Religions, who were endued with so much light, leave it for a rule? and why did not some Saints embrace this frequency? Saint Mark the Evangelist cut off his Thumb, that they might not make him ordain. Saint Francis of Assise would never be a Priest. Saint Benet was a long time without Communicating. Before I come to answer, I will ask whether be well, that a man in health should not eat something every day, because the Law does not command it? why have some Saints abstained from food some days?

whether single life be good and not Marriage, as S. Paul says, because the Law commands it not? and why some Saints have not been Married? whether it be a good and holy thing to hear Mass daily, because the Church does not command it? and why some Saints have retired into the desert, where they could not hear it? Again, before I come to answer, I will suppose that some examples of the Saints are more to be admired than imitated, and that therefore they do not make a general rule; that if some have not Communicated, they were only a few; and they that did Communicate, numberless: and therefore it will be more safe to follow the most and not the fewest. I answer the difficulty and the question; that things necessary ought to be commanded, that which is evil ought to be prohibited, and that which is good and holy ought to be advised. The holy Church does always act rightly, and therefore she does not command the faithful to Communicate daily: because how holy and good a thing so ever it be, yet its not essentially necessary: and the precept of the Church, always looks at the benefit of the faithful, and so great is our luke-warmness, and the frailty of our times, that a precept of Daily Communion would be an occasion of sin and ruin, and therefore the Church does not enjoin Christians by precept any more than one Communion in a year, though the desires that through devotion men would Communicate every day. Many men shift off their coming daily to this Divine Banquet, that they may not be taken notice of for it, and that they may give no occasion to others to grumble: and the Ministers hearing this reason, hold their tongues and rest satisfied. O hurtful silence! must they permit, for worldly respects, that the faithful should lose so great a benefit? Is it possible that they should let them live at a distance, and separate from God and his sweet and loving friendship, because the world should not censure them? if there should be any great account made of what the world says, not only the soul would be lost, but also the judgment. Is it not known, that the world makes it its business to speak ill of what good is, and to persecute those that do not take part with it? All those that serve great men, do make open show of the degree of their office, greatness and dignity; and shall a Christian think it a shame to himself to communicate, and be seen in the service of Jesus Christ? If it were an evil work to Communicate every day, it might breed scandal; but if it be the best work that a Christian can do, why should he keep from it through an idle fear of offending his neighbor? The Jews were offended at the good works of Jesus Christ, but for all that, his Majesty never left off doing them. He that does ill and interprets the good that others do in an evil sense, its he that gives cause for the scandal: but to do well, was never a scandal, much less can so great good, as Communicating be one. If a man should take offence by seeing us eat, surely we would not for all that be such fools as to starve ourselves. We ought to take great heed of following vanities and worldly pleasures, that we many not by them offend or scandalize our Neighbor: from these vices we ought to keep our selves, not from Daily Communion, because this cannot cause scandal, but will rather edify our Neighbor, and by our good example, it may be, he may come to change his life and resolve himself to frequent the Sacraments. O how many people are there that are cheated by these worldly respects! O unhappy men! they are not ashamed to be base in their lives, and yet they are ashamed to be Christians and to be known for such!

Chapter Three

Wherein are shown some of the great benefits, of which a faithful man is deprived, by being prohibited the Communion, when he is sufficiently disposed for it. That the Minister may see and take good notice of the hurt which he does, by depriving the faithful of the Communion, that desire and ask it without the guilt of Mortal Sin, it will be necessary to lay before him some of those infinite benefits of which he defrauds them, only in one Communion, that he may undeceive himself that deprives them of infinite good for mortification sake.

First he deprives such a one of the increase of grace and glory which he receives in the Communion, whose effect is infallible, though he should have venial sins about him. He also deprives him of the mortification of all his five senses and powers, which he therein performs, while his Eyes, his Smelling, his Taste, his Touch, his Imagination, his Understanding and all his knowledge and capacity do tell him that that Host is Bread: by all this he is humbled, mortified, and subdued, while he belies that it is not that which he feels and tastes, but that his God and Lord is in it. He deprives him also, by taking the Communion from him, of the cleansing of his sins and evil habits, and being preserved from them for the time to come; of many helps which are therein administered to him for the performance of every good thing, and avoiding every evil one? and it may happen that the Eternal Salvation of Damnation of a Soul may depend upon one of these helps. He deprives him of the lessening the pains of Purgatory, which is participated in every Communion. He deprives him of the highest acts of Faith, Hope and Charity, which he exercises, by believing that he receives that God, who he sees not, nor feels, and hoping in him, whom he had not seen and being united with him by love. God is goodness itself, and he is willing to be communicated through love to Souls, by means of the Divine and Sacramental Bread: Is there a greater happiness in the world? can there be a greater felicity? and shall there be any Minister to deprive the Soul of this benefit? In this wonderful Sacrament Christ is united to the Soul, and becomes one and the same thing with it. In which fineness of love is the most profound, admirable and worthy of consideration and gratitude, because there is not more to give nor to receive: and what Minister shall deprive the soul of this boundless grace? All Blessings do here meet together in this precious Food, here all desires of God are fulfilled, here is the loving and sacramental Union, here's the Peace, the Conformity, the Transformation of God, with the Soul, and the Soul with God. By receiving Jesus in this Sacrament, the Eternal Father and the Divine Spirit is also received; here are all the Virtues, Charity, Hope, Purity, Patience, and Humility: because Christ our Lord begets all Virtue in the Soul, by means of this heavenly Food: and what a Heart must the Ministers have to forbid the Soul so great a Happiness. If one only degree of Grace is a gift of inestimable Value and so precious, that its not to be bought for a thousand Worlds being a particle of God himself, and a formal participation of the Divine Nature, which makes us his Children and Friends, Heirs of Heaven, and the Habitation of the most Holy Trinity: and if never so little Grace be worth more than all the Virtues, Alms, and Penances, and the removing Mountains (as St. Paul says) and giving all away to the Poor, is a mere Nothing without Grace: How then can it be well to deprive the Faithful of the increase of Grace, which he might find only in one Communion? How can the Minister deprive him of that and of many others that follow it, without giving them other things equivalent to those they lose? What can be of equal value with habitual Grace, which a faithful Man might receive? neither can the Humility which he may exercise, nor the Reverence, nor the Mortification, upon the account of which he leaves off the Communion, be worth so much; nor are they equivalent to that Grace only, which he loses, and which he might have had by receiving that Communion. And now lets make up this Account. If Restitution ought to be (as all the Doctors say) conformable to the Good, which was taken from one's Neighbor, what can he restore, which deprives a faithful Man of God himself? Would it not be great want of Charity to take from a Man a Mount of Gold, only to gather up a little Grain? Only for one Grain of Mortification, (if yet there is any in it) the Ministers do deprive a Christian of a whole Mount of Blessings, which are heaped up together in the Communion: If there were no other way to mortify and try the Soul, but this, it ought not to be used; because by this Mortification they deprive him of a greater good: but there are infinite ways of proving and mortifying the Soul besides, without doing it so great a Spiritual Prejudice. The Blessings of this Sacrament don't end here; because, besides, the increase of Grace, it sustains and gives new strength to the Soul, to resist Temptations; it satisfies the desires, takes away the hunger of temporal things, unites with Christ and his Members, who are the Just and Righteous, breaks the power of Satan, gives strength to suffer Martyrdom, pardons the Venial Sins, to which he that Communicates does not stand affected; and keeps from Mortal Sins, by virtue of the aid which it does contribute. The Body of Christ (says St. Bernard,) is Medicine to the Sick, Provision for the Pilgrim, fresh Strength to the Weary, it delights the Strong, it heals the wounded, it preserves the Health of Soul and Body. And whoever is a worthy Communicant, is made more strong to receive Contempt, more patient to suffer Reproof, more fit to endure Troubles, more ready for Obedience, and to return the Lord Thanks. St. Leo Pope says, that when a man is Communicated, Christ comes to honor him with his

Presence, to anoint him with his Grace, to cure him with his Mercy, to heal him with his Blood, to raise him by his Death, to illuminate him with his Light, to inflame him with his Love, to comfort him with his infinite Sweetness, to be united and espoused with his Soul, to make him partaker of his Divine Spirit, and of all the Blessings which he purchased us by his Cross. Do you seek (says St. Bonaventure,) where God is? you must expect to find him in this Divine Sacrament, which being worthily received, does pardon Sins, mitigate Passions, gives light to the Understanding, satiates the Soul, revives Faith, encourages Hope, enkindles Charity, increases Devotion, fills with Grace, and is the rich Pledge of Glory. This Sacrament (says St. Thomas) drives away evil Spirits, defends us from Concupiscence, washes off the Stains of the Heart, appeases Gods Anger, illuminates the Understanding, to know him inflames the Will, to love him, delights the memory with Sweetness, confirms the whole man in Goodness, frees him from Punishment Everlasting, multiplies the merits of good Life, and brings him to his Eternal Country. The Body of the Lord (as he pursues it) produces Three principal Effects. First, it destroys Sin. Secondly, it increases Spiritual Blessings. Thirdly, it comforts men's Souls; and in Chap. 25 he says, it satiates the Spirit to follow what is good; it comforts and strengthens the Soul, to shun what is evil, it preserves the Life always to praise the Lord. As it is a Sacrifice, it remits the Sins of those who are alive, and lightens the punishment of those who are in Purgatory, and augments the accidental Glory of those who are in Heaven. Lastly, the Body of Christ is called the Sacrament of Charity; because it makes us partakers of the Spirit Divine, of the sweet Abode of Christ himself, and the rich Transformation of God. It would be an endless thing to relate the Blessings, which, according to the saying of Saints, they do receive from this Sacrament, who come to partake of it without Mortal Sin: and of all these does the Minister deprive a Christian, when he only forbids him one Communion. But more than this, depriving them of the Communion, he deprives all the Saints of Heaven, all the Angels, the most holy Virgin, and Christ himself of that accidental glory which accrues to them by every Communion received in grace. If the Saints in Heaven have a special accidental glory, by every good work, though never so small, that is done here below, as many pious Authors are of opinion, with how much more reason will they have it by a work so sublime as the Communion is, wherein there is included an immensity of all the wonderful works of God? And if from one only Communion there are so many blessings, as are specified before, to be obtained, what will there be of the sacrifice of the Mass, the gravest, the highest work that is in Heaven or Earth? And shall there then be, Ministers, who under pretence of Penance, Mortification, or the old way, must hinder Priests so great, so holy, and so fruitful a sacrifice? Saint Jerom said, that at the least the Soul suffers not in Purgatory, while Mass is said for it [it was well the Author did not point to us where this blind passage is, in Saint Jeromes Works.] Saint Austin assures us, that the Divine Sacrifice is never Celebrated, but one of these two things follow upon it, either the Conversion of a sinner, or the letting loose of some Soul out of Purgatory, [this is as much Saint Austins saying, as the other is Saint Jeromes.] William Altisiodorensis was not contented with one Soul; but affirmed, that by every Mass there were the Lord knows how many Souls that got away from thence. Severius in St. Martin's Life gives an account that he set as many souls at liberty with his Masses, as persons assisted at the hearing of them. Venerable Bede says, that the Priest, who, being not lawfully hindered, does neglect to say Mass, deprives the most holy Trinity of glory and praise, the Angels of joy, Sinners of pardon, the Righteous of grace and help, the souls in Purgatory of cooling and refreshment, the Church of the heavenly benefit of Jesus Christ our Lord, and the Priest himself of Medicine and help. If every Mass therefore has all this of its own, what Minister under the color of zeal shall be so bold as to hinder and defraud the Trinity, the Angels, the Virgin, the Church, the Righteous, Sinners, the Souls in Purgatory, and the Priests themselves that desire to celebrate, so much glory and so much good? without doubt though this be done with zeal, yet 'its want of consideration, and it will be well, to premeditate and consider it better, before any goes about to hinder it.

The End.

FRANCOIS FENELON

SPIRITUAL PROGRESS

First Preface

The Providence of God among the Churches seems to call to the present time for further light upon the subject of a higher experience than that usually attained by the members of our Christian societies. Among the teachers who have been from time to time anointed for this work, Fenelon is justly held in high estimation. While some, perhaps, have had a more interior experience, few, if any, have so joined to the deepest devotion, a power of spiritual analysis that eminently fitted them for the office of instructors. And now, beloved reader, one word in conclusion, from the love of God to you. God has led you, in his Providence, to open this book that He may do you good. If through his infinite mercy you have had a personal experience of the matters herein written, your heart will be filled with thanksgiving and praise as you read. What has God wrought! If not, you will find many things strange, and it would not be surprising if you should be ready to pronounce some untrue. But ah! beware of being wise in your own conceit! The Spirit of God that searches the deep things of God, alone can decide. Do not distrust the reports of these spies whom God has sent before you into the promised land. It is a land flowing with milk and honey; true, the children of Anak are there, in whose sight we are but as grasshoppers, but they are bread for us. The Lord God, He it is that shall fight for us, and He will surely bring us into that exceeding good land. The natural man receives not the things of God, for they are foolishness unto him; neither can he know them, because they are spiritually discerned. If, then, you have not experienced the things that follow, think it not strange that they should seem foolish and false; in Gods own time they shall be perceived, if you follow on to know. If you will be advised by one who knows nothing, and who is least in the household of faith, you will deny nothing, reject nothing, despise nothing, lest haply you be found fighting against God: you will receive nothing but what is accompanied by the Amen of the Spirit of God in your heart; all else shall be as the idle wind. Reading thus, in absolute dependence, not upon mans wisdom or teaching, but upon the utterances of the blessed Spirit within, you shall infallibly be guided into all Truth. Such is the promise of Him who cannot lie. And may His blessing rest upon you!

I counsel you to buy of me gold tried in the fire, that you may be rich; and white raiment that you may be clothed, and that the shame of your nakedness does not appear; and anoint your eyes with eye-salve, that you may see. Rev. 3:18

Of The Little Knowledge Of God There Is In The World

What men stand most in need of, is the knowledge of God. They know, to be sure, by dint of reading, that history gives an account of a certain series of miracles and marked providences; they have reflected seriously on the corruption and instability of worldly things; they are even, perhaps, convinced that the reformation of their lives on certain principles of morality is desirable in order to their salvation; but the whole of the edifice is destitute of foundation; this pious and Christian exterior possesses no soul. The living principle which animates every true believer, God, the all and in all, the author and the sovereign of all, is wanting. He is, in all things, infinite in wisdom power and love, and what wonder, if everything that comes from his hand should partake of the same infinite character and set at nought the efforts of human reason. When He works, his ways and his thoughts are declared by the prophet to be as far above our ways and our thoughts as the heavens are above the earth. He makes no effort when He would execute what He has decreed; for to Him all things are equally easy; He speaks and causes the heavens and the earth to be created out of nothing, with as little difficulty as he causes water to descend or a stone to fall to the ground. His power is co-extensive with his will; when He wills, the thing is already accomplished. When the Scriptures represent

Him as speaking in the creation of the world, it is not to be understood as signifying that it was necessary that the word of command should issue from Him, in order that the universe he was about to create should hear and obey his will; that word was simple and interior, neither more nor less than the thought which he conceived of what He was about to do and the will to do it. The thought was fertile, and without being rendered exterior, begat from Him as the fountain of all life, the sum of the things that are. His mercy, too, is but his pure will; He loved us before the creation of the world; He saw and knew us, and prepared his blessings for us; He loved and chose us from all Eternity. Every new blessing we receive is derived from this Eternal origin; He forms no new will respecting us; it is not He that changes, but we. When we are righteous and good, we are conformable to his will and agreeable to Him; when we depart from well doing and cease to be good, we cease to be conformable to Him and to please Him. This is the immutable standard which the changeable creature is continually approaching and leaving. His justice against the wicked and his love towards the righteous are the same thing; it is the same quality that unites Him to everything that is good, and is incompatible with everything that is evil. Mercy is the goodness of God, beholding our wickedness and striving to make us good; perceived by us in time, it has its source in the eternal love of God for his creature. From Him alone proceeds true goodness; alas! for that presumptuous soul that seeks it in itself! It is Gods love towards us that gives us everything; but the richest of his gifts is that we may love Him with that love which is his due. When He is able by his love to produce that love in us, He reigns within; He constitutes there our life, our peace, our happiness, and we then already begin to taste that blissful existence which He enjoys. His love towards us is stamped with his own character of infinity: it is not like ours, bounded and constrained; when He loves, all the measures of his love are infinite. He comes down from Heaven to earth to seek the creature of clay whom he loves; He becomes creature and clay with him; He gives him his flesh to eat. These are the prodigies of Divine love in which the Infinite outstrips all the affection we can manifest. He loves like a God, with a love utterly incomprehensible. It is the height of folly to seek to measure infinite love by human wisdom. Far from losing any element of its greatness in these excesses, He impresses upon his love the stamp of his own grandeur, while He manifests a delight in us bounded only by the infinite. O! how great and lovely is He in his mysteries! But we want eyes to see them, and have no desire to behold God in everything.

Of The Necessity Of Knowing And Loving God

It is not astonishing that men do so little for God and that the little which they do costs them so much. They do not know Him; scarcely do they believe that He exists; and the impression they have is rather a blind deference for general opinion than a lively and distinct conviction of the Divinity. They suppose it is so, because they do not dare to examine, and because they are indifferent in the matter, their souls being distracted by the inclination of their affections and passions for other objects; but their only idea of Him is of something wonderful, far off and unconnected with us. They think of Him as a stern and powerful Being, ever making requisitions upon us, thwarting our inclinations, threatening us with great evils, and against whose terrible judgment it behooves every one to be on his guard. Such is the inward thought of those who think seriously about religion, and their number even is small enough. He is one who fears God, say they; and in truth such an one fears only, but does not love; as the child is in awe of the master who punishes him, or as the servant is in dread of the blows of one whom he serves from fear, and of whose interests is he utterly regardless. Would he like to be treated by a son or a servant as he treats God? It is because God is not known; if He were known, He would be loved. God is love, says the apostle John; he who loves Him not, does not know Him, for how could we know love without loving it? It is plain, then, that all those who have hitherto only feared God, have not known Him. But who shall know You, O! my God? He who shall seek with his whole heart to know You, who shall know himself with approbation no longer, and to whom all that is not You shall be as though it were not! The world cannot receive this saying because it is full of self, and vanity, and lies, and is empty of God; but I trust that there will always be souls hungering for God, who will relish the truth which I am about to set forth. O my God! before You made the Heavens and the earth, there was none other but You. You were, because of your years there was no beginning; but You were alone. Out of You there was nothing, and You did rejoice in this blessed solitude; You are all sufficient in Yourself, and you had no need of anything out of Yourself, for none can give unto You, and it is You that gives to all by your all-powerful word, that is, by your simple will. To it, nothing is difficult, and it does whatsoever it will from its own labor. You did cause that this world, which was not as yet, should begin to be; not as the workmen of the earth, who find the materials for their work ready made to their hands, and whose art consists in bringing them together, and arranging them by slow degrees in the requisite order; You did find nothing ready made, but did create all the materials for your work. It was to nothing that You did say, Let the world be, and it was. You did only speak and it was done. But why did You create all these things? They were all made for man and man was made for You. This is the order which is of your appointment, and woe to him who inverts it, who would that all should be for him and shuts himself in self! He breaks the fundamental law of creation. No! Lord, You can not yield the essential prerogatives of a creator; it would degrade You. You can pardon the guilty soul that has warred against You, because You can fill it with your pure love; but you can not cease to be at variance with the soul which refers all your gifts to itself, and refuses to embrace You as its Creator with a sincere and disinterested affection. To have no feeling but fear, is not to refer to itself to You, but on the contrary, to think of You solely with reference to self. To love You with a single eye to the good You can bestow, is not to lose ones self in You, but to lose You in self! What then must be done in order that we may be lost in You? We must renounce, forget and forever lose sight of self, take part with You and shine, O God, against ourselves and ours; have no longer any will, glory or peace, but yours only; in a word, we must love You without loving self except in and for You. God who made us out of nothing, re-creates us, as it were, every moment. It does not follow that because we were yesterday, we shall of course be today; we should cease to exist and return into the nothingness out of which He formed us, did not the same all-powerful hand prevent. Of ourselves we are nothing; we are but what God has made us, and for so long time only as He pleases. He has but to withdraw the hand that sustains us and we plunge into the abyss of annihilation, as a stone held in the air falls by its own weight when its support is removed. Existence and life, then, are only ours because they are conferred by God. There are blessings, however, of a purer and higher order than these; a well-ordered life is better than life; virtue is of higher price than health; uprightness of heart and the love of God are as far above temporal goods as the heavens are above the earth. If then these lower and baser gifts are held only through the mercy and at the pleasure of God, with how much more reason must it be true of the sublime gift of his love! They know You not, then, O my God, who regard You as an all-powerful Being, separate from themselves, giving laws to all nature, and creator of everything which we behold; they know You but in part! they know not that which is most marvelous and which most nearly concerns your rational creatures! To know that You are the God of my heart, that You do what pleases You, this it is that elevates and affects me! When I am good, it is because You render me so; not only do You turn my heart as pleases You, but You give me one like your own! It is Yourself that You love in me; You are the life of my soul as my soul is the life of my body; You are more intimately present to me than I am to myself; this I, to which I am so attached and which I have so ardently loved, ought to be strange to me in comparison with You; You are the giver of it; without You it never would have been; therefore it is that You desire that I should love You better than it. O incomprehensible power of my Creator! O rights of the Creator over the creature which the creature will never sufficiently comprehend! O prodigy of love which God alone could perform! God interposes himself as it were, between me and myself; He separates me from myself; He desires to be nearer to me by his pure love than I am to myself. He would have me look upon this me as a stranger; He would have me escape from its walls, sacrifice it whole to Him, returning it absolutely and unconditionally to Him from whom I received it. What I am ought certainly to be less precious to me than He by whom I am. He made me for himself and not to be my own; that is, to love Him and to will what He wills, and not to seek my own will. Does any one feel his heart revolt at this total sacrifice of self to Him who has created us? I weep for his blindness; I compassionate his bondage to self, and pray God to deliver him from it, by teaching him to love Him above every other object. O my God! in these souls, offended at your pure love, I behold the darkness and rebellion resulting from the fall! You did not make mans heart will this monstrous passion of appropriation. The uprightness wherein the scriptures teach us he was originally created consisted in this, that he had no claim upon himself but acknowledged that he belonged to his Creator. O Father! your children are sadly changed, and no longer bear your image! They are enraged, they are discouraged when they are told they should belong to You as You belong to Yourself! They desire to reverse this holy order, and would madly raise themselves into Gods; they desire to be their own, to do everything for self, or at least, to surrender themselves with certain reservations and conditions, and for their own advantage. O monstrous usurpation! O unknown rights of God! O the ingratitude and insolence of the creature! Miserable nothing! what have you to keep for yourself! What have you which belongs to you? What have you which did not come from on high, and ought not to return thither? Everything, yes, even this which I would divide with God his gifts, is a gift of God, and was only made for Him; everything within you cries out against you and for your Creator. Be still, then, you who, having been created, would deny your Creator, and surrender yourself wholly to Him. But alas! O my God! what a consolation is it to know that everything within as well as without me, is the work of your hand! You are ever with me. When I do wrong, You are within me, reproaching me with the evil which I do, raising within me regrets for the good which I abandon, and opening to me your arms of mercy. When I do good, You inspire the desire, and do it in me and with me; it is You who loves good and hates evil in my heart, who suffers and prays, who does good to the neighbor and gives alms: I do all these things but by your means; You causes me to do them; it is You who putts them in me. These good works, which are your gifts, become my works; but they do not cease to be your gifts; and they cease to be good works if I look at them for a moment as emanating from myself, or if I forget that they are good only because they come from You. You, then, (it is my delight to believe it!) are incessantly working within me; there You labor invisibly like a miner in the bowels of the earth. You do everything and yet the world beholds You not, attributes nothing to You; and even I myself wandered everywhere vainly searching for You outside of myself; I ran over all the wonders of nature that I might form some conception of your greatness; I asked your creatures of You and not once thought of finding You in the depths of my heart where You had never ceased to dwell. No, O my God! it is not necessary to descent into the depths nor to pass beyond the seas; it is not necessary to ascend into the heavens to find You; You are nearer to us than we are to ourselves. O my God! who are at once so great and so condescending, so high above the heavens and so accommodating to the misery of the creature, so infinite and so intimately enclosed in the depths of my heart, so terrible and so lovely, so jealous and so easy to be entreated of those who converse with You with the familiarity of pure love, when will your children cease to be ignorant of You? Where shall I find a voice loud enough to reproach the whole world with its blindness, and to tell it with authority all that You are? When we bid men look for You in their own hearts, it is as though we bade them search for You in the remotest and most unknown lands! What territory is more distant or more unknown to the greater part of them, vain and dissipated as they are, than the ground of their own hearts? Do they ever know what it is to enter within themselves? Have they ever endeavored to find the way? Can they even form the most distant conception of the nature of that interior sanctuary, that impenetrable depth of the soul where You desire to be worshipped in spirit and in truth? They are ever outside of themselves in the objects of their ambition or of their pleasure. Alas! how can they understand heavenly truths, since, as our Lord says, they cannot even comprehend those which are earthly? They cannot conceive what it is to enter within themselves by serious reflection; what would they say if they were told bid to come out of themselves that they might be lost in God? As for me, my Creator, I shut my eyes to all exterior things, which are but vanity and vexation of spirit, that I may enjoy in the deepest recesses of my heart an intimate companionship with You through Jesus Christ your Son, who is your Wisdom and Eternal Understanding. He became a child that by his childhood and the folly of his cross, he might put to shame our vain and lying wisdom. Cost what it may, and in spite of my fears and speculations, I desire to become lowly and a fool, still more despicable in my own eyes than in those of the wise in their own conceit. Like the apostles, I would become drunk with the Holy Spirit, and be content with them to become the sport of the world. I find You everywhere within. It is You that does every good thing which I seem to do. I have a thousand times experienced that I could not of myself govern my temper, overcome my habits, subdue my pride, follow my reason nor will again the good which I had once willed. It is You that must both bestow the will and preserve it pure; without You I am but a reed shaken by the wind. You are the author of all the courage, the uprightness and the truth which I possess; You have given me a new heart which longs after your righteousness, and which is athirst for your eternal truth; You have taken away the old man full of filth and corruption, and which was jealous, vain, ambitious, restless, unrighteous and devoted to its own pleasure. In what a state of misery did I live. Ah! could I ever have believed that I should be enabled thus to turn to You, and shake off the yoke of my tyrannical passions? But, behold a marvel that eclipses all the rest! Who but You could ever have snatched me from myself, and turned all my hatred and contempt against mine own bosom? I have not done this; for it is not by our own power that we depart from self; no! You, O Lord, did shine with your own light into the depth of my heart which could not be reached by any other, and did there reveal the whole of my foulness. I know that, even after beholding, I have not changed it; that I am still filthy in your sight, that my eyes have not been able to discover the extent of my pollution; but I have, at least, seen a part, and I desire to behold the whole. I am despised in my own sight, but the hope that I have in You causes me to live in peace; for I will neither flatter my defects nor suffer them to discourage me. I take your side, O God, against myself; it is only by your strength that I am able to do this. Behold what has God wrought within me! and You continue your work from day to day in cleansing me from the old Adam and in building up the new. This is the new creation which is gradually going on. I leave myself, Father, in your hands; make and re-make this clay, shape it or grind it to atoms; it is your own, it has nought to say; only let it always be subservient to your ever-blessed designs, and let nothing in me oppose your good pleasure for which I was created. Require, command, forbid; what would You have me do? what not do? Exalted, or abased, rejoicing or suffering, doing your work or laid aside, I will always praise You alike, ever yielding up all my own will to Yours! Nothing remains for me but to adopt the language of Mary: Be it unto me according to your words, Let me, O my God, stifle forever in my heart, every thought that would tempt me to doubt your goodness. I know that You can not but be good. O merciful Father! let me no longer reason about grace, but silently abandon myself to its operation. Grace performs everything in us, but does it with and through us; it is by it, therefore, that I act, that I forbear, that I suffer, that I wait, that I resist, that I believe, that I hope, and that I love, all in co-operation with grace. Following its guidance, it will do all things in me, and I shall do all things through it; it moves the heart, but the heart must move; there is no salvation without mans action. I must work, then, without losing a moment, that I may put no hindrance in the way of that grace which is incessantly working within me. All the good is of grace, all the evil is of self; when I do right, it is grace that does it; when I do wrong, it is because I resist grace. I pray God that I may not seek to know more than this; all else will but serve to nourish a presumptuous curiosity. O my God! keep me ever in the number of those babes to whom You reveal your mysteries, while You conceal them from the wise and prudent! You cause me clearly to understand that You make use of the evils and imperfections of the creature to do the good which you have determined beforehand. You conceal yourself under the importunate visitor, who intrudes upon the occupation of your impatient child, that he may learn not to be impatient, and that he may die to the gratification of being free to study or work as he pleases. You avail yourself of slanderous tongues to destroy the reputation of your innocent children, that, beside their innocence, they may offer You the sacrifice of their too highly-cherished reputation. By the cunning artifices of the envious, You lay low the fortunes of those whose were too much set upon their prosperity. It is your hand that sends death upon him to whom life is a constant source of danger, and the tomb a harbor of refuge. It is You that makes his death a remedy, bitter enough, it is true, but effectual, for those who were too fondly attached to him, and thus, while saving one, by removing him from life, You prepare the others, by that very act, for a happy death. Thus You mercifully strew bitterness over everything that is not Yourself, to the end that our hearts, formed to love You and to exist upon your love, may be, as it were, constrained to return to You by a want of satisfaction in everything else. And this is because You are all Love, and consequently all Jealousy. O jealous God! (for thus are you called!) a divided heart displeases You; a wandering one excites your pity. You are infinite in all things, in love as well as in wisdom and power. You love like an infinite God when you love; You move heaven and earth to save your loved ones; You become man, a babe, the vilest of men, covered with reproaches, dying with infamy and under the pangs of the cross; all this is not too much for an infinite love. Our finite love and limited wisdom cannot understand it; how should the finite comprehend the Infinite? it has neither eyes to see it nor a heart to take it in; the debased and narrowed soul of man and his vain wisdom are offended, and can perceive no trace of God in this excess of love. But for myself, it is by this very character of infinity that I recognize it: this is the love that does all things; that brings to pass even the evils we suffer, so shaping them that they are but the instruments of preparing the good which, as yet, has not arrived. But ah! when shall we return love for Love? When shall we seek Him who seeks us and constantly carries us in his arms? When He bears us along in his tender and paternal bosom, then it is that we forget Him; in the sweetness of his gifts, we forget the Giver; his ceaseless blessings, instead of melting us into love, distract our attention and turn it away from Him.

On Pure Love

The Lord has made all things for Himself, says the Scripture; everything belongs to Him, and He will never release his right to anything. Free and intelligent creatures are his as much as those which are otherwise. He refers every unintelligent thing totally and absolutely to Himself, and He desires that his intelligent creatures should voluntarily make the same disposition of themselves. It is true that He desires our happiness, but that is neither the chief end of his work, nor an end to be compared with that of his glory. It is for his glory only that He wills our happiness; the latter is a subordinate consideration, which He refers to the final and essential end of his glory. That we may enter into his designs in this respect, we must prefer God before ourselves, and endeavor to will our own happiness for his glory; in any other case, we invert the order of things. And we must not desire his glory on account of our own salvation, but, on the other hand, the desire for his glory should impel us to seek our own happiness as a thing which He has been pleased to make a part of his glory. It is true that all holy souls are not capable of exercising this explicit preference for God over themselves, but there must at least be an implicit preference; the former, which is more perfect, is reserved for those whom God has endowed with light and strength to prefer Him to themselves, to such a degree as to desire their own happiness simply because it adds to his glory. Men have a great repugnance to this truth, and consider it to be a very hard saying, because they are lovers of self from self-interest. They understand, in a general and superficial way, that they must love God more than all his creatures, but they have no conception of loving God more than themselves, and loving themselves only for Him. They can utter these great words without difficulty, because they do not enter into their meaning, but they shudder when it is explained to them, that God and his glory are to be preferred before ourselves and everything else to such a degree that we must love his glory more than our own happiness, and must refer the latter to the former, as a subordinate means to an end.

On Prayer And The Principal Exercises Of Piety

True prayer is only another name for the love of God. Its excellence does not consist in the multitude of our words; for our Father knows what things we have need of before we ask Him.

The true prayer is that of the heart, and the heart prays only for what it desires. To pray, then is to desire but to desire what God would have us desire. He who asks what he does not from the bottom of his heart desire, is mistaken in thinking that he prays. Let him spend days in reciting prayers, in meditation or in inciting himself to pious exercises, he prays not once truly, if he really desire not the things he pretends to ask.

O! how few there are who pray! for how few are they who desire what is truly good! Crosses, external and internal humiliation, renouncement of our own wills, the death of self and the establishment of Gods throne upon the ruins of self love, these are indeed good; not to desire these, is not to pray; to desire them seriously, soberly, constantly, and with reference to all the details of life, this is true prayer; not to desire them, and yet to suppose we pray, is an illusion like that of the wretched who dream themselves happy. Alas! how many souls full of self, and of an imaginary desire for perfection in the midst of hosts of voluntary imperfections, have never yet uttered this true prayer of the heart! It is in reference to this that St. Augustine says: He that loves little, prays little; he that loves much, prays much.

On the other hand, that heart in which the true love of God and true desire exist, never ceases to pray. Love, hid in the bottom of the soul, prays without ceasing, even when the mind is drawn another way. God continually beholds the desire which He has himself implanted in the soul, though it may at times be unconscious of its existence; his heart is touched by it; it ceaselessly attracts his mercies; it is that Spirit which, according to St. Paul, helps our infirmities and makes intercession for us with groans which cannot be uttered.

Love desires of God that he would give us what we need, and that He would have less regard to our frailty than to the purity of our intentions. It even covers over our trifling defects, and purifies us like a consuming fire; He makes intercession for the Saints, according to the will of God. For we know not what we should pray for as we ought, and, in our ignorance, frequently request what would be injurious; we should like fervor of devotion, distinct sensible joys and apparent perfections, which would serve to nourish within us the life of self and a confidence in our own strength; but love leads us on, abandons us to all the operations of grace, puts us entirely at the disposal of Gods will, and thus prepares us for all his secret designs.

Then we will all things and yet nothing. What God gives, is precisely what we should have desired to ask; for we will whatever He wills and only that. Thus, this state contains all prayer: it is a work of the heart which includes all desire. The Spirit prays within us for those very things which the Spirit himself wills to give us. Even when we are occupied with outward things, and our thoughts drawn off by the providential engagements of our position, we still carry within us a constantly burning fire, which not only cannot be extinguished, but nourishes a secret prayer, and is like a lamp continually lighted before the throne of God, I sleep but my heart wakes. Blessed are those servants, whom the Lord when he comes, shall find watching.

There are two principal points of attention necessary for the preservation of this constant spirit of prayer which unites us with God: we must continually seek to cherish it, and we must avoid everything that tends to make us lose it. In order to cherish it, we should pursue a regulated course of reading; we must have appointed seasons of secret prayer, and frequent states of recollection during the day; we should make use of retirement when we feel the need of it, or when it is advised by those of greater experience, and unite in the ordinances appropriate to our condition. We should greatly fear and be exceedingly cautious to avoid all things that have a tendency to make us lose this state of prayer. Thus we should decline those worldly occupations and associates which dissipate the mind, pleasures which excite the passions, and everything calculated to awaken the love of the world and those old inclinations that have caused us so much trouble. There is an infinity of detail in these two heads; general directions only can be given, because each individual case presents features peculiar to itself.

We should choose those works for reading which instruct us in our duty and in our faults; which, while they point out the greatness of God, teach us what is our duty to Him, and how very far we are from performing it; not those barren productions which melt and sentimentalize the heart; the tree must bear fruit; we can only judge of the life of the root by its fecundity.

The first effect of a sincere love is an earnest desire to know all that we ought to do to gratify the object of our affection. Any other desire is a proof that we love ourselves under a pretence of loving God; that we are seeking an empty and deceitful consolation in Him; that we would use God as an instrument for our pleasure, instead of sacrificing that for his glory. God forbid that his children should so love Him! Cost what it may, we must both know and do without reservation what he requires of us.

Seasons of secret prayer must be regulated by the leisure, the disposition, the condition, and the inward impulse of each individual. Meditation is not prayer, but it is its necessary foundation; it brings to mind the truths which God has revealed. We should be conversant not only with all the mysteries of Jesus Christ, and the truths of his Gospel, but also with everything they ought to operate in us for our regeneration; we should be colored and penetrated by them as wool is by the dye.

So familiar should they become to us, that, in consequence of seeing them at all times and ever near to us, we may acquire the habit of forming no judgment except in their light; that they may be to us our only guide in matters of practice, as the rays of the sun are our only light in matters of perception. When these truths are once, as it were, incorporated in us, then it is that our praying begins to be real and fruitful. Up to that point it was but the shadow; we thought we had penetrated to the inmost recesses of the gospel, when we had barely set foot upon the vestibule all our most tender and lively feelings, all our firmest resolutions, all our clearest and farthest views, were but the rough and shapeless mass from which God would hew in us his likeness.

When his celestial rays begin to shine within us, then we see in the true light; then there is no truth to which we do not instantaneously assent, as we admit, without any process of reasoning, the splendor of the sun, the moment we behold his rising beams. Our union with God must be the result of our faithfulness in doing and suffering all his will.

Our meditations should become every day deeper and more interior. I say deeper, because by frequent and humble meditation upon Gods truth, we penetrate farther and farther in search of new treasures; and more interior, because as we sink more and more to enter into these truths, they also descend to penetrate the very substance of our souls. Then it is that a simple word goes farther than whole sermons.

The very things which had been, fruitlessly and coldly, heard a hundred times before, now nourish the soul with a hidden manna, having an infinite variety of flavors for days in succession. Let us beware, too, of ceasing to meditate upon truths which have heretofore been blessed to us, so long as there remains any nourishment in them, so long as they yet yield us anything; it is a certain sign that we still need their ministration; we derive instruction from them without receiving any precise or distinct impression; there is an indescribable something in them, which helps us more than all our reasoning. We behold a truth, we love it and repose upon it; it strengthens the soul and detaches us from ourselves; let us dwell upon it in peace as long as possible.

As to the manner of meditating, it should not be subtle, nor composed of long reasoning; simple and natural reflections derived immediately from the subject of our thoughts are all that is required. We need take a few truths; meditate upon these without hurry, without effort, and without seeking for far-fetched reflections. Every truth should be considered with reference to its practical bearing. To receive it without employing all means to put it faithfully in practice at whatever cost, is to desire to hold the truth in unrighteousness; it is a resistance to the truth impressed upon us, and of course, to the Holy Spirit. This is the most terrible of all unfaithfulness.

As to a method in prayer, each one must be guided by his own experience. Those who find themselves profited in using a strict method, need not depart from it, while those who cannot so confine themselves, may make use of their own mode, without ceasing to respect that which has been useful to many, and which so many pious and experienced persons have highly recommended. A method is intended to assist; if it be found to embarrass, instead of assisting, the sooner it is discarded the better.

The most natural mode, at first, is to take a book, and to cease reading whenever we feel so inclined by the passage upon which we are engaged, and, whenever that no longer ministers to our interior nourishment, to begin again. As a general rule, those truths which we highly relish, and which shed a degree of practical light upon the things which we are required to give up for God, are leadings of Divine Grace, which we should follow without hesitation. The Spirit blows where it wills, and where the Spirit of the Lord is, there is liberty. In the course of time the proportion of reflection and reasoning will diminish, and that of tender feelings, affecting views and desires, will increase as we become sufficiently instructed and convinced by the Holy Spirit. The heart is satisfied, nourished, warmed, set on fire; a word only will give it employment for a long time.

Finally, increase of prayer is indicated by an increase of simplicity and steadiness in our views, a great multitude of objects and considerations being no longer necessary. Our intercourse with God resembles that with a friend; at first, there are a thousand things to be told, and as many to be asked; but after a time, these diminish, while the pleasure of being together does not. Everything has been said, but the satisfaction of seeing each other, of feeling that one is near the other, or reposing in the enjoyment of a pure and sweet friendship, can be felt without conversation; the silence is eloquent and mutually understood. Each feels that the other is in perfect sympathy with him, and that their two hearts are incessantly poured one into the other, and constitute but one.

Thus it is that in prayer, our communion with God becomes a simple and familiar union, far beyond the need of words. But let it be remembered that God himself must alone institute this prayer within us; nothing would be more rash nor more dangerous, than to dare to attempt it of ourselves. We must suffer ourselves to be led step by step, by some one conversant with the ways of God, who may lay the immovable foundations of correct teaching, and of the complete death of self in everything.

As regards retirement and attending upon ordinances, we must be governed by the advice of some one in whom we have confidence. Our own necessities, the effect produced upon us, and many other circumstances, are to be taken into consideration.

Our leisure and our needs must regulate our retirements; our needs, because it is with the soul as with the body; when we can no longer work without nourishment, we must take it; we shall otherwise be in danger of fainting. Our leisure, because, this absolute necessity of food excepted, we must attend to duty before we seek enjoyment in spiritual exercises. The man who has public duties and spends the time appropriate to them in meditating in retirement, would miss of God while he was seeking to be united to Him. True union with God is to do his will without ceasing, in spite of all our natural disinclination and in every duty of life, however disagreeable or mortifying.

As precautions against wanderings we must avoid close and intimate intercourse with those who are not pious, especially when we have been before led astray by their infectious maxims. They will open our wounds afresh: they have a secret correspondence deep in our souls; there is there a soft and insinuating counselor who is always ready to blind and deceive us.

Would you judge of a man? says the Holy Spirit. Observe who are his companions. How can he who loves God, and who loves nothing except in and for God, enjoy the intimate companionship of those who neither love, nor know God, and who look upon love to Him as a weakness? Can a heart full of God and sensible of its own frailty, ever rest, and be at ease with those who have no feelings in common with it, but are ever seeking to rob it of its treasure? Their delights, and the pleasures of which Faith is the source, are incompatible.

I am well aware that we cannot, nay, that we ought not to break with those friends to whom we are bound by esteem of their natural amiability, by their services, by the tie of sincere friendship, or by the regard consequent upon mutual good offices. Friends whom we have treated with a certain familiarity and confidence, would be wounded to the quick, were we to separate from them entirely; we must gently and imperceptibly diminish our intercourse with them, without abruptly declaring our alteration of sentiment; we may see them in private, distinguish them from our less intimate friends, and confide to them those matters in which their integrity and friendship enable them to give us good advice, and to think with us, although our reasons for so thinking are more pure and elevated than theirs. In short, we may continue to serve them, and to manifest all the attentions of a cordial friendship, without suffering our hearts to be embarrassed by them.

How perilous is our state without this precaution! If we do not, from the first, boldly adopt all measures to render our piety entirely free and independent of our unregenerate friends, it is threatened with a speedy downfall. If a man surrounded by such companions be of a yielding disposition and inflammable passions, it is certain that his friends, even the best-intentioned ones, will lead him astray. They may be good, honest, faithful, and possessed of all those qualities which render friendship perfect in the eye of the world; but, for him, they are infected, and their amiability only increases the danger. Those who have not this estimable character, should be sacrificed at once; blessed are we, when a sacrifice that ought to cost us so little, may avail to give us so precious a security for our eternal salvation!

Not only, then, should we be exceedingly careful whom we will see, but we must also reserve the necessary time that we may see God alone in prayer. Those who have stations of importance to fill, have generally so many indispensable duties to perform, that without the greatest care in the management of their time, none will be left to be alone with God. If they have ever so little inclination for dissipation, the hours that belong to God and their neighbor disappear altogether. We must be firm in observing our rules. This strictness seems excessive, but without it everything falls into confusion; we become dissipated, relaxed and lose strength; we insensibly separate from God, surrender ourselves to all our pleasures, and only then begin to perceive that we have wandered, when it is almost hopeless to think of endeavoring to return. Prayer, prayer! this is our only safety. Blessed be God which has not turned away my prayer, nor his mercy from me. And to be faithful in prayer it is indispensable that we should dispose all the employments of the day, with a regularity nothing can disturb.

On Conformity To The Life Of Jesus Christ

We must imitate Jesus; live as He lived, think as He thought, and be conformed to his image, which is the seal of our sanctification. What a contrast! Nothingness strives to be something, and the Omnipotent becomes nothing! I will be nothing with You, my Lord! I offer You the pride and vanity which have possessed me hitherto. Help my will; remove from me occasions of my stumbling; turn away my eyes from beholding vanity; let me behold nothing but You and myself in your presence, that I may understand what I am and what You are. Jesus Christ was born in a stable; he was obliged to fly into Egypt; thirty years of his life were spent in a workshop; he suffered hunger, thirst, and weariness; he was poor, despised and miserable; he taught the doctrines of Heaven, and no one would listen. The great and the wise persecuted and took him, subjected him to frightful torments, treated him as a slave and put him to death between two malefactors, having preferred to give liberty to a robber, rather than to suffer him to escape. Such was the life which our Lord chose; while we are horrified at any kind of humiliation, and cannot bear the slightest appearance of contempt. Let us compare our lives with that of Jesus Christ, reflecting that he was the Master and that we are the servants; that He was all-powerful, and that we are but weakness; that he was abased and that we are exalted. Let us so constantly bear our wretchedness in mind, that we may have nothing but contempt for ourselves. With what face can we despise others, and dwell upon their faults, when we ourselves are filled with nothing else? Let us begin to walk in the path which our Savior has marked out, for it is the only one that can lead us to Him. And how can we expect to find Jesus if we do not seek Him in the states of his earthly life, in loneliness and silence, in poverty and suffering, in persecution and contempt, in annihilation and the cross? The saints find him in heaven, in the splendors of glory and in unspeakable pleasures; but it is only after having dwelt with Him on earth in reproaches, in pain and in humiliation. To be a Christian is to be an imitator of Jesus Christ. In what can we imitate Him if not in his humiliation? Nothing else can bring us near to Him. We may adore him as Omnipotent, fear him as just, love him with all our heart as good and merciful, but we can only imitate him as humble, submissive, poor and despised. Let us not imagine that we can do this by our own efforts; everything that is written is opposed to it; but we may rejoice in the presence of God. Jesus has chosen to be made partaker of all our weaknesses; He is a compassionate high-priest who has voluntarily submitted to be tempted in all points like as we are; let us, then, have all our strength in Him who became weak that he might strengthen us; let us enrich ourselves out of his poverty, confidently exclaiming, I can do all things through Christ which strengthens me. Let me follow in your footsteps, O Jesus! I would imitate You, but cannot without the aid of your grace! O humble and lowly Savior, grant me the knowledge of the true Christian, and that I may willingly despise myself; let me learn the lesson, so incomprehensible to the mind of man, that I must die to myself by an abandonment that shall produce true humility. Let us earnestly engage in this work, and change this hard heart, so rebellious to the heart of Jesus Christ. Let us make some approaches toward the holy soul of Jesus; let Him animate our souls and destroy all our repugnancies. O lovely Jesus! who has suffered so many injuries and reproaches for my sake, let me esteem and love them, and let me desire to share your life of humiliation!

On Humility

What a mercy is humiliation to a soul that receives it with a steadfast faith! There are a thousand blessings in it for ourselves and for others; for our Lord bestows his grace upon the humble. Humility renders us charitable towards our neighbor; nothing will make us so tender and indulgent to the faults of others as a view of our own. Two things produce humility when combined; the first is a sight of the abyss of wretchedness from which the all-powerful hand of God has snatched us, and over which he still holds us, as it were, suspected in the air, and the other is the presence of that God who is ALL. Our faults, even those most difficult to bear, will all be of service to us, if we make use of them for our humiliation, without relaxing our efforts to correct them. It does no good to be discouraged; it is the result of a disappointed and despairing self-love. The true method of profiting by the humiliation of our faults, is to behold them in all their deformity, without losing our hope in God, and without having any confidence in ourselves. We must bear with ourselves without either flattery or discouragement, a mean seldom attained; for we either expect great things of ourselves and of our good intentions, or wholly despair. We must hope nothing for self, but wait for everything from God. Utter despair of ourselves, in consequence of a conviction of our helplessness, and unbounded confidence in God, are the true foundations of the spiritual edifice. That is a false humility, which, acknowledging itself unworthy of the gifts of God, dares not confidently expect them; true humility consists in a deep view of our utter unworthiness, and in an absolute abandonment to God, without the slightest doubt that He will do the greatest things in us. Those who are truly humble, will be surprised to hear anything exalted of themselves. They are mild and peaceful, of a contrite and humble heart, merciful and compassionate; they are quiet, cheerful, obedient, watchful, fervent in spirit and incapable of strife; they always take the lowest place, rejoice when they are despised, and consider every one superior to themselves; they are lenient to the faults of others in view of their own, and very far from preferring themselves before any one. We may judge of our advancement in humility, by the delight we have in humiliations and contempt.

On Prayer

Many are tempted to believe that they no longer pray, when they cease to enjoy a certain pleasure in the act of prayer. But, if they will reflect that perfect prayer is only another name for love to God, they will be undeceived. Prayer, then, does not consist in sweet feelings, nor in the charms of an excited imagination, nor in that illumination of the intellect that traces with ease the most sublime truths in God; nor even in a certain consolation in the view of God: all these things are external gifts from his hand, in the absence of which, love may exist even more purely, as the soul may then attach itself immediately and solely to God, instead of to his mercies. This is that love by naked faith which is the death of nature, because it leaves it no support; and when we are convinced that all is lost, that very conviction is the evidence that all is gained. Pure love is in the will alone; it is no sentimental love, for the imagination has no part in it; it loves, if we may so express it, without feeling, as faith believes without seeing. We need not fear that this love is an imaginary thing nothing can be less so than the mere will separate from all imagination: the more purely intellectual and spiritual are the operations of our minds, the nearer are they, not only to reality but to the perfection which God requires of us: their working is more perfect; faith is in full exercise while humility is preserved. Such love is chaste: for it is the love of God in and for God; we are attached to Him, but not for the pleasure which he bestows on us; we follow Him, but not for the loaves and fishes. What! some may say, can it be that a simple will to be united with God, is the whole of piety? How can we be assured that this will is not a mere idea, a trick of the imagination, instead of a true willing of the soul? I should indeed believe that it was a deception, if it were not the parent of faithfulness on all proper occasions; for a good tree brings forth good fruit; and a true will makes us truly earnest and diligent in doing the will of God; but it is still compatible in this life with little failings which are permitted by God that the soul may be humbled. If, then, we experience only these little daily frailties, let us not be discouraged, but extract from them their proper fruit, humility. True virtue and pure love reside in the will alone. Is it not a great matter always to desire the Supreme Good whenever He is seen; to keep the mind steadily turned towards Him, and to bring it back whenever it is perceived to wander; to will nothing advisedly but according to his order; in short, in the absence of all sensible enjoyment, still to remain the same in the spirit of a submissive, irreclaimable burnt-offering? Think you it is nothing to repress all the uneasy reflections of self-love; to press forward continually without knowing whither we go, and yet without stopping; to cease from self-satisfied thoughts of self, or at least, to think of ourselves as we would of another; to fulfill the indications of Providence for the moment, and no further? Is not this more likely to be the death of the Old Adam than fine sentiments, in which we are, in fact, thinking only of self, or external acts, in the performance of which we congratulate self on our advancement? It is a sort of infidelity to simple faith when we desire to be continually assured that we are doing well; it is, in fact, to desire to know what we are doing, which we shall never know, and of which it is the will of God that we should be ignorant. It is trifling by the way in order to reason about the way. The safest and shortest course is to renounce, forget and abandon self, and through faithfulness to God to think no more of it. This is the whole of religion to get out of self and of self-love in order to get into God. As to involuntary wanderings, they are no hindrance to love, inasmuch as love is in the will, and the will only wanders when it wills to wander. As soon as we perceive that they have occurred, we drop them instantly and return to God, and thus, while the external senses of the spouse are asleep, the heart is watching; its love knows no intermission. A tender parent does not always bear his son distinctly in mind; he thinks and imagines a thousand things disconnected with him, but they do not interfere with the paternal affection; the moment that his thoughts rest again upon his child, he loves, and feels in the depths of his soul that though he has ceased to think of him he has not for an instant failed to love him. Such should be our love to our Heavenly Father; a love simple, trustful, confident and without anxiety. If our imagination take wing and our thoughts wander, let us not be perplexed; all these things are not that hidden man of the heart in that which is not corruptible, even the ornament of a meek and quiet spirit, of which St. Peter speaks. Let us only turn our thoughts, whenever we can, towards the face of the Well-beloved without being troubled at our wanderings. When He shall see fit to enable us to preserve a more constant sense of his presence with us, He will do so. He sometimes removes it for our advancement; it amuses us with too many reflections which are true distractions, diverting the mind from a simple and direct look toward God and withdrawing us from the shades of naked faith. We often seek in these reflections a resting-place for our self-love and consolation in the testimony we endeavor to extract from them for self; and thus the warmth of our feelings causes us to wander. On the contrary, we never pray so purely as when we are tempted to believe that we do not pray at all; we fear that we pray ill, but we should only fear being left to the desolation of sinful nature, to a philosophical infidelity, seeking perpetually a demonstration of its own operations in faith; in short, to impatient desires for consolation in sight and feeling. There is no more bitter penance than this state of pure faith without sensible support; and hence it seems to me the most effective, the most crucifying, and the least illusive. Strange temptation! We look impatiently for sensible consolation from the fear of not being penitent enough! Ah! why do we not consider the renouncement of that consolation which we are so strongly tempted to seek, as a proof of our penitence? Remember our Lord abandoned by his Father on the cross: all feeling, all reflection withdrawn that his God might be hidden from him; this was indeed the last blow that fell upon the man of sorrows, the consummation of the sacrifice! Never should we so abandon ourselves to God as when He seems to abandon us. Let us enjoy light and consolation when it is his pleasure to give it to us, but let us not attach ourselves to his gifts, but to Him; and when He plunges us into the night of Pure Faith, let us still press on through the agonizing darkness. Moments are worth days in this tribulation; the soul is troubled and yet at peace; not only is God hidden from it, but it is hidden from itself, that all may be of faith; it is discouraged, but feels nevertheless an immovable will to bear all that God may choose to inflict; it wills all, accepts all, even the troubles that try its faith, and thus in the very height of the tempest, the waters beneath are secretly calm and at peace, because its Will is one with Gods. Blessed be the Lord who performs such great things in us, notwithstanding our unworthiness!

On Meditation

When the solid foundations of a perfect conversion of heart, a scrupulous repentance and a serious meditation of all the Christian virtues have been laid, both theoretically and practically, we become gradually so accustomed to these truths, that we regard them at last with a simple and steady look, without the necessity of going back to examine and convince ourselves of each of them in detail. They are then all embraced in a certain enjoyment of God, so pure and so intimate, that we find everything in Him. It is no longer the intellect that examines and reasons; it is the will which loves and plunges into the infinite Good. But this is not your state. You must walk for a long while in the way of the sinners who are beginning to seek God; ordinary meditation is your lot, too happy that God condescends to admit you to it. Walk then in the spirit, like Abraham, without knowing whither you go; be content with your daily bread, and remember that in the desert the manna of to-day could not be preserved until tomorrow without corrupting. The children of God must be shut up to the grace of the present moment, without desiring to foresee the designs of Providence concerning them. Meditate, then, since now is your opportunity, upon all the mysteries of Jesus Christ and upon all the Gospel truths which you have for so long a time ignored and rejected. When God shall have entirely effaced from your mind the impression of all your worldly maxims, and the Spirit shall have left there no trace of your old prejudices, then it will be necessary to ascertain the direction in which you are attracted by grace, and to follow step by step without anticipating. In the meantime, dwell in peace in the bosom of God, like a little child on the breast of its mother; be satisfied with thinking on your chosen subject simply and easily; suffer yourself to be led gently to the truths which affect you, and which you find to nourish your heart. Avoid all exertions that excite the intellect, which often tempt us to believe that there is more piety in a dangerous vivacity of the imagination, than in a pure and upright intention of abandonment to God. Avoid likewise all refined speculation; confine yourself to simple reflections, and recur to them frequently. Those who pass too rapidly from one truth to another, feed their curiosity and restlessness; they even distract their intellect by too great a multiplicity of views. Give every truth time to send down deep roots into the heart; the main point is to love. Nothing gives rise to such severe fits of indigestion as eating too much and too hastily. Digest every truth leisurely, if you would extract the essence of it for your nourishment, but let there be no restless self-reflective acts. Be sure that your exercise will not be acceptable unless performed without agitation or tumult. I am well aware that you will have distractions enough; bear them without impatience, dismiss them and recur quietly to your subject as soon as you perceive that your imagination has wandered. In this way these involuntary distractions will produce no injurious effects, and the patience with which you bear them without being discouraged, will advance you farther than a more continuous meditation, in which you might take more self-satisfaction. The true method of conquering wandering thoughts, is never to attack them directly with bitterness, and never to be discouraged by their frequency or duration. Suffer yourself, then, to be quietly occupied by the subject you have chosen; only let the exercise be as holy as you can make it, to which end take the following directions: Do not encumber yourself with a great number of thoughts upon a subject; but dwell upon each sufficiently long to allow it to afford its proper nourishment to the heart. You will gradually become accustomed to regard each truth steadily by itself, without flitting from one to another; this habit will serve to fix them deeply in your soul. You will thus, also, acquire a habit of dwelling upon your themes with pleasure and peaceful acquiescence, instead of considering them rapidly and intellectually as most persons do. Thus the foundations will be firmly laid for all that God intends to do in you; he will thus mortify the natural activity of the mind, that ever inclines it to seek novelties, instead of deeply imprinting the truths already in some degree familiar. You must not, however, forcibly restrain your mind to a subject which no longer seems to afford any nourishment; I would advise only that you should not abandon it so long as it still ministers food. As to your affections, retain all which the view of your subject naturally and quietly induces; but do not attempt to stir yourself up to great efforts, for they will exhaust and agitate you, and even cause aridity; they will occupy you too much with your own exertions, and implant a dangerous confidence in your own power; in short, they will attach you too firmly to sensible pleasures, and will thus prepare you great trouble in a time of dryness. Be content, then, to follow with simplicity, and without too many reflections, the emotions which

God shall excite in view of your subject, or of any other truth. As for higher things, have no thoughts of them; there is a time for everything, and it is of the greatest importance that nothing should be precipitated. One of the cardinal rules of the spiritual life is, that we are to live exclusively in the present moment, without casting a look beyond. You remember that the Israelites in the desert followed the pillar of fire, or of cloud, without knowing whither it was leading them; they had a supply of manna but for one day; all above that became useless. There is no necessity now for moving rapidly; think only of laying a solid foundation; see that it is deep and broad by an absolute renunciation of self, and by an abandonment without reserve to the requirements of God. Let God, then, raise upon this foundation such a building as He pleases. Shut your eyes and commit yourself to Him. How wonderful is this walking with Abraham in pure faith, not knowing whither we go! and how full of blessings is the path! God will then be your guide; He himself will travel with you, as we are told He did with the Israelites, to bring them step by step across the desert to the promised land. Ah! what will be your blessedness if you will but surrender yourself into the hands of God, permitting him to do whatever He will, not according to your desires, but according to His own good pleasure!

On Mortification

God calls us hourly and momentarily to the exercise of mortification; but nothing can be more false than the maxim that we should always choose that which mortifies us the most. Such a plan would soon destroy our health, our reputation, our business, our intercourse with our relatives and friends, and the good works which Providence requires of us. I have no hesitation in saying that we ought to avoid certain things which experience has shown us to injure our health, such as certain kinds of food, etc. This course will, no doubt, spare us some suffering; but it does not tend to pamper the body nor require the employment of expensive or delicious substitutes; on the contrary, it conduces to a sober, and, therefore, in many respects, mortified life. Failures in regimen are owing to a want of mortification; they are not due either to courage in enduring pain, or to indifference to life, but to a weak hankering for pleasure, and impatience of anything that annoys. Submitting to regimen for the purpose of preserving health, is a great constraint; we would much rather suffer and be sick, than be constantly restraining our appetites; we love liberty and pleasure more than health. But God arranges all that in the heart which is devoted to Him; He causes us to fall in quietly with every regulation, and takes away a certain want of pliability in the will, and a dangerous confidence in ourselves; He blunts the desires, cools the passions, and detaches the man, not only from exterior things, but from self, renders him mild, amiable, simple, lowly, ready to will or not, according to His good pleasure. Let it be so with us; God desires it, and is ready to effect it; let us not resist his will. The mortification which comes in the order of God, is more serviceable than any enjoyment in devotion which should result from our own affection and choice. In regard to austerities, every one must regard his attraction, his state, his need and his temperament. A simple mortification, consisting in nothing more than an unshaken fidelity in providential crosses, is often far more valuable than severe austerities which render the life more marked, and tempt to a vain self-complacency. Whoever will refuse nothing which comes in the order of God, and seek nothing out of that order, need never fear to finish his days work without partaking of the cross of Jesus Christ. There is an indispensable Providence for crosses as well as for the necessities of life; they are a part of our daily bread; God never will suffer it to fail. It is sometimes a very useful mortification to certain fervent souls, to give up their own plans of mortification, and adopt with cheerfulness those which are momentarily revealed in the order of God. When a soul is not faithful in providential mortifications, there is reason to fear some illusion in those which are sought through the fervor of devotion; such warmth is often deceitful, and it seems to me that a soul in this case would do well to examine its faithfulness under the daily crosses allotted by Providence.

On Self-Abandonment

If you would fully comprehend the meaning of self-abandonment, recall the interior difficulty which you felt, and which you very naturally testified when I directed you always to count as nothing this self which is so dear to us. To abandon ones self is to count ones self as nought; and he who has perceived the difficulty of doing it, has already learned what that renunciation is, which so revolts our nature. Since you have felt the blow, it is evident that it has fallen upon the sore spot in your heart; let the all-powerful hand of God work in you as he well knows how, to tear you from yourself. The origin of our trouble is, that we love ourselves with a blind passion that amounts to idolatry. If we love anything beyond, it is only for our own sakes. We must be undeceived respecting all those generous friendships, in which it appears as though we so far forgot ourselves as to think only of the interests of our friend. If the motive of our friendship be not low and gross, it is nevertheless still selfish; and the more delicate, the more concealed, and the more proper in the eyes of the world it is, the more dangerous does it become, and the more likely to poison us by feeding our self-love. In those friendships which appear, both to ourselves and to the world, so generous and disinterested, we seek, in short, the pleasure of loving without recompense, and by the indulgence of so noble a sentiment, of raising ourselves above the weak and sordid of our race. Besides the tribute which we pay to our own pride, we seek from the world the reputation of disinterestedness and generosity; we desire to be loved by our friends, although we do not desire to be served by them; we hope that they will be charmed with what we do for them without any expectation of return; and in this way we get that very return which we seem to despise: for what is more delicious to a delicate self-love, than to hear itself applauded for not being self-love? You may have seen some one who seemed to think of every one but himself, who was the delight of good people, who was well disciplined, and seemed entirely forgetful of self. The self-oblivion is so great that self-love even would imitate it, and finds no glory equal to that of seeming to seek none at all. This moderation and self-renunciation which, if genuine, would be the death of nature, become, on the other hand, the most subtle and imperceptible food of a pride which despises all ordinary forms of glory, and desires only that which is to be secured by trampling under foot all the gross objects of ambition which captivate ordinary minds. But it is not a difficult matter to unmask this modest arrogance this pride which seems no pride at all, so much does it appear to have renounced all the ordinary objects of desire. Condemn it and it cannot bear to be found fault with; let those whom it loves fail to repay it with friendship, esteem, and confidence, and it is stung to the quick. It is easy to see that it is not disinterested, though it tries so hard to seem so: it does not indeed accept payment in as gross coin as others; it does not desire insipid praise, or money, or that good fortune which consists in office and dignities. It must be paid, nevertheless; it is greedy of the esteem of good people; it loves that it may be loved again and be admired for its disinterestedness; it seems to forget self, that, by that means, it may draw the attention of the whole world upon self alone. It does not, indeed, make all these reflections in full detail; it does not say in so many words, I will deceive the whole world with my generosity, in order that the world may love and admire me; no, it would not dare to address such a gross and unworthy language to itself; it deceives itself with the rest of the world; it admires itself in its generosity, as a belle admires her beauty in a mirror; it is affected by perceiving that it is more generous and more disinterested than the rest of mankind; the illusion it prepares for others extends to itself; it passes with itself for what it passes itself upon others, that is, for generosity, and this is what pleases it more than anything else. However little we may have looked within to study the occasions of our pleasure and our grief, we shall have no difficulty in admitting that pride, as it is more or less delicate, has various tastes. But give it what taste you will, it is still pride; and that which appears the most restrained and the most reasonable is the most devilish; in esteeming itself, it despises others; it pities those who are pleased with foolish vanities; it recognizes the emptiness of greatness and rank; it cannot abide those who are intoxicated with good fortune; it would, by its moderation, be above fortune, and thus raise itself to a new height, by putting under foot all the false glory of men; like Lucifer, it would become like to the Most

High. It would be a sort of divinity, above all human passions and interests, and it does not perceive that it seeks to place itself above men by this deceitful pride which blinds it. We may be sure, then, that it is the love of God only that can make us come out of self. If his powerful hand did not sustain us, we should not know how to take the first step in that direction. There is no middle course; we must refer everything either to God or to self; if to self, we have no other God than self; if to God, we are then in order, and regarding ourselves only as one among the other creatures of God, without selfish interests, and with a single eye to accomplish his will, we enter into that self-abandonment which you desire so earnestly to understand. But let me say again, that nothing will so shut your heart against the grace of abandonment, as that philosophic pride and self love in the disguise of worldly generosity, of which you should be especially in fear, on account of your natural disposition towards it. The greater our inherent endowment of frankness, disinteredness, pleasure in doing good, delicacy of feeling, love of honor, and generous friendship, the more lively should be our distrust of self, and our fear lest we take complacency in these gifts of nature. The reason why no creature can draw us out of ourselves is, that there is none that deserves to be preferred before ourselves. There is none which has the right so to detach us, nor the perfection which would be necessary to unite us to them without reference to ourselves, nor the power to satisfy the soul in such an attachment. Hence it is that we love nothing out of ourselves, except for the reference it has to self; we choose under the direction of our coarse and brutal passions, if we are low and boorish, or under the guidance of a refined desire for glory, if we are so delicate as not to be satisfied with what is gross and vulgar. But God does two things, which He only has the power to do. He reveals himself to us, with all his rights over the creature, and in all the charms of his goodness. Then we feel that, not having made ourselves, we are not made for ourselves; that we are created for the glory of Him whom it has pleased to form us; that He is too great to make anything except for Himself, and that thus all our perfection and our happiness should be to be lost in Him. This is what no created thing, dazzling though it may be, can make us realize in respect to itself. Far from finding in them that infinity which so fills and transports us in God, we discover only a void, a powerlessness to fill our hearts, an imperfection that continually drives us into ourselves. The second miracle which God works is, to operate in our hearts that which He pleases, after having enlightened our understanding. He is not satisfied with having displayed his own charms; He makes us love Him by producing, by his grace, his love in our hearts; and He thus himself performs within us, what He makes us see we owe to Him. You desire, perhaps, to know more in detail in what this self-abandonment consists. I will endeavor to satisfy you. There is little difficulty in comprehending that we must reject criminal pleasures, unjust gains, and gross vanities, because the renouncement of these things consists in a contempt which repudiates them absolutely, and forbids our deriving any enjoyment from them; but it is not so easy to understand that we must abandon property honestly acquired, the pleasures of a modest and well-spent life, and the honors derivable from a good reputation, and a virtue which elevates us above the reach of envy. The reason why we do not understand that these things must be given up, is, that we are not required to discard them with dislike, but, on the contrary, to preserve them to be used according to the station in which the Divine Providence places us. We have need of the consolation of a mild and peaceful life, to console us under its troubles; in respect to honors, we must regard that which is convenient, and we must keep the property we possess to supply our wants. How then are we to renounce these things at the very moment when we are occupied in the care of preserving them? We are, moderately and without inordinate emotion, to do what is in our power to retain them, in order to make a sober use of them, without desiring to enjoy them or placing our hearts upon them. I say, a sober use of them, because, when we are not attached to a thing for the purposes of self-enjoyment and of seeking our happiness in it, we use only so much of it as we are necessarily obliged to; as you may see a wise and faithful steward study to appropriate only so much of his masters property as is precisely requisite to meet his necessary wants. The abandonment of evil things then, consists in refusing them with horror; of good things, in using them with moderation for our necessities, continually studying to retrench all those imaginary wants with which greedy nature would flatter herself. Remember that we must not only renounce evil, but also good things; for Jesus has said, Whatsoever he be of you that forsakes not all he has, he cannot be my disciple. It follows, then, that the Christian must abandon everything that he has, however innocent; for, if he do not renounce it, it ceases to be innocent. He must abandon those things which it is his duty to guard with the greatest possible care, such as the good of his family, or his own reputation, for he must have his heart on none of these things; he must preserve them for a sober and moderate use; in short, he must be ready to give them all up whenever it is the will of Providence to deprive him of them. He must give up those whom he loves best, and whom it is his duty to love; and his renouncement of them consists in this, that he is to love them for God only; to make use of the consolation of their friendship soberly, and for the supply of his wants; to be ready to part with them whenever God wills it, and never to seek in them the true repose of his heart. This is that chastity of true Christian friendship which seeks in the mortal and earthly friend, only the heavenly spouse. It is thus that we use the world and the creature as not abusing them, according to Saint Paul. We do not desire to take pleasure in them; we only use what God gives us, what he wills that we should love, and what we accept with the reserve of a heart, receiving it only for necessities sake, and keeping itself for a more worthy object. It is in this sense that Christ would have us leave father and mother, brothers and sisters, and friends, and that he is come to bring a sword upon earth. God is a jealous God; if, in the recesses of your soul, you are attached to any creature, your heart is not worthy of Him: He must reject it as a spouse that divides her affections between her bridegroom and a stranger. Having abandoned everything exterior, and which is not self, it remains to complete the sacrifice by renouncing everything interior, including self. The renouncement of the body is frightful to most delicate and worldly-minded persons. They know nothing, so to speak, that is more themselves than this body, which they flatter and adorn with so much care; and even when deprived of its graces, they often retain a love for its life amounting to a shameful cowardice, so that the very name of death makes them shudder. Your natural courage raises you above these fears, and I think I hear you say, I desire neither to flatter my body, nor to hesitate in consenting to its destruction, whenever it shall be the will of God to waste and consume it to ashes. You may thus renounce the body, and yet there may remain great obstacles in the way of your renouncing the spirit. The more we are able, by the aid of our natural courage, to despise the clay tenement, the more apt are we to set a higher value upon that which it contains, by the aid of which we are enabled to look down upon it. We feel towards our understanding, our wisdom, and our virtue, as a young and worldly woman feels towards her beauty. We take pleasure in them; it gives us a satisfaction to feel that we are wise, moderate, and preserved from the excitement which we see in others; we are intoxicated with the pleasure of not being intoxicated with pleasure; we renounce with courageous moderation the most flattering temptations of the world, and content us with the satisfaction derived from a conviction of our self-control. What a dangerous state! What a subtle poison! How recreant are you to God, if you yield your heart to this refinement of self-love! You must renounce all satisfaction and all natural complacency in your own wisdom and virtue. Remember, the purer and more excellent the gifts of God, the more jealous He is of them. He showed mercy to the first human rebel, and denied it to the angels. Both sinned by the love of self, but as the angel was perfect, and regarded as a sort of divinity, God punished his unfaithfulness with a fiercer jealousy than He did mans disobedience. We may infer from this, that God is more jealous of his most excellent gifts than He is of the more common ones; He would have us attached to nothing but Himself, and to regard his gifts, however excellent, as only the means of uniting us more easily and intimately to Him. Whoever contemplates the grace of God with a satisfaction and sort of pleasure of ownership, turns it into poison. Never appropriate exterior things to yourself then, such as favor or talents, nor even things the most interior. Your good will is no less a gift of Gods mercy, than the life and being which you receive direct from his hands. Live, as it were, on trust; all that is in you, and all that you are, is only loaned you; make use of it according to the will of Him who lends it, but never regard it for a moment as your own. Herein consists true self-abandonment; it is this spirit of self-divesting, this use of ourselves and of ours with a single eye to the movements of God, who alone is the true proprietor of his creatures. You will desire to know, probably, what should be the practice of this renouncement in detail. But I answer that the feeling is no sooner established in the interior of the soul, than God himself will take you by the hand, that you may be exercised in self-renunciation in every event of every day. Self-abandonment is not accomplished by means of painful reflections and continual struggles; it is only by refraining from self-contemplation, and from desiring to master ourselves in our own way, that we lose ourselves in God. The terms abandonment, annihilation and death of itself, and the correlative expressions, union with God, oneness, and others of similar import, are frequently used by writers on the higher life, as a most concise and convenient form of designating a state of experience indicated throughout the New Testament, by such texts as the following: Wherefore, if you be dead with Christ, etc. (Col. 2:20) If you then be risen with Christ, etc. (Col. 3:1) For you are dead and your life is hid with Christ in God. (Col. 3:3) And they that are Christ's have crucified the flesh with the affections and lusts. (Gal. 5:24) For it is God which works in you both to will and to do of his good pleasure. (Phil. 2:13) That they all may be one: as You, Father, are one in me and I in You, that they also may be one in us. (John 17:21) It has been objected by some, that this abnegation of self, recommended in such glowing terms by these pious authors, involved two exceedingly dangerous errors. That on the one hand it necessarily implied an abandonment and loss of our identity, by a sort of Pagan transfusion into God, and on the other, that it bordered upon, if it did not constitute, a very pernicious form of perfectionism, in that it made God the author of all our willing and doing whatever their moral character. It can scarcely be necessary to say to anyone who has made himself familiar with the subject, that such doctrines would be a melancholy perversion of the teachings of the writers in question. By the death of self, and annihilation of the will, they simply mean to express, in the strongest manner possible, that the soul, on every occasion, and under all circumstances, wills only what God wills, retaining perfectly its identity, and of course, its power to will. By union with, or absorption into God, they intend to convey the idea of the state of Oneness referred to by Christ, wherein the soul is made partaker of the perfect Holiness of God; but none are more earnest in insisting that the smallest appearance of evil is unanswerable evidence that such an attainment is still at a distance. By their fruits you shall know them, is constantly asserted to be the inexorable standard of judgment for this, as for all other states of experience.

On Temptations

I know of but two resources against temptations. One is, faithfully to follow the interior light in sternly and immediately cutting off everything we are at liberty to dismiss, and which may excite or strengthen the temptation. I say everything which we are at liberty to dismiss, because we are not always permitted to avoid the occasions of evil. Such as are unavoidable connected with the particular position in which Providence has placed us, are not considered to be within our power. The other expedient consists in turning towards God in every temptation, without being disturbed or anxious to know if we have not already yielded a sort of half consent, and without interrupting our immediate recourse to God. By examining too closely whether we have not been guilty of some unfaithfulness, we incur the risk of being again entangled in the temptation. The shortest and surest way is to act like a little child at the breast; when we show it a frightful monster, it shrinks back and buries its face in its mothers bosom, that it may no longer behold it. The sovereign remedy is the habit of dwelling continually in the presence of God. He sustains, consoles, and calms us. We must never be astonished at temptations, be they never so outrageous. On this earth all is temptation. Crosses tempt us by irritating our pride, and prosperity by flattering it. Our life is a continual combat, but one in which Jesus Christ fights for us. We must pass on unmoved, while temptations rage around us, as the traveler, overtaken by a storm, simply wraps his cloak more closely about him, and pushes on more vigorously towards his destined home. If the thought of former sins and wretchedness should be permitted to come before us, we must remain confounded and abashed before God, quietly enduring in his adorable presence all the shame and ignominy of our transgressions. We must not, however, seek to entertain or to call up so dangerous a recollection. In conclusion, it may be said that in doing what God wills, there is very little to be done by us; and yet there is a wonderful work to be accomplished, no less than that of reserving nothing, and making no resistance for a moment, to that jealous love, which searches inexorably into the most secret recesses of the soul for the smallest trace of self, for the slightest intimations of an affection of which itself is not the author. So, on the other hand, true progress does not consist in a multitude of views, nor in austerities, trouble and strife; it is simply willing nothing and everything, without reservation and without choice, cheerfully performing each days journey as Providence appoints it for us; seeking nothing, refusing nothing; finding everything in the present moment, and suffering God, who does everything, to do his pleasure in and by us, without the slightest resistance. O how happy is he who has attained to this state! and how full of good things is his soul, when it appears emptied of everything! Let us pray the Lord to open to us the whole infinitude of his paternal heart, that our own may be there submerged and lost, so that it may make but one with His! Such was the desire of Paul for the faithful, when he longed for them in the bowels of Jesus Christ.

On Wandering Thoughts And Dejection

Two things trouble you; one is, how you may avoid wandering thoughts; the other, how you may be sustained against dejection. As to the former, you will never cure them by set reflections; you must not expect to do the work of grace by the resources and activity of nature. Be simply content to yield your will to God without reservation; and whenever any state of suffering is brought before you, accept it as his will, in an absolute abandonment to his guidance. Do not go out in search of these crucifixions, but when God permits them to reach you without your having sought them, they need never pass without your deriving profit from them. Receive everything that God presents to your mind, notwithstanding the shrinking of nature, as a trial by which He would exercise and strengthen your faith. Never trouble yourself to inquire whether you will have strength to endure what is presented, if it should actually come upon you, for the moment of trial will have its appointed and sufficient grace; that of the present moment is to behold the afflictions presented tranquilly, and to feel willing to receive them whenever it should be the will of God to bestow them. Go on cheerfully and confidently in this trust. If this state of the will should not change in consequence of a voluntary attachment to something out of the will of God, it will continue forever. Your imagination will doubtless wander to a thousand matters of vanity; it will be subject to more or less agitation, according to your situation and the character of the objects presented to its regard. But what matter? The imagination, as St. Theresa declares, is the fool of the household; it is constantly busy in making some bustle or other, to distract the mind which cannot avoid beholding the images which it exhibits. The attention is inevitable, and is a true distraction, but, so long as it is involuntary, it does not separate us from God; nothing can do that but some distraction of the will. You will never have wandering thoughts if you never will to have them, and may then say with truth that you have prayed without ceasing. Whenever you perceive that you have involuntarily strayed away, return without effort, and you will tranquilly find God again without any disturbance of soul. As long as you are not aware of it, it is no wandering of the heart; when it is made manifest, look to God at once with fidelity, and you will find that this simple faithfulness to Him will be the occasion of blessing you with his more constant and more familiar indwelling. A frequent and easy recollection is one of the fruits of this faithful readiness to leave all wanderings as soon as they are perceived; but it must not be supposed that it can be accomplished by our own labors. Such efforts would produce trouble, scrupulosity, and restlessness in all those matters in which you have most occasion to be free. You will be constantly dreading lest you should lose the presence of God and continually endeavoring to recover it; you will surround yourself with the creations of your own imagination, and thus, the presence of God, which ought, by its sweetness and illumination, to assist us in everything which comes before us in his providence, will have the effect of keeping us always in a tumult, and render us incapable of performing the exterior duties of our condition. Be never troubled, then, at the loss of the sensible presence of God; but, above all, beware of seeking to retain Him by a multitude of argumentative and reflective acts. Be satisfied during the day, and while about the details of your daily duties, with a general and interior view of God, so that if asked, at any moment, whither your heart is tending, you may answer with truth that it is toward God, though the attention of your mind may then be engrossed by something else. Be not troubled by the wanderings of your imagination which you cannot restrain; how often do we wander through the fear of wandering and the regret that we have done so! What would you say of a traveler who, instead of constantly advancing in his journey, should employ his time in anticipating the falls which he might suffer, or in weeping over the place where one had happened? On! on! you would say to him, on! without looking behind or stopping. We must proceed, as the Apostle bids us, that we may abound more and more. The abundance of the love of God will be of more service in correcting us than all our restlessness and selfish reflections. This rule is simple enough; but nature, accustomed to the intricacies of reasoning and reflection, considers it as altogether too simple. We want to help ourselves, and to communicate more impulse to our progress; but it is the very excellency of the precept that it confines us to a state of naked faith, sustained by God alone in our absolute abandonment to Him, and leads us to the death of self by stifling all remains of it whatever. In this way we shall not be led to increase the external devotional practices of such as are exceedingly occupied, or are feeble in body, but shall be contented with turning them all into simple love; thus, we shall only act as constrained by love, and shall never be overburdened, for we shall only do what we love to do. Dejection often arises from the fact that, in seeking God, we have not so found Him as to content us. The desire to find Him, is not the desire to possess Him: it is simply a selfish anxiety to be assured, for our own consolation, that we do possess Him. Poor Nature, depressed and discouraged, is impatient of the restraints of naked faith, where every support is withdrawn; it is grieved to be traveling, as it were, in the air, where it cannot behold its own progress towards perfection. Its pride is irritated by a view of its defects, and this sentiment is mistaken for humility. It longs, from self-love, to behold itself perfect; it is vexed that it is not so already; it is impatient, haughty, and out of temper with itself and everybody else. Sad state! As though the work of God could be accomplished by our ill-humor! As though the peace of God could be attained by means of such interior restlessness! Martha, Martha! why are you troubled and anxious about many things? One thing is needful, to love Him and to sit attentively at his feet! When we are truly abandoned to God, all things are accomplished without the performance of useless labor; we suffer ourselves to be guided in perfect trust; for the future, we will whatever God wills, and shut our eyes to everything else; for the present, we give ourselves up to the fulfillment of his designs. Sufficient for every day is the good and the evil thereof. This daily doing of the will of God is the coming of his kingdom within us, and at the same time our daily bread. We should be faithless indeed, and guilty of heathen distrust, did we desire to penetrate the future, which God has hidden from us; leave it to Him: let Him make it short or long, bitter or sweet; let Him do with it even as it shall please Himself. The most perfect preparation for this future, whatever it may be, is to die to every will of our own, and yield ourselves wholly up to his; we shall in this frame of mind, be ready to receive all the grace suitable to whatever state it shall be the will of God to develop in and around us. When we are thus prepared for every event, we begin to feel the Rock under our feet at the very bottom of the abyss; we are ready to suppose every imaginable evil of ourselves, but we throw ourselves blindly into the arms of God, forgetting and losing everything else. This forgetfulness of self is the most perfect renouncement of self and acceptance of God; it is the sacrifice of self-love; it would be a thousand times more agreeable to accuse and condemn ourselves, to torment body and mind, rather than to forget. Such an abandonment is an annihilation of self-love, in which it no longer finds any nourishment. Then the heart begins to expand; we begin to feel lighter for having thrown off the burden of self, which we formerly carried; we are astounded to behold the simplicity and straightness of the way. We thought there was a need of strife and constant exertion, but we now perceive that there is little to do; that it is sufficient to look to God with confidence, without reasoning either upon the past or the future, regarding Him as a loving Father, who leads us every moment by the hand. If some distraction or other should hide Him for a moment, without stopping to look at it, we simply turn again to Him from whom we had departed. If we commit faults, we repent with a repentance wholly of love, and, returning to God, he makes us feel whatever we ought. Sin seems hideous, but we love the humiliation of which it is the cause, and for which God permitted it. As the reflections of our pride upon our defects are bitter, disheartening and vexatious, so the return of the soul towards God is recollected, peaceful and sustained by confidence. You will find by experience how much more your progress will be aided by this simple, peaceful turning to God, than by all your chagrin and spite at the faults that exist in you. Only be faithful in turning quietly towards God alone, the moment you perceive what you have done; do not stop to argue with yourself; you can gain nothing from that quarter; when you accuse yourself of your misery, I see but you and yourself in consultation; poor wisdom that will issue from where God is not! Whose hand is it that must pluck you out of the mire? Your own? Alas! you are buried deeper than thought, and cannot help yourself; and more, this very slough is nothing but self; the whole of your trouble consists in the inability to leave yourself, and do you expect to increase your chances by dwelling constantly upon your defects, and feeding your sensitiveness by a view of your folly? You will in this way only increase your difficulties, while the gentlest look towards God would calm your heart. It is his presence that causes us to go forth from self, and when He has accomplished that, we are in peace. But how are we to go forth? Simply by turning gently towards God, and gradually forming the habit of so doing, by a faithful persistence in it, whenever we perceive that we have wandered from Him. As to that natural dejection which arises from a melancholic temperament, it belongs purely to the body, and is the province of the physician. It is true that it is constantly recurring, but let it be borne in peace, as we receive from his hands a fever or any other bodily ailment. The question is not, what is the state of our feelings, but what is the condition of our will. Let us will to have what is the condition of our will. Let us will to have whatever we have, and not to have whatever we have not. We would not even be delivered from our sufferings, for it is Gods place to apportion to us our crosses and our joys. In the midst of affliction we rejoice, as did the Apostle; but it is not joy of the feelings, but of the will. The wicked are wretched in the midst of their pleasures, because they are never content with their state; they are always desiring to remove some thorn, or to add some flower to their present condition. The faithful soul, on the other hand, has a will which is perfectly free; it accepts, without questioning, whatever bitter blessings God develops, wills them, from them, and embraces them; it would not be freed from them, if it could be accomplished by a simple wish; for such a wish would be an act originating in self, and contrary to its abandonment to Providence, and it is desirous that this abandonment should be absolutely perfect. If there be anything capable of setting a soul in a large place, it is this absolute abandonment to God. It diffuses in the soul a peace which flows as a river, and a righteousness which is as the waves of the sea. If there be anything that can render the soul calm, dissipate its scruples and dispel its fears, sweeten its sufferings by the anointing of love, impart strength to it in all its actions, and spread abroad the joy of the Holy Spirit in its countenance and words, it is this simple, free, and child-like repose in the arms of God.

On Confidence In God

The best rule we can ever adopt, is to receive equally, and with the same submission, everything that God sends us during the day, both within and without. Without, there are things disagreeable that must be met with courage, and things pleasant that must not be suffered to arrest our affections. We resist the temptations of the former by accepting them at once, and of the latter by refusing to admit them into our hearts. The same curse is necessary in regard to the interior life; whatever is bitter serves to crucify us, and works all its benefit in the soul, if we receive it simply, with a willingness that knows no bounds, and a readiness that seeks no alleviation. Pleasant gifts, which are intended to support our weakness by giving us a sensible consolation in our external acts, must be accepted with equal satisfaction, but in a different way. They must be received, because God sends them, and not because they are agreeable to our own feelings; they are to be used, like any other medicine, without self-complacency, without attachment to them, and without appropriation. We must accept them, but not hold on to them; so that when God sees fit to withdraw them, we may neither be dejected nor discouraged. The source presumption lies in attachment to these transitory and sensible gifts. We imagine we have no regard to anything but the gift of God, while we are really looking to self, appropriating his mercy and mistaking it for Him. And thus we become discouraged whenever we find that we have been deceived in ourselves; the soul, however, that is sustained upon God, is not surprised at its own misery; it is delighted to find new proof that it can do nothing of itself, and that God must do everything. I am never in the least troubled at being poor, when I know that my Father has infinite treasures which He will give me. We shall soon become independent of trust in ourselves, if we suffer our hearts to feed upon absolute confidence in God. We must count less upon sensible delights and the measures of wisdom which devise for our own perfection, than upon simplicity, lowliness, renunciation of our own efforts, and perfect pliability to all the designs of grace. Everything else tends to emblazon our virtues, and thus inspire a secret reliance upon our own resources. Let us pray God that he would root out of our hearts everything of our own planting, and set out there, with his own hands, the tree of life, bearing all manner of fruits.

In What Manner We Are To Watch Ourselves

The following seem to me to be useful practical directions as to the manner in which we ought to watch ourselves, without being too much occupied with the duty. The wise and diligent traveler watches all his steps, and keeps his eyes always directed to that part of the road which is immediately before him; but he does not incessantly look backwards to count his steps and examine his footmarks, he would lose time and hinder his progress by so doing. The soul which God truly leads by the hand (for I do not now speak of those who are learning to walk, and who are yet looking for the road), ought to watch its path, but with a simple, tranquil vigilance confined to the present moment, and without restlessness from love of self. Its attention should be continually directed to the will of God, in order to fulfill it every instant, and not be engaged in reflex acts upon itself in order to be assured of its state, when God prefers it should be uncertain. Thus the Psalmist exclaims, My eyes are ever toward the Lord; for he shall pluck my feet out of the net. Observe how, in order to keep his feet in safety in a way sown with snares, instead of fixing his eyes upon the ground to scrutinize every step, he raises them to the Lord. We never watch so diligently over ourselves as when we walk in the presence of God, as He commanded Abraham. And, in fact, what should be the end of all our vigilance? To follow step by step the will of God. He who conforms to that in all things, watches over himself and sanctifies himself in everything. If, then, we never lost sight of the presence of God, we should never cease to watch, and always with a simple, lovely, quiet and disinterested vigilance; while, on the other hand, the watchfulness which is the result of a desire to be assured of our state, is harsh, restless, and full of self. We must walk not by our own light, but by that of God. We cannot behold the holiness of God without feeling horror at the smallest of our transgressions. In addition to the presence of God and a state of recollection, we may add, the examination of conscience according to our need, but conducted in a way that grows more and more simple, easy, and destitute of restless self-contemplations. We examine ourselves not for our own satisfaction, but to conform to the advice we receive, and to accomplish the will of God. In short, we abandon ourselves into the hands of God, and are just as happy in knowing ourselves there, as we should be miserable if we were in our own. We desire to see nothing of what it pleases Him to conceal. As we love Him infinitely more than we do ourselves, we make an unconditional sacrifice of ourselves to his good pleasure; desiring only to love Him and to forget ourselves. He who thus generously loses his soul, shall find it again with eternal life.

On The Inward Teaching Of The Spirit Of God

It is certain from the Holy Scriptures that the Spirit of God dwells within us, acts there, prays without ceasing, groans, desires, asks for us what we know not how to ask for ourselves, urges us on, animates us, speaks to us when we are silent, suggests to us all truth, and so unites us to Him that we become one spirit. This is the teaching of faith, and even those instructors who are farthest removed from the interior life, cannot avoid acknowledging so much. Still, notwithstanding these theoretical principles, they always strive to maintain that in practice the external law, or at least a certain light of learning and reason, illuminates us within, and that then our understanding acts of itself from that instruction. They do not rely sufficiently upon the interior teacher, the Holy Spirit, who does everything in us. He is the soul of our soul; we could not form a thought or a desire without Him. Alas! what blindness is ours! We reckon ourselves alone in the interior sanctuary, when God is much more intimately present there than we are ourselves. What, then! you will say, are we all inspired? Yes, doubtless; but not as were the prophets and apostles. Without the actual inspiration of the Spirit of grace, we could neither do, nor will, nor believe any good thing. We are, then, always inspired, but we incessantly stifle the inspiration. God does not cease to speak, but the noise of the creatures without, and of our passions within, confines us and prevents our hearing. We must silence every creature, including self, that in the deep stillness of the soul we may perceive the ineffable voice of the Bridegroom. We must lend an attentive ear, for his voice is soft and still, and is only heard of those who hear nothing else! Ah, how rare is it to find a soul still enough to hear God speak! The slightest murmur of our vain desires, or of a love fixed upon self, confounds all the words of the Spirit of God. We hear well enough that he is speaking, and that he is asking for something, but we cannot distinguish what is said, and are often glad enough that we cannot. The least reserve, the slightest self-reflective act, the most imperceptible fear of hearing too clearly what God demands, interferes with the interior voice. Need we be astonished, then, if so many people, pious indeed, but full of amusements, vain desires, false wisdom, and confidence in their own virtues, cannot hear it, and consider its existence as a dream of fanatics? Alas! what would they with their proud reasoning? Of what efficacy would be the exterior word of pastors, or even of the Scriptures themselves, if we had not within, the word of the

Holy Spirit giving to the others all their vitality? The outward word, even of the Gospel, without the fecundating, vivifying, interior word would be but an empty sound. It is the letter that alone kills, and the Spirit alone can give us life. O! eternal and omnipotent word of the Father, it is you that speaks in the depth of our souls! The word that proceeded from the mouth of the Savior, during the days of his mortal life, has only had energy to produce such wondrous fruits, because it has been animated by that Spirit of life which is The Word itself. Hence it is that St. Peter says: Lord, to whom shall we go? You have the words of eternal life. It is not, then, the outward law of the Gospel alone which God shows us internally, by the light of reason and faith; it is his Spirit that speaks, touches, operates in and animates us; so that it is the Spirit which does in us and with us whatever we do that is good, as it is our soul that gives life to our body, and regulates all its movements. It is, then, true, that we are continually inspired, and that we do not lead a gracious life, except so far as we act under this interior inspiration. But O God! how few Christians feel it! how few are they, who do not annihilate it by their voluntary distractions, or by their resistance! Let us recognize, then, the fact that God is incessantly speaking in us. He speaks in the impenitent also, but, stunned by the noise of the world and their passions, they cannot hear Him; the interior voice is to them a fable. He speaks in awakened sinners; they are sensible of remorse of conscience, which is the voice of God reproaching them inwardly for their sins. When they are deeply moved, they have no difficulty in understanding about this interior voice, for it is it that pierces them so sharply. It is in them that two-edged sword of which Paul speaks as piercing even to the dividing asunder of soul and spirit. God causes himself to be perceived, enjoyed, followed; they hear that sweet voice that buries a reproach in the bottom of the heart, and causes it to be torn in pieces. Such is true and pure contrition. God speaks, too, in wise and enlightened persons, whose life, outwardly correct, seems adorned with many virtues; but such are often too full of themselves and their lights, to listen to God. Everything is turned into reasoning; they substitute the principles of natural wisdom and the plans of human prudence, for what would come infinitely better through the channel of simplicity and docility to the word of God. They seem good, sometimes better than others; they are so, perhaps, up to a certain point, but it is a mixed goodness. They are still in possession of themselves, and desire always to be so, according to the measure of their reason; they love to be in the hands of their own counsel, and to be strong and great in their own eyes. I thank you, O my God with Jesus Christ, that You have hid your ineffable secrets from these great and wise ones, while You take pleasure in revealing them to feeble and humble souls! It is with babes alone that You are wholly unreserved; the others You treat in their own way; they desire knowledge and great virtues, and You give them dazzling illuminations, and convert them into heroes. But this is not the better part; there is something more hidden for your dearest children; they lie with John on your breast. As for these great ones who are constantly afraid of stooping and becoming lowly, You leave them in all their greatness; they shall never share your caresses and your familiarity, for to deserve these, they must become as little children, and play upon your knees. I have often observed that a rude, ignorant sinner, just beginning to be touched by a lively sense of the love of God, is much more disposed to listen to this inward language of the Spirit of Grace, than those enlightened and learned persons who have grown old in their own wisdom. God, whose sole desire is to communicate Himself, cannot, so to speak, find where to set his foot in souls so full of themselves, who have grown fat upon their own wisdom and virtues; but, as says the Scripture, his secret is with the simple. But where are they? I do not find them; God sees them and loves to dwell in them; My Father and I, says Jesus Christ, will come unto him and make our abode with him. Ah! a soul delivered from self, and abandoned to grace, counting itself as nothing, and walking, without thought, at the will of that pure love which is its perfect guide, has an experience which the wise can neither receive nor understand! I was once as wise as any; thinking I saw everything, I saw nothing; I crept along feeling my way by a succession of reasoning, but there was no ray to enlighten my darkness; I was content to reason. But when we have silenced everything within, that we may listen to God, we know all things without knowing anything, and then perceive that, until then, we were utterly ignorant of all that we thought we understood. We lose all that we once had, and care not for it; we have then no more that belongs to self; all things are lost, and we with them. There is something within that joins with the spouse in the Canticles in saying; Let me see your countenance, let he hear your voice; for sweet is your voice and your countenance is comely. Ah! how sweet is that voice, it makes me all tremulous within! Speak, O beloved, and let none other dare to speak but You! Be still, my soul; speak, Love! Then it is that we know all things without knowing anything. Not that we have the presumption to suppose that we possess in ourselves all truth. No! on the contrary, we feel that we see nothing, can do nothing, and are nothing: we feel it and are delighted at it. But in this unreserved abandonment, we find everything we need from moment to moment, in the infinity of God. There we find the daily bread of knowledge, as of everything else, without lying up; then the unction from above teaches us all truth, while it takes away our own wisdom, glory, interest, even our own will; it makes us content with our powerlessness, and with a position below every creature; we are ready to yield to the merest worms of the dust, and to confess our most secret miseries before the whole world, fearing unfaithfulness more than punishment and confusion of face. Here it is, I say, that the Spirit teaches us all truth; for all truth is eminently contained in this sacrifice of love, where the soul strips itself of everything to present it to God.

On Daily Faults And The Toleration Of Ourselves

You understand that many of our faults are voluntary in different degrees, though they may not be committed with a deliberate purpose of failing in our allegiance to God. One friend sometimes reproaches another for a fault not expressly intended to be offensive, and yet committed with the knowledge that it would be so. In the same way, God lays this sort of faults to our charge. They are voluntary, for although not done with an express intention, they are still committed freely and against a certain interior light of conscience, which should have caused us to hesitate and wait. Of these offences, pious souls are often guilty; as to those of deliberate purpose, it would be strange indeed if a soul consecrated to God should fall into such. Little faults become great, and even monstrous in our eyes, in proportion as the pure light of God increases in us; just as the sun in rising, reveals the true dimensions of objects which were dimly and confusedly discovered during the night. Be sure that, with the increase of the inward light, the imperfections which you have hitherto seen, will be beheld as far greater and more deadly in their foundations, than you now conceive them, and that you will witness, in addition, the development of a crowd of others, of the existence of which you have not now the slightest suspicion. You will there find the weaknesses necessary to deprive you of all confidence in your own strength; but this discovery, far from discouraging, will serve to destroy your self-reliance, and to raze to the ground the edifice of pride. Nothing marks so decidedly the solid progress of a soul, as that it is enabled to view its own depravity without being disturbed or discouraged. It is an important precept to abstain from doing a wrong thing whenever we perceive it in time, and when we do not, to bear the humiliation of the fault courageously. If a fault is perceived before it is committed, we must see to it that we do not resist and quench the Spirit of God, advising us of it inwardly. The Spirit is easily offended, and very jealous; He desires to be listened to and obeyed; He retires if He be displeased; the slightest resistance to Him is a wrong, for everything must yield to Him, the moment He is perceived. Faults of haste and frailty are nothing in comparison with those where we shut our ears to the voice of the Holy Spirit beginning to speak in the depths of the heart. Restlessness and an injured self-love will never mend those faults which are not perceived until after they are committed; on the contrary, such feelings are simply the impatience of wounded pride at beholding what confounds it. We must quietly humble ourselves in peace; I say in peace, for it is no humiliation to do it in a vexed and spiteful way. We must condemn our faults, mourn over them, repent of them, without seeking the slightest shadow of consolation in any excuse, and behold ourselves covered with confusion in the presence of God; and all this without being bitter against ourselves or discouraged; but peacefully reaping the profit of our humiliation. Thus from the serpent itself we draw the antidote to his venom. It often happens that what we offer to God, is not what he most desires to have of us; that we are frequently the most unwilling to give, and the most fearful He will ask. He desires the sacrifice of the Isaac, the well-beloved son; all the rest is as nothing in his eyes, and he permits it to be offered in a painful unprofitable manner, because He has no blessings for a divided soul. He will have everything, and until then there is no rest. Who has hardened himself against Him and has prospered? Would you prosper, and secure the blessing of God upon your labors? Reserve nothing, cut to the quick and burn, spare nothing, and the God of peace will be with you. What consolation, what liberty, what strength, what enlargedness of heart, what increase of grace, will follow when there remains nothing between God and the soul, and when the last sacrifices have been offered up without hesitation! We must neither be astonished nor disheartened. We are not more wicked than we were; we are really less so; but while our evil diminishes, our light increases, and we are struck with horror at its extent. But let us remember, for our consolation, that the perception of our disease is the first step to a cure; when we have no sense of our need, we have no curative principle within; it is a state of blindness, presumption and insensibility, in which we are delivered over to our own counsel, and commit ourselves to the current, the fatal rapidity of which we do not realize, until we are called to struggle against it. We must not be discouraged either by experience of our weakness, or by dislike of the constant activity which may be inseparable from our condition in life. Discouragement is not a fruit of humility, but of pride; nothing can be worse. Suppose we have stumbled, or even fallen, let us rise and run again; all our falls are useful, if they strip us of a disastrous confidence in ourselves, while they do not take away a humble and salutary trust in God. The repugnancies which we feel towards our duties, come, no doubt, of imperfections; if we were perfect, we should love everything in the order of God, but since we are born corrupt, and with a nature revolting against his laws, let us praise Him that He knows how to evolve good from evil, and can make use even of our repugnancies as a source of virtue. The work of grace does not always advance as regularly as that of nature, says St. Theresa. Carefully purify your conscience, then, from daily faults; suffer no sin to dwell in your heart; small as it may seem, it obscures the light of grace, weighs down the soul, and hinders that constant communion with Jesus Christ which it should be your pleasure to cultivate; you will become lukewarm, forget God, and find yourself growing in attachment to the creature. A pure soul, on the other hand, which is humiliated, and rises promptly after its smallest faults, is always fervent and always upright. God never makes us sensible of our weakness except to give us of His strength; we must not be disturbed by what is involuntary. The great point is, never to act in opposition to the inward light, and to be willing to go as far as God would have us.

On Fidelity In Small Matters

St. Francis of Sales says that great virtues and fidelity in small things are like sugar and salt; sugar is more delicious, but of less frequent use, while salt enters into every article of our food. Great virtues are rare; they are seldom needed, and when the occasion comes, we are prepared for it by everything which has preceded, excited by the greatness of the sacrifice, and sustained either by the brilliancy of the action in the eyes of others, or by self-complacency in our ability to do such wonderful things. Small occasions, however, are unforeseen; they recur every moment, and place us incessantly in conflict with our pride, our sloth, our self-esteem, and our passions; they are calculated thoroughly to subdue our wills, and leave us no retreat. If we are faithful in them, nature will have no time to breathe, and must die to all her inclinations. It would please us much better to make some great sacrifices, however painful and violent, on condition of obtaining liberty to follow our own pleasure, and retain our old habits in little things. But it is only by this fidelity in small matters that the grace of true love is sustained and distinguished from the transitory excitements of nature. It is with piety as it is with our temporal goods; there is more danger from little expenses than from larger disbursements, and he who understands how to take care of what is insignificant, will soon accumulate a large fortune. Everything great owes its greatness to the small elements of which it is composed; he that loses nothing, will soon be rich. Consider, on the other hand, that God does not so much regard our actions, as the motive of love from which they spring, and the pliability of our wills to his. Men judge our deeds by their outward appearance; with God, that which is most dazzling in the eyes of man, is of no account. What he desires is a pure intention, a will ready for anything, and ever pliable in his hands, and an honest abandonment of self; and all this can be much more frequently manifested on small than on extraordinary occasions; there will also be much less danger from pride, and the trial will be far more searching. Indeed, it sometimes happens, that we find it harder to part with a trifle than with an important interest; it may be more of a cross to abandon a vain amusement, than to bestow a large sum in charity. We are the more easily deceived about these small matters, in proportion as we imagine them to be innocent, and ourselves indifferent to them. Nevertheless, when God takes them away, we may easily recognize, in the pain of the deprivation, how excessive and inexcusable were both the use and the attachment. If we are in the habit of neglecting little things, we shall be constantly offending our families, our domestics, and the public. No one can well believe that our piety is sincere, when our behavior is loose and irregular in its little details. What ground have we for believing that we are ready to make the greatest sacrifices, when we daily fail in offering the least? But the greatest danger of all consists in this, that by neglecting small matters, the soul becomes accustomed to unfaithfulness. We grieve the Holy Spirit, we return to ourselves, we think it a little thing to be wanting towards God. On the other hand, true love can see nothing small; everything that can either please or displease God, seems to be great; not that true love disturbs the soul with scruples, but it puts no limits to its faithfulness. It acts simply with God; and as it does not concern itself about those things which God does not require from it, so it never hesitates an instant about those which He does, be they great or small. Thus it is not by incessant care that we become faithful and exact in the smallest things, but simply by a love which is free from the reflections and fears of restless and scrupulous souls. We are, as it were, drawn along by the love of God; we have no desire to do anything but what we do, and no will in respect to anything which we do not do. At the very moment when God is following the soul, relentlessly pursuing it into the smallest details, and seemingly depriving it of all its liberty, it finds itself in a large place, and enjoys a perfect peace in Him. Happy soul! Those persons who are by nature less strict in small matters, should lay down and preserve inviolate the most rigid laws in respect to them. They are tempted to despise them; they habitually think little of them, and do not sufficiently estimate their importance; they do not consider the insensible progress of our passions, and even forget their own sad experience on the subject. They prefer rather to be deluded by the promise of an imaginary firmness, and to trust to their own courage that has so often deceived them, than to subject themselves to a never-ceasing fidelity. It is a small matter, say they; true, but it is of amazing consequence to you; it is a matter that you love well enough to refuse to give it up to God; a matter which you sneer at in words, that you may have a pretence to retain it; a small matter, but one that you withhold from your Maker, and which will prove your ruin. It is no nobility of soul that despises small things; on the contrary, it is a contracted spirit that regards as unimportant, what it cannot trace to its necessary and overwhelming results. The more trouble it occasions us to be on our guard against small matters, the more need have we to fear negligence, to distrust our strength, and to interpose impregnable barriers between ourselves and the least remissness. Finally, judge by your own feelings. What would you think of a friend who owed everything to you, and who was willing from a sense of duty to serve you on those rare occasions which are called great, but who should manifest neither affection nor the least regard for your wishes in the common intercourse of life? Do not be frightened at this minute attention to small matters. It needs courage at first; but this is a penance which you deserve, which you need, and which will work out for you peace and security; without it, all is trouble and relapse. God will gradually make it pleasant and easy to you, for true love is obedient without constraint, and without strife or effort.

On Transitory Emotions, Fidelity, And Simplicity

We must not be surprised if we frequently perceive in ourselves emotions of pride, of self-complacency, of confidence in ourselves, of desire to follow our own inclination contrary to right, of impatience at the weakness of others, or at the annoyances of our own state. In such cases we must instantly let them drop like a stone to the bottom of the sea, recollect ourselves in God, and wait, before acting, until we are in such a frame as our recollection should induce in us. If the distraction of business, or of vivacity of imagination, should hinder us from calmly and easily entering into such a state, we must at least endeavor to be quiet by the rectitude of the will, and by the desire for recollection. In such a case, the will to be recollected, answers to deprive the soul of its own will, and to render it docile in the hands of God. If perchance in your excitement, some emotion too nearly allied to depraved nature, should have escaped you, be not discouraged; go straight on; quietly bear the humiliation of your fault before God, without being delayed by the smarting of self-love at the betrayal of its weakness. Proceed confidently, without being troubled by the anguish of a wounded pride that cannot bear to see itself imperfect. Your fault will be of service in causing you to die to self, and to become nothing before Him. The true method of curing this defect is to become dead to the sensitiveness of self-love, without hindering the course of grace, which had been a little interrupted by this transitory unfaithfulness. The great point is to renounce your own wisdom by simplicity of walk, and to be ready to give up the favor, esteem, and approbation of every one, whenever the path in which God leads you passes that way. We are not to meddle with things which God does not lay upon us, nor uselessly utter hard sayings which those about us are not able to bear. We must follow after God, never precede Him; when He gives the signal, we must leave all and follow Him. If, after an absolute consecration to Him, and a conviction in conscience that he requires something of us, we hesitate, delay, lose courage, dilute what He would have us do, indulge fears for our own comfort or safety, desire to shield ourselves from suffering and obloquy, or seek to find some excuse for not performing a difficult and painful duty, we are truly guilty in his sight. God keep you from such unfaithfulness! Nothing is more dreadful than this inward resistance to Him; it is that sin against the Holy Ghost of which our Lord assures us that it shall not be forgiven, neither in this world, neither in the world to come. Other faults committed in the simplicity of your good intentions, will be of service if they produce humility, and render you of less account in your own eyes. But resistance to the Spirit of God through pride and a pusillanimous worldly wisdom, tender of its own comfort in performing the work of God, is a fault which will insensibly quench the Spirit of Grace in your heart. God, jealous and rejected after so much mercy, will depart and leave you to your own resources; you will then turn round in a kind of circle instead of advancing with rapid strides along the Kings highway; your inward life will grow dim and dimmer, without your being able to detect the sure and deep-seated source of your disease. God would behold in you a simplicity which will contain so much the more of his wisdom as it contains less of your own; He desires to see you lowly in your own eyes, and as docile in his hands as a babe. He desires to create in your heart that child-like disposition so distasteful to the spirit of man, but so agreeable to the spirit of the Gospel, in spite of the infection of a scornful and contemptuous world. By this very simplicity and lowliness He will heal all the remains of haughty and self-confident wisdom in you, and you shall say with David, And I will yet be more vile than this, and will be base in mine own sight, from the moment that you give yourself to the Lord.

On The Advantages Of Silence And Recollection

You must endeavor to be as silent as the proprieties of human intercourse will permit. This grace cherishes the presence of God, saves us many proud and rude expressions, and suppresses a great multitude of idle words and dangerous judgments of our neighbor. Silence humbles our spirit, and gradually detaches it from the world; it constitutes in the heart a sort of solitude like that you so much long after, and will supply all your wants in the many perplexities that surround you. If we never unnecessarily open our mouths, we may enjoy many moments of communion even when unavoidably detained in society. You desire to be at liberty, that you may pray to God; and God, who knows so much better than we do, what we really want, sends perplexity and restraint, that you may become mortified. This trial from the hand of God, will be far more serviceable to you, than the self-sought sweetness of prayer. You know very well that constant retirement is not necessary, in order to love God. When He gives you the time, take it and profit by it, but until then, wait in faith, well persuaded that what He orders is best. Frequently raise your heart to Him in abstraction from the world; speak only when obliged to; bear with patience whatever happens to cross you. You are already acquainted with religion, and God treats you according to your necessity; you have more need of mortification than of illumination. The only thing I fear for you in this state, is wanderings, and you may avoid those by silence. Only be faithful in keeping silence, when it is not necessary to speak, and God will send grace to preserve you from dissipation when it is. When you are not permitted to enjoy long seasons of leisure, economize the short ones; ten minutes thus faithfully employed before God, in the midst of your distractions, will be as valuable to you as whole hours devoted to Him, in your more unoccupied moments. Farther, these little odds and ends of time, will amount to quite a sum in the course of the day, and present this advantage, that God will very likely have been more in mind than if you had given it to Him all at once. Love, silence, suffering, yielding our own pleasure to the will of God, and to the love of our neighbor, such is our portion; too happy in bearing the burden which God himself lays upon us in the order of his Providence! The crosses which originate with ourselves, are not near as efficient in eradicating self-love, as those which come in the daily allotments of God. These latter contribute no ailment for the nourishment of our own wills, and as they proceed immediately from a merciful Providence, they are accompanied by grace sufficient for all our needs. We have nothing to do, then, but to surrender ourselves to God each day, without looking farther; He will carry us in his arms as a tender mother bears her child. Let us believe, hope, and love with all the simplicity of babes; in every necessity turning a loving and trusting look towards our Heavenly Father. For the Scripture says, Can a woman forget her sucking child that she should not have compassion on the son of her womb? Yes, they may forget, yet will I not forget you!

Privation & Annihilation

There is scarce any one who desires to serve God, but does so for selfish reasons; we expect gain and not loss, consolation and not suffering, riches and not poverty, increase and not diminution. But the whole interior work is of an opposite character; to be lost, sacrificed, made less than nothing, and despoiled of an excessive delight, even in the gifts of God, that we may be forced to cling to Him alone. We are like a patient eagerly desiring returning health, who feels his own pulse forty times a day, and requires his physician to prescribe frequent doses of various remedies, and to give him a daily assurance that he is getting better. Such is almost the only use we make of our spiritual conductors. We travel in a little round of every-day virtues, never gathering sufficient courage to pass generously beyond it, and our guides, like the doctor, flatter, console, encourage and strengthen our selfish sensitiveness, and administer pleasant remedies, to the effects of which we soon become insensible. The moment we find ourselves deprived of the delights of grace, that milk for babes, we are at once in despair; a manifest proof that we were looking to the means, instead of to the end, and solely for selfish gratification. Privations are meat for men; by them the soul is rendered hardy, is separated from self, and offered in a pure sacrifice to God; but we give up all, the moment they commence. We cannot but think that everything is going to ruin, when, in fact, the foundations are just beginning to be solidly laid. Nothing would give us more delight than that God should do all his pleasure with us, provided it should always be to magnify and perfect us in our own eyes. But if we are not willing to be destroyed and annihilated, we shall never become that whole burnt offering, which is entirely consumed in the blaze of Gods love. We desire to enter into a state of pure faith, and retain our own wisdom! To be a babe, and great in our own eyes! Ah! what a sad delusion!

On The Proper Use Of Crosses

We are hardly to be persuaded of the goodness of God in loading those whom He loves with crosses. Why, we say, should

He take pleasure in causing us to suffer? Could he not render us good without making us miserable? Yes, doubtless, He could, for all things are possible with God. He holds in his omnipotent hands the hearts of men, and turns them as He will; as the skill of the workman can give direction to the stream on the summit of a hill. But able as He was to save us without crosses, He has not chosen to do it; as he has not seen fit to create men at once in the full vigor of manhood, but has suffered them to grow up by degrees amid all the perils and weaknesses of infancy and youth. In this matter, He is the Master; we have only to adore in silence the depths of His wisdom, without comprehending it. Nevertheless, we see clearly that we never could become wholly good without becoming humble, unselfish, and disposed to refer everything to God, without any restless self-reflective acts. The work of grace, in detaching us from self and destroying our self-love, could not be otherwise than painful, without a miracle. Neither in his gracious nor providential dealings does God work a miracle lightly. It would be as great a wonder to see a person full of self become in a moment dead to all self-interest and all sensitiveness, as it would be to see a slumbering infant wake in the morning a fully-developed man. God works in a mysterious was in grace as well as in nature, concealing his operations under an imperceptible succession of events, and thus keeps us always in the darkness of faith. He not only accomplishes his designs gradually, but by means that seem the most simple, and the most competent to the end, in order that human wisdom may attribute the success to the means, and thus his own working be less manifest; otherwise every act of God would seem to be a miracle, and the state of faith, wherein it is the will of God that we should live, would come to an end. This state of faith is necessary, not only to stimulate the good, causing them to sacrifice their reason in a life so full of darkness, but also to blind those who, by their presumption, deserve such a sentence. They behold the works of God, but do not understand them; they can see nothing in them but the effects of material laws; they are destitute of true knowledge, for that is only open to those who distrust their own abilities; proud human wisdom is unworthy to be taken into the counsels of God. God renders the working of grace slow and obscure, then, that he may keep us in the darkness of faith. He makes use of the inconstancy and ingratitude of the creature, and of the disappointments and surfeits which accompany prosperity, to detach us from them both; He frees us from self by revealing to us our weaknesses, and our corruptions, in a multitude of backslidings. All this dealing appears perfectly natural, and it is by this succession of natural means that we are burnt as by a slow fire. We should like to be consumed at once by the flames of pure love, but such an end would scarce cost us anything; it is only an excessive self-love that desires thus to become perfect in a moment and at so cheap a rate. Why do we rebel against the length of the way? Because we are wrapped up in self; and God must destroy an infatuation which is a constant hindrance to his work. Of what, then, can we complain? Our trouble is, that we are attached to creatures, and still more to self; God prepares a series of events which gradually detaches us from creatures, and separates us from self. The operation is painful, but is rendered necessary by our corruption, and the same cause makes it distressing; if our flesh were sound, the surgeon would use no knife; he only cuts in proportion to the depth of the wound, and the diseased condition of the parts; if we suffer greatly, it is because the evil is great; is the surgeon cruel because he cuts to the quick? Nay, on the contrary, it is both love and skill; he would treat in the same way his only and well-beloved son. It is the same with God. He never afflicts us, if we may so say, except against his own inclination; his paternal heart is not gratified by the sight of our misery, but he cuts to the quick, that He may heal the disease in our souls. He must snatch away from us whatever we cling to too fondly, and all that we love irregularly and to the prejudice of his rights. He acts in this as we do by children; they cry because we take away the knife, which was their amusement, but might have been their death. We weep, we become discouraged, we cry aloud; we are ready to murmur against God, as children get angry with their mothers. But God lets us weep, and secures our salvation; He afflicts only to amend; even when He seems to overwhelm, He means nothing but good; it is only to spare us the evils we were preparing for ourselves. The things we now lament for a little space, would have caused us to mourn forever; what we think lost, was indeed lost when we seemed to have it, but now God has laid it aside for us, that we may inherit it in the eternity so near at hand. He only deprives us of what we cherish, to teach us how to love it purely, solidly, and moderately, and to secure to us its eternal enjoyment in his own bosom; to do us a thousand times more good than we could ask or think of ourselves. With the exception of sin, nothing happens, in this world, out of the will of God. It is He who is the author, ruler, and giver of all; He has numbered the hairs of our head, the leaves of every tree, the sand upon the sea-shore, and the drops of the ocean. When He made the universe, his wisdom weighed and measured every atom. It is he that breathes into us the breath of life, and renews it every moment; He it is that knows the number of our days, and that holds in his all-powerful hand, the keys of the tomb to open or to shut. What we admire, is as nothing in the eyes of God: a little more or less of life, is a difference that disappears in the light of eternity. What matter whether this fragile vessel, this clay tabernacle, be broken and reduced to ashes, a little sooner or later? Ah! what short-sighted and deceitful views are ours! We are thrown into consternation at the death of a man in the prime of life. What a dreadful loss! exclaims the world. Who has lost anything? The dead? He has lost some years of vanity, illusion, and danger to his immortal soul; God has snatched him from the midst of his iniquities, and separated him from a corrupt world and his own weakness. The friends whom he has left? They are deprived of the poison of worldly felicity; they lose a perpetual intoxication; they get rid of the forgetfulness of God and themselves, in which they lay sunk say, rather, they gain the bliss of detachment from the world, through the virtue of the cross. The same blow that saves the dying, prepares the survivors, by their suffering, to labor courageously for their own salvation. O! is it not true that God is good, tender, compassionate towards our misery, even when He seems to launch his thunders at us, and we are open-mouthed in our complaints of his severity! What difference can we discover between two persons who lived a century ago? The one died twenty years before the other, but now they are both gone; the separation which then seemed so abrupt and so long, appears as nothing to us, and was, in fact, but short. Those things which are severed, shall soon be reunited, and no trace of the separation will be visible. We look upon ourselves as immortal, or at least as having a duration of ages. O folly and madness! those who die from day to day, tread upon the heels of those that are already dead; life flows like a torrent; that which is gone is but a dream, and even while we contemplate that which now is, it vanishes and is lost in the abyss of the past. So will it be with the future; days, months, and years, glide like the billows of a torrent, each hurrying along the other. A few moments more, and all is over! Alas! how short will that existence then appear, which now wearies us with its sad and tedious length! The disgust of life is the result of the weakness of our self-love. The sick man thinks the night will never end, because he sleeps not, but it is no longer than others; we exaggerate all our sufferings by our cowardice; they are great, it is true, but they are magnified by timidity. The way to lessen them is to abandon ourselves courageously into the hands of God; we must suffer, but the end of our pain is to purify our souls, and make us worthy of Him.

On The Interior Operations Of God

In the beginning God attacked us in externals; little by little he withdrew such of his creatures as we loved too much, and contrary to his law. But this outward work, though essential in laying the foundation of the building, goes but a little way towards the completion of the whole edifice. The interior operation, although invisible, is beyond comparison, greater, more difficult, and more wonderful! There comes a time, when God, having completely stripped us, having mortified the flesh as to the creatures to which it clung, commences an interior work for the purpose of forcing from us our hold upon Self. External objects are now no longer the subjects of his spoliations: he would tear from us the I, which is the centre of our self-love. It was only for the sake of this I that we loved all the rest; and He now pursues it relentlessly and without cessation. To deprive a man of his clothing, would be harsh treatment enough; but that is nothing in comparison with the discipline which should strip off his skin and muscles, and reduce him to a skeleton of bones. Trim up the branches of a tree, and far from killing it, you even add to its vigor, and it shoots out again on every side; but attack the trunk, wither the root, and it fades, languishes and dies. It is the good will of God towards us, thus to make us die to self. As to the external mortification of the senses, He causes us to accomplish it be certain courageous efforts against ourselves. The more the senses are destroyed by the courage of the soul, the more highly does the soul estimate its own virtue, and live by its own labor. But in process of time, God reserves for his own hand the work of attacking the soul in its depths, and depriving it finally of the last vestige of the life of Self. It is no longer the strength of the soul that is then employed against the things without, but its weakness that is turned against itself. It looks at self; it is shocked at what it sees: it remains faithful, but it no longer beholds its own fidelity. Every defect in its previous history rises up to view, and often new faults, of which it had never before even suspected the existence. It no longer finds those supports of fervor and courage which formerly nourished it. It faints; like Jesus, it is heavy even unto death. All is taken away but the will to retain nothing, and to let God work without reservation. It has not even the consolation of perceiving that it has such a will. It is no longer a perceptible, designed will, but simple, without reflex acts, and so much the more hidden, as it is deeper and more intimate in the soul. In such a state, God sees to everything that is necessary to detach the soul from self. He strips it little by little, removing one after another all the investments in which it was wrapped. The last operations, though not always the greatest, are, nevertheless, the most severe. Though the outside garments may be more costly than those within, yet the removal of the latter is more painful than that of the former. During the first, we are consoled by reflecting upon what is left us; during the last, nothing remains but bitterness, nakedness, and confusion. I shall perhaps be asked, in what these deprivations consist; but I cannot say. They are as various as the characters of men. Each man suffers according to his necessity, and the designs of God. How is it possible to know what will be taken off from us, when we do not know what we have on? We cling to an infinity of things which we should never suspect; we only feel that they are a part of us when they are snatched away, as I am only conscious that I have hairs when they are pulled from my head. God develops to us, little by little, what is within us, of which we are, until then, entirely ignorant, and we are astonished at discovering in our very virtues, defects of which we should never have believed ourselves capable. It is like a grotto which appears perfectly dry, but in which the water suddenly sprout out from every point, even from those that were least suspended. These spoliations are not commonly such as could have been anticipated. That which we expect, finds us prepared, and is scarce proper to hasten the death of self. God surprises us in the most unlooked-for quarters. They are nothings, but nothings which desolate us and crucify self-love. Great and striking virtues are no longer appropriate; they would nourish pride, and communicate a certain degree of strength and interior assurance contrary to the design of God, which is, to make us lose ground. Then it is a simple, single way; everything is commonplace. Others see nothing great, and the person himself discovers within, only what seems natural, weak, and feeble; but he would rather a hundred times, fast all his life on bread and water, and practice the greatest austerities, than suffer what is going on within him. Not because he enjoys a certain taste of fervor in austerities; not at all, that delight is gone; but he finds in the pliability which God requires in an infinity of little things, more of self-abandonment and death than there would be in great sacrifices. Nevertheless, God never leaves the soul until He has rendered it supple and pliable, by twisting it all manner of ways. At one time the person must speak frankly; at another be still; he must be praised, then blamed, then forgotten, and then examined anew; he must be low, he must be high, he must suffer condemnation without uttering a word in self-defense, and again he must speak well of himself. He must be willing to find himself weak, restless, and irresolute in the merest trifles; manifesting the waywardness of a little child; shocking his friends by his coldness; becoming jealous and suspicious without reason; even relating his most foolish jealousies to those in regard to whom he feel them; speaking with patience and labor to persons, contrary to their desire and his own, and without fruit; appearing artificial and faithless; in short, to find himself arid, languishing, weary of God, dissipated in mind, and so far separated from every gracious thought as to be tempted to despair. Such are examples of some of the spoliations which now desolate myself; but there is an infinity of others which God apportions to each one according to his own wise purposes. Let no one tell me that these are only empty imaginations. Can we doubt that God acts immediately in the soul? that He so acts as to make it die to self? that, after having subdued the grosser passions, He attacks all the subtle resources of self-love within, especially in those souls who have generously and without reserve delivered themselves up to the operations of his grace? The more He would purify them, the more He exercises them interiorly. The world has neither eyes to see nor ears to hear these trials; but the world is blind; its wisdom is dead; it cannot coexist with the Spirit of truth. The things of God, says the Apostle, no man knows but the Spirit of God; the Spirit searches the deep things of God. We are not, at first, accustomed to this interior supervision, which thus tends to raze us to the foundation. We are willing to be silent and recollected; to suffer all things; to be at the disposal of Providence, like a man passively trusting himself to the current of a river; but we dare not yet risk listening to the interior voice, calling us to the sacrifices which God is preparing. We are like the child Samuel, who did not yet know the Lord; when the Lord called, he thought it was Eli, but he was told that he had been dreaming, and that no one spoke to him. Just so, we are uncertain whether it may not be some imagination which would carry us too far. Often the high-priest Eli, that is, our spiritual advisers, tell us that we have been dreaming, and bid us lie down again. But God does not leave us, and continues to wake us, until we lend an ear to what He has to say. If it were a matter of visions, apparitions, revelations, extraordinary illuminations, miracles, things contrary to true teaching, we should be right in not being detained by them. But when God has led us to a certain point of abandonment, and we subsequently have an interior conviction that He still desires us to give up certain innocent things, the tendency of all which is only to make us more simple and more profoundly dead to self, can it be an illusion to yield to such drawings? Probably no one follows them without good counsel. The repugnance which our wisdom and self-love manifest to them, is a sufficient evidence that they are of grace; for we see that we are only hindered from following them by selfish considerations. The more we fear to do these things, the more we have need to do them; for it is a fear which arises only from delicacy, want of pliability and attachment either to our pleasures or our views. We must die to all the sentiments of the natural life. Thus every pretext for retreat is cut off by the conviction in the depths of the soul, that the sacrifices required will assist in causing us to die. Ease and promptness in yielding to these movements, are the means by which souls make the greatest advances. Those who are ingenuous enough never to hesitate, soon make incredible progress. Others argue, and never fail to find a sufficient reason for not following the interior monitor. They are willing and not willing; they want to wait for certainties; they search about for advisers, who will bid them not do what they are afraid of doing; they stop at every step, and look back; then languish in irresolution, and insensibly estrange the Spirit of God. At first they grieve Him by their hesitation; then they irritate Him by formal resistance, and finally quench his operations by repeated opposition. While they thus resist, they find pretexts both to conceal and justify the resistance; but they insensibly grow dry; they lose their simplicity, and, make what effort they may to deceive themselves, they are not at peace; there is always at the bottom of the conscience, a feeling of reproach that they have been wanting toward God. But as God becomes more distant, because they are departing from Him, the soul becomes hardened by degrees. It is no longer peaceful; but it no longer seeks true peace; on the contrary, it wanders farther and farther from it, by seeking it where it is not; like a dislocated bone, a continual source of pain, and out of its natural position, yet, it manifests no tendency to resume its place, but, on the contrary, binds itself fast in its false relations. Ah! how much to be pitied is that soul which is just beginning to reject the secret invitations of God, when he demands that it shall die to all! At first, it is but an atom; but the atom becomes a mountain, and soon forms a sort of chaos between it and God. We play deaf when God demands a lowly simplicity; we are afraid to listen; we should be glad enough to be able to convince ourselves that we had not heard; we say so, but are not persuaded. We get into a tumult; we doubt all our past experience; and the graces which had served the most effectually to make us humble and simple before God, begin to look like illusions. We seek without, for spiritual advisers who may calm the trouble within; we readily find them, for there are so many, gifted even with much knowledge and piety, who have yet but little experience. In this condition, the more we strive to recover, the sicker we get. We are like the wounded deer, bearing in his side the fatal arrow; the more he struggles through the woods to be delivered of his enemy, the more deeply he buries it in his body. Alas! Who has hardened himself against Him and has prospered. Can God, who is Himself the true Peace, leave that heart peaceful which opposes itself to his designs? Such a person is like one with an unknown disorder. Physicians employ their art in vain to give him any solace. You behold him sad, depressed, languishing; no food, no remedy can avail to do him good; he dies day by day. Can we wonder that, wandering from the true way, we should ceaselessly continue to stray farther and farther from the right course? But, as you will say, the commencement of these things is a small matter; true, but the end is deplorable. In the sacrifice which we made when we devoted ourselves wholly to God, we reserved nothing and felt happy in so doing, while we were looking at things with a general view and at a distance; but when God takes us at our word and accepts our offer in detail, we are made aware of a thousand repugnances, the existence of which we had not so much as suspected before. Our courage fails; frivolous excuses are suggested to flatter our feeble and tempted souls; then we hesitate and doubt whether it is our duty to obey; we do only the half of what God requires of us, and we mix with the divine influence a something of self, trying still to secure some nutriment for that corrupt interior which wills not to die. A jealous God retires: the soul begins to shut its eyes, that it may not see that it has no longer the courage to act, and God leaves it to its weakness and corruption, because it will be so left. But think of the magnitude of its error! The more we have received of God, the more ought we to render. We have received love and singular grace: we have received the gift of pure and unselfish love, which so many pious souls have never tasted; God has spared nothing to possess us wholly; He has become the interior Bridegroom; He has taken pains to do everything for his bride but He is infinitely jealous. Do not wonder at the exacting nature of his jealousy! What is its object? Is it talents, illuminations, the regular practice of external virtues? Not at all; He is easy and condescending in such matters. Love is only jealous about love;

the whole of his scrutiny falls upon the state of the will. He cannot share the heart of the spouse with any other; still less can He tolerate the excuses by which she would convince herself that her heart is justly divided; this it is that lights the devouring fires of his jealousy. As long, O spouse! as pure and disinterested love shall guide you, so long the Bridegroom will bear with inexhaustible patience all your wrong doing through weakness or inadvertence, without prejudice to the purity of your love; but from the moment that you refuse anything that God asks, and begin to deceive yourself in the refusal, from that moment He will regard you as a faithless spouse, and one seeking to conceal her infidelity! How many souls, after having made great sacrifices, fall into these ways! False wisdom is the source of the whole difficulty; it is not so much through defect of courage as through excess of reason, that we are arrested at this point. It is true that when God has called souls to this state of absolute sacrifice, he treats them in accordance with the gifts He has lavished upon them; He is insatiable for deaths, losses, renunciation; He is jealous of his own gifts even, because the excellence of the blessings secretly breeds within us a sort of self-confidence. All must be destroyed, every vestige must perish! We have abandoned everything and He comes now to take everything, leaving us absolutely nothing. If there be the smallest thing to which we cling, however good it may appear, there He comes sword in hand, and cuts into the remotest corner of the soul. If we are still fearful in any recess, to that spot He comes, for He always attacks us in our weakest points. He pushes hard, without giving us time to breathe. Do you wonder? Can we be dead while we yet breathe? We desire that God would give us the death-stroke; but we long to die without pain; we would die to our own will by the power of the will itself; we want to lose all and still hold all. Ah! what agony, what distress, when God has brought us to the end of our strength! We faint like a patient under a painful surgical operation. But the comparison is nothing, for the object of the surgeon is to give us life that of God to make us die. Poor souls! weak in spirit! how these last blows overwhelm you! The very apprehension of them makes you tremble and fall back! How few are there who make out to cross the frightful desert! Scarcely shall two or three behold the promised land! Woe to those from whom God had reason to expect everything, and who do not accept the grace! Woe to him who resists the interior guidance! strange sin, that against the Holy Spirit! Unpardonable either in this world or in the next, what is it but resistance to the divine monitor within? He who resists the Spirit, striving for his conversion shall be punished in this world by affliction, and in the next by the pains of hell. Happy is he who never hesitates; who fears only that he follows with too little readiness; who would rather do too much against self than too little! Blessed is he who, when asked for a sample, boldly presents his entire stock, and suffers God to cut from the whole cloth! happy he who, esteeming himself as nothing, puts God to no necessity of sparing him! Thrice happy he whom all this does not affright! It is thought that this state is a painful one; it is a mistake; here is peace and liberty; here the heart, detached from everything, is immeasurably enlarged, so as to become illimitable; nothing cramps it; and in accordance with the promise, it becomes, in a certain sense, one with God himself. You only O my God! can give the peace which is then enjoyed! The less timid the soul is in the sacrifice of itself, the greater liberty does it acquire! At length, when it no longer hesitates to lose all and forget self, it possesses all. It is true that it is not a conscious possession, so that the soul addressed itself as happy, for that would be to return to self after having quitted it forever; but it is an image of the condition of the blessed, who will be always ravished by the contemplation of God, without having a moment, during the whole of eternity, to think of themselves and their felicity. They are so satisfied in these transports, that they will be eternally rejoicing, without once saying to themselves that they are happy. You grant to those souls who never resist you, O bridegroom of souls! even in this life, a foretaste of this felicity. They will all things and nothing. As it is things created which hem up the heart, these souls, being restrained by no attachment to the creature, and no reflections of self, enter as it were into your immensity! Nothing stops them; they become continually more and more lost; but though their capacity should increase to an infinite extent, You would fill it; they are always satisfied. They do not say that they are happy, but feel that they are so; they do not posses happiness, but their happiness possesses them. Let any one ask them at any moment,

Do you will to suffer what you suffer? Would you have what you have not? They will answer without hesitation and without reflection, I will to suffer what I suffer, and to want that which I have not; I will everything which God wills; I will nothing else. Such, my God, is true and pure worship in spirit and in truth. You seek such to worship You, but scarce find them! There are few but seek self in your gifts, instead of seeking You alone in the cross and in spoliation. Most seek to guide You instead of being guided by You. They give themselves up to You, that they may become great, but withdraw when they are required to become little. They say they are attached to nothing, and are overwhelmed by the smallest losses. They desire to possess You, but are not willing to lose self, that they may be possessed by You. This is not loving You; it is desiring to be loved by You. O God, the creature knows not to what end You have made him; teach him, and write in the depths of his soul, that the clay must suffer itself to be shaped at the will of the potter!

On Christian Perfection

Christian Perfection is not that rigorous, tedious, cramping thing that many imagine. It demands only an entire surrender of everything to God from the depths of the soul, and the moment this takes place, whatever is done for Him becomes easy. They who are Gods without reserve, are in every state content; for they will only what He wills, and desire to do for Him whatever he desires them to do; they strip themselves of everything, and in this nakedness find all things restored a hundred fold. Peace of conscience, liberty of spirit, the sweet abandonment of themselves and theirs into the hand of God, the joy of perceiving the light always increasing in their hearts, and finally the freedom of their souls from the bondage of the fears and desires of this world, these things constitute that return of happiness which the true children of God receive a hundred fold in the midst of their crosses, while they remain faithful. They are sacrificed, it is true, but it is to that which they love best; they suffer, but they will to endure all that they do receive, and prefer that anguish to all the false joys of the world; their bodies are subject to excruciating pain; their imaginations are troubled; their minds become languid and weak, but the will is firm and peacefully quiet in the interior of the soul, and responds a joyful Amen! to every stroke from the hand that would perfect the sacrifice. What God requires of us, is a will which is no longer divided between Him and any creature; a simple, pliable state of will which desires what He desires, rejects nothing but what He rejects, and wills without reserve what He wills, and under no pretext wills what He does not. In this state of mind, all things are proper for us; our amusements, even, are acceptable in his sight. Blessed is he who thus give himself to God! He is delivered from his passions, from the opinions of men, from their malice, from the tyranny of their maxims, from their cold and miserable raillery, from the misfortunes which the world attributes to chance, from the infidelity and fickleness of friends, from the artifices and snares of enemies, from the wretchedness and shortness of life, from the horrors of an ungodly death, from the cruel remorse that follows sinful pleasures, and finally from the everlasting condemnation of God! The true Christian is delivered from this innumerable multitude of evils, because, putting his will into the hands of God, he wills only what He wills, and thus finds comfort in the midst of all his suffering in the way of faith, and its attendant hope. What weakness it is, then, to be fearful of consecrating ourselves to God, and of getting too far into so desirable a state! Happy those who throw themselves, as it were, headlong, and with their eyes shut, into the arms of the Father of mercies, and the God of all comfort! Their whole desire then, is to know what is the will of God respecting them; and they fear nothing so much as not perceiving the whole of his requirements. So soon as they behold a new light in his law, they are transported with joy, like a miser at the finding of a treasure. No matter what cross may overwhelm the true child of God, he wills everything that happens, and would not have anything removed which his Father appoints; the more he loves God, the more is he filled with content; and the most stringent perfection, far from being a burthen, only renders his yoke the lighter. What folly to fear to be too devoted to God! to fear to be happy! to fear to love the will of God in all things! to fear to have too much courage under inevitable crosses, too much consolation in the love of God, and too great a detachment from the passions which make us miserable! Let us refuse, then, to set our affections upon things of the earth that we may set them exclusively upon God. I do not say, that we must abandon them entirely; for if our lives be already moral and well ordered, we have only to change the secret motive of our actions into Love, and we may continue almost the same course of life. God does not overturn our conditions nor the duties attached to them, but we may go on doing that now for the service of God which we did formerly to satisfy the world, and to please ourselves. There will only be this difference: instead of being harassed by pride, by overbearing passion, and by the malicious censures of the world, we shall act with liberty, with courage, and with hope in God. We shall be animated with confidence; the expectation of things eternal, which advance as things temporal recede from us, will support us in the midst of suffering; the love of God, who will cause us to perceive how great is his love toward us, will lend us wings to fly in his ways, and to raise us above all our miseries. Is this hard to believe? Experience will convince us. O taste and see that the Lord is good! says the Psalmist. The Son of God says to every Christian without exception, If any man will come after me, let him deny himself, and take up his cross and follow me. The broad way leads unto destruction; we must walk in the strait way, though there be few that travel therein. It is only the violent who take the Kingdom by force. We must be born again, renounce and hate ourselves, become children, be poor in spirit, mourn that we may be comforted, and not be of this world, which is cursed because of offences. Many are affrighted at these truths, and their fear arises from this: that while they know the exacting nature of religion, they are ignorant of its gifts, and of the spirit of love which renders everything easy. They are not aware that religion leads to the highest perfection, while bestowing peace through a principle of love that smoothes every rough place. They who are in truth and indeed wholly consecrated to God, are ever happy. They prove that the yoke of our Redeemer is easy and his burden light; that in Him is the peace of the soul, and that He gives rest to them that are weary and heavy laden, according to his own blessed promise. But how unhappy are those poor, weak souls, who are divided between God and the world! They will and they do not will; they are lacerated at once by their passions and their remorse; they are afraid of the judgments of God and of the opinions of men; they dislike the evil, but are ashamed of the good; they suffer the pains of virtue, without enjoying its consolations. Ah! could they but have a little courage, just enough to despise the vain conversation, the cold sneers, and the rash judgments of men, what peace would they not enjoy in the bosom of God! It is dangerous to our salvation, unworthy of God and of ourselves, and destructive even of our peace of mind, to desire to remain always in our present position. Our whole life is only given us that we may advance with rapid strides towards our heavenly country. The world recedes like a deceptive shadow, and eternity already approaches to receive us. Why do we linger and look behind, while the light of the Father of Mercies is shining upon us from before? Let us make haste to reach the Kingdom of God. All the vain pretexts which are used to cover our reservations toward God are instantly dissipated by the first commandment of the law: You shall love the Lord your God with all your heart, and with all your soul, and with all your strength, and with all your mind. Notice how many expressions are here brought together by the Holy Spirit, to forestall all the reservations the soul might make to the prejudice of this jealous Love; not only with the whole extent and strength of the soul, but with all the intensity of the intellect. How then can we conclude that we love Him if we cannot make up our minds to receive his law, and to apply ourselves at once to fulfill all his blessed will? They who fear that they shall discover too clearly what this love demands, are very far indeed from possessing the active and incessant affection required by this commandment. There is but one way in which God should be loved, and that is to take no step except with Him and for Him, and to follow, with a generous self-abandonment, everything which He requires. They who live in some self-denial, but have still a wish to enjoy a little of the world, think that this is a small matter; but they run the risk of being included in the number of those lukewarm ones whom God will spew out of his mouth. God is not pleased with the souls that say, thus far will I go and no farther. Should the creature prescribe laws to the Creator? What would a master say of his servants, or a king of his subjects, who should be willing to serve him, but only after their own fashion? who should be afraid of becoming too much interested in his service and his interests, and who should be ashamed publicly to acknowledge themselves attached to him? Or rather, what will the King of kings say to us if we serve Him in this wicked manner? The time is not far distant; it is near, it is even at hand; let us hasten to anticipate it; let us love that eternal beauty which never grows old, and which preserves in endless youth those who love nothing but it; let us despise this miserable world which is already falling to pieces on every side! Have we not beheld for years, that they, who today are high in honor and in the esteem of men, tomorrow, surprised by death, are laid side by side in the tomb? This poor world, the object of so much insane attachment, we are daily about to leave; it is but misery, vanity and folly; a phantom, the very fashion of which passes away!

The Way Of Naked Faith And Pure Love

Those who are attached to God, only so far as they enjoy pleasure and consolation, resemble those who followed the Lord, not to hear his teaching, but because they did eat of the loaves and were filled. They are ready to say with Peter, Master, it is good for us to be here; and let us make three tabernacles; but they know not what they say. After being intoxicated with the joys of the mountain they deny the Son of God and refuse to follow him to Calvary. Not only do they desire delights, but they seek illuminations also; the mind is curious to behold, while the heart requires to be filled with soft and flattering emotions. Is this dying to self? Is this the way in which the just shall live by faith? They desire to have extraordinary revelations, which may be regarded as supernatural gifts, and a mark of the special favor of God. Nothing is so flattering to self-love; all the greatness of the world at once could not so inflate the heart; these supernatural gifts nourish in secret the life of nature. It is an ambition of the most refined character, as it is wholly spiritual; but it is merely ambition; a desire to feel, to enjoy, to posses God and his gifts, to behold his light, to discern spirits, to prophesy, in short, to be an extraordinarily gifted person; for the enjoyment of illuminations and delights, leads the soul little by little towards a secret coveting of all these things. Yet the apostle shows us a more excellent way, for which he inspires us with a holy emulation; it is the way of charity which seeks not her own, and desires not to be clothed upon, if we may adopt the apostles language, but suffers herself to be unclothed. She is less in search of pleasure than of God, whose will she longs to fulfill. If she finds pleasure in devotion, she does not rest in it, but makes it serve to strengthen her weakness, as a convalescent uses a staff to aid in walking, but throws it aside on his restoration. In the same way the tender and child-like soul that God fed with milk in the beginning, suffers itself to be weaned when He sees it is time that it should be nourished upon strong meat. We must not be ever children, always hanging upon the breast of heavenly consolations; we must put away childish things with St. Paul. Our early joys were excellent to attract us, to detach us from gross and worldly pleasures by others of a purer kind, and to lead us into a life of prayer and recollection; but to be constantly in a state of enjoyment that takes away the feeling of the cross, and to live in a fervor of devotion, that continually keeps paradise open, this is not dying upon the cross and becoming nothing. This life of illumination and sensible delights, is a very dangerous snare, if we become so attached to it as to desire nothing farther; for he who has no other attraction to prayer, will quit both it and God, whenever this source of his gratification is dried up. St. Theresa says, you know, that a vast number of souls leave off praying at the very moment when their devotion is beginning to be real. How many are there who, in consequence of too tender rearing in Jesus Christ, and too great fondness for the milk of his word, go back and abandon the interior life as soon as God undertakes to wean them! We need not be astonished at this, for they mistake the portico of the temple for the very sanctuary itself; they desire the death of their gross external passions, that they may lead a delicious life of self-satisfaction within. Hence so much infidelity and disappointment, even among those who appeared the most fervent and the most devoted; those who have talked the loudest of abandonment, of death to self, of the darkness of faith and of desolation, are often the most surprised and discouraged, when they really experience these things, and their consolation is taken away. O how excellent is the way pointed out by John of the Cross, who would have us believe without seeing, and love without desiring to feel! This attachment to sensible delights, is the fruitful source of all our illusions; souls are earthly in desiring something tangible, as it were, before they can feel firm. But this is all wrong; it is these very things of sense that produce vacillation; we think, while the pleasure lasts, that we shall never desert God; we say in our prosperity, that we shall never be moved; but the moment our intoxication is over, we give up all for lost, thus substituting our own pleasure and imagination in place of God. Naked faith, alone, is a sure guard against illusion. When our foundation is not upon any imagination, feeling, pleasure, or extraordinary illumination; when we rest upon God only in pure and naked faith, in the simplicity of the gospel receiving the consolations which He sends, but dwelling in none; abstaining from judging, and ever obedient; believing that it is easy to be deceived, and that others may be able to set us right; in short, acting every moment with simplicity and an upright intention, following the light of the faith of the present moment; then we are indeed in a way that is but little subject to illusion. Experience will demonstrate, better than anything else, how much more certain this path is than that of illuminations and sensible delights. Whoever will try it, will soon find that this way of naked faith, rigidly followed, is the profoundest and most complete death of self. Interior delights and revelations indemnify our self-love for all its external sacrifices, and cherish a secret and refined life of nature; but to suffer ourselves to be stripped within and without at once, without by Providence, and within by the night of pure faith, this is a total sacrifice, and a state the farthest possible from self-deception. Those, then, who seek to guard against being deceived by a constant succession of emotions and certainties, are by that very course exposing themselves most surely to such a result. On the other hand, those who follow the leadings of the love that strips them and the faith that walks in darkness, without seeking any other support, avoid all the sources of error and illusion. The author of the Imitation of Christ tells you, that if God takes away your inward delights, it should be your pleasure to remain without pleasure. O how beloved of God is a soul thus crucified, that rests calmly upon the cross, and desires only to expire with Jesus! It is not true to say that we are afraid of having lost God, on being deprived of feeling; it is impatience under the trial, the restlessness of a pampered and dainty nature, a search for some support for self-love, a weariness of abandonment, and a secret return to self, after our consecration to God. O God, where are they who stop not in the road to death? If they persevere unto the end, they shall receive a crown of life.

On The Presence Of God

The true source of all our perfection is contained in the command of God in Abraham, Walk before me, and be perfect. The presence of God calms the soul, and gives it quiet and repose even during the day, and in the midst of occupation but we must be given up to God without reserve. When we have once found God, we have nothing to seek among men; we must make the sacrifice of our dearest friendships; the best of friends has entered into our hearts, that jealous Bridegroom who requires the whole of it for himself. It takes no great time to love God, to be refreshed by his presence, to elevate our hearts to Him, or to worship Him in the depths of our soul, to offer to Him all we do and all we suffer; this is the true kingdom of God within us, which cannot be disturbed. When the distraction of the senses and the vivacity of the imagination hinder the soul from a sweet and peaceful state of recollection, we should at least be calm as to the state of the will: in that case, the will to be recollected is a sufficient state of recollection for the time being. We must return toward God, and do everything which He would have us do with a right intention. We must endeavor to awake within ourselves, from time to time, the desire of being devoted to God in all the extent of our powers; in our intellect, to know him and think on him, and in our will, to love him. We must desire too, that our outward senses may be consecrated to him in all their operations. Let us be careful how we voluntarily engage, either externally or internally, in matters which cause such distraction of the will and intellect, and so draw them out of themselves that they find difficulty in re-entering and finding God. The moment we discover that anything causes excessive pleasure or joy within us, let us separate our heart from it, and, to prevent it from seeking its repose in the creature, let us present it to God, the true object of love, the sovereign good. If we are faithful in breaking up all attachment to the creature, that is, if we prevent its entering into those depths of the soul which our Lord reserves for Himself, to dwell there and to be there respected, adored, and loved, we shall soon experience that pure joy which He never fails to give to a soul freed and detached from all human affections. Whenever we perceive within us anxious desires for anything, whatever it may be, and find that nature is hurrying us with too much haste to do what is to be done, whether it be to say something, see something, or to do something, let us stop short, and repress the precipitancy of our thoughts and the agitation of our actions for God has said, that his Spirit does not dwell in disquiet. Be careful not to take too much interest in what is going on around you, nor to be much engaged in it is a fruitful source of distraction. As soon as we have found what it is that God requires of us in anything that comes up, let us stop there and separate ourselves from all the rest. By that means we shall always preserve the depths of the soul free and equable, and rid ourselves of many things that embarrass our hearts, and prevent them from turning easily toward God. An excellent means of preserving our interior solitude and liberty of soul, is to make it a rule to put an end, at the close of every action, to all reflections upon it, all reflex acts of self-love, whether of a vain joy or sorrow. Happy is he whose mind contains only what is necessary, and who thinks of nothing except when it is time to think of it! so that it is God who excites the impression, by calling us to perform his will as soon as it is exhibited, rather than the mind laboriously foreseeing and seeking it. In short, let us be accustomed to recollect ourselves during the day and in the midst of our occupations, by a simple view of God. Let us silence by that means all the movements of our hearts, when they appear in the least agitated. Let us separate ourselves from all that does not come from God. Let us suppress our superfluous thoughts and reveries. Let us utter no useless word. Let us seek God within us, and we shall find Him without fail, and with Him, joy and peace. While outwardly busy, let us be more occupied with God than with everything else. To be rightly engaged, we must be in his presence and employed for Him. At the sight of the Majesty of God, our interior ought to become calm and remain tranquil. Once a single word of the Savior suddenly calmed a furiously agitated sea: one look of his at us, and of ours toward Him, ought always to perform the same miracle within us. We must often raise our hearts to God. He will purify, enlighten, and direct them. Such was the daily practice of the sacred Psalmist: I have set the Lord always before me. Let us often employ the beautiful words of the same holy prophet, Whom have I in heaven but you? And there is none upon earth that I desire beside you! God is the strength of my heart and my portion forever! We must not wait for a leisure hour, when we can bar our doors; the moment that is employed in regretting that we have no opportunity to be recollected, might be profitably spent in recollection. Let us turn our hearts toward God in a simple, familiar spirit, full of confidence in him. The most interrupted moments, even while eating or listening to others, are valuable. Tiresome and idle talk in our presence, instead of annoying, will afford us the delight of employing the interval in seeking God. Thus all things work together for good to them that love God. We must read according to our necessity and desire, but with frequent interruptions, for the purpose of recollection. A word or two, simple and full of the Spirit of God, will be to us as hidden manna. We forget the words, but the effect remains; they operate in secret, and the soul is fed and enriched. The reader will not understand by this, that the soul, in a state of true abandonment, does not exhibit affection for those about it. As, by that process, it commences to see God as He is, it also begins to be like Him, and is all love. Its whole existence, like that of God, may be summed up in the single word Love. But its love is divine, not human; its affection for all creatures of God, in their respective relations, is higher, and deeper, and holier than it ever was before.

On Conformity To The Will Of God

The essence of virtue consists in the attitude of the will. This is what the Lord would teach us when he said, The kingdom of God is within you. It is not a question of extensive knowledge, of splendid talents, nor even of great deeds; it is a simple matter of having a heart and loving. Outward works are the fruits and consequences of loving, and the spring of all good things is at the bottom of the soul. There are some virtues which are appropriate to certain conditions, and not to others; some are good at one time, and some at another; but an upright will is profitable for all times and all places. That kingdom of God which is within us, consists in our willing whatever God wills, always, in everything, and without reservation; and thus his kingdom comes; for his will is then done as it is in Heaven, since we will nothing but what is dictated by his sovereign pleasure. Blessed are the poor in spirit! Blessed are they who are stripped of everything, even of their own wills, that they may no longer belong to themselves! How poor in spirit does he become who has given up all things to God! But how is it that our will becomes right, when it unreservedly conforms to that of God? We will whatever He wills; what He does not will, we do not; we attach our feeble wills to that all-powerful one that regulates everything. Thus nothing can ever come to pass against our wishes; for nothing can happen contrary to the will of God, and we find in his good pleasure an inexhaustible source of peace and consolation. The interior life is the beginning of the blessed peace of the saints, who eternally cry, Amen, Amen! We adore, we praise, we bless God in everything; we see Him incessantly, and in all things his paternal hand is the sole object of our contemplation. There are no longer any evils; for even the most terrible that come upon us, work together for good, as St. Paul says, to those that love God. Can the suffering that God destines to purify and make us worthy of himself, be called an evil? Let us cast all our cares, then, into the bosom of so good a Father, and suffer Him to do as He pleases. Let us be content to adopt his will in all points, and to abandon our own absolutely and forever. How can we retain anything of our own, when we do not even belong to ourselves? The slave has nothing; how much less, then, should we own anything, who in ourselves are but nothingness and sin, and who are indebted for everything to pure grace! God has only bestowed upon us a will, free and capable of self-possession, that we may the more generously recompense the gift by returning it to its rightful owner. We have nothing but our wills only; all the rest belongs elsewhere. Disease removes life and health; riches make to themselves wings; intellectual talents depend upon the state of the body. The only thing that really belongs to us is our will, and it is of this, therefore, that God is especially jealous, for He gave it to us, not that we should retain it, but that we should return it to Him, whole as we received it, and without the slightest reservation. If the least desire remain, or the smallest hesitation, it is robbing God, contrary to the order of creation; for all things come from Him, and to Him they are all due. Alas! how many souls there are full of self, and desirous of doing good and serving God, but in such a way as to suit themselves; who desire to impose rules upon God as to his manner of drawing them to Himself. They want to serve and possess Him, but they are not willing to abandon themselves to Him, and be possessed by Him. What a resistance they offer to Him, even when they appear so full of zeal and fervor! It is certain that in one sense, their spiritual abundance becomes an obstacle to their progress; for they hold it all, even their virtues, in appropriation, and constantly seek self, even in good. O how superior to such fervid and illuminated souls, walking always in virtue, in a road of their own choice, is that humble heart that renounces its own life, and every selfish movement, and dismisses all will except such as God gives from moment to moment, in accordance with his Gospel and Providence! Herein lies the meaning of those words of the Lord; If any man will come after me, let him deny himself and take up his cross and follow me. We must follow Jesus Christ, step by step, and not open up a path for ourselves. We can only follow Him by denying ourselves; and what is this but unreservedly abandoning every right over ourselves? And so St. Paul tells us; You are not your own: no, not a thing remains that belongs to us! Alas for him that resumes possession of anything after once abandoning it! To desire to serve God in one place rather than in another, in this way rather than in that, is not this desiring to serve Him in our own way rather than in his? But to be equally ready for all things, to will everything and nothing, to leave ourselves in his hands, like a toy in the hands of a child, to set no bounds to our abandonment, inasmuch as the perfect reign of God cannot abide them, this is really denying ourselves; this is treating Him like a God, and ourselves like creatures made solely for his use.

General Directions For Attaining Inward Peace

There is no peace to them that resist God: if there be joy in the world, it is reserved for a pure conscience; the whole earth is full of tribulation and anguish to those who do not possess it. How different is the peace of God from that of the world! It calms the passions, preserves the purity of the conscience, is inseparable from righteousness, unites us to God and strengthens us against temptations. The peace of the soul consists in an absolute resignation to the will of God. Martha, Martha, you are careful and troubled about many things; but one thing is needful. The pain we suffer from so many occurrences, arises from the fact that we are not entirely abandoned to God in everything that happens. Let us put all things, then, into his hands, and offer them to Him in our hearts, as a sacrifice beforehand. From the moment that you cease to desire anything according to your own judgment, and begin to will everything just as God wills it, you will be free from your former tormenting reflections and anxieties about your own concerns; you will no longer have anything to conceal or take care of. Until then, you will be troubled, vacillating in your views and enjoyments, easily dissatisfied with others and but little satisfied with yourself, and full of reserve and distrust. Your good intentions, until they become truly humble and simple, will only torment you; your piety, however sincere, will be the occasion of more internal reproach then of support or consolation. But if you will abandon your whole heart to God, you will be full of peace and joy in the Holy Ghost. Alas for you, if you will regard man in the work of God! In our choice of a guide, men must be counted as nothing; the slightest respect for their opinion dries up the stream of grace, and increases our indecision. We suffer and we displease God besides. How can we refuse to bestow all our love upon God, who first loved us with the tender love of a Father, pitying our frailty, and well knowing the mire from which we have been dragged? When a soul is filled with this love, it enjoys peace of conscience, it is content and happy, it requires neither greatness nor reputation, nor pleasure, nor any of the perishing gifts of time; it desires only the will of God, and watches incessantly in the joyful expectation of its Spouse.

Pure Love Only Can Suffer Aright And Love Its Sufferings

We know that we must suffer, and that we deserve it; nevertheless, we are always surprised at affliction, as if we thought we neither merited nor had need of it. It is only true and pure love that delights to endure, for nothing else is perfectly abandoned. Resignation induces us to bear pain, but there is a something in it which is afflicted in suffering, and resists. The resignation that measures out its abandonment to God with selfish reflection, is willing to suffer, but is constantly examining to ascertain whether it suffers acceptably. In fact, the resigned soul is composed as it were of two persons; one keeping the other in subjection, and watching lest it should revolt. In pure love, unselfish and abandoned, the soul is fed in silence on the cross, and on union with the crucified Savior, without any reflections on the severity of its sufferings. There exists but a single, simple will, which permits God to see it just as it is, without endeavoring to behold itself. It says nothing, does nothing. What then does it do? It suffers. And is this all? Yes, all; it has nothing else to do but to suffer. Love can be heard easily enough, without speech or thought. It does all that it is required to do, which is, to have no will when it is stripped of all consolation. The purest of all loves is a will so filled with that of God, that there remains nothing else. What a consolation is it to think that we are then rid of so many anxieties about our exercise of patience and the other virtues in the sight of those about us? It is enough to be humbled and abandoned in the midst of suffering. This is not courage; it is something both more and less; less in the eyes of the ordinary class of Christians, more in the eyes of pure faith. It is a humiliation which raises the soul into all the greatness of God; a weakness which strips it of every resource, to bestow upon it his omnipotence. When I am weak, says St. Paul, then I am strong; I can do all things through Christ who strengthen me. It suffices then, to feed upon some short sentences suited to our state and our taste, with frequent interruptions to quiet the senses and make room for the inward spirit of recollection. We sometimes suffer, scarcely knowing that we are in distress; at other times we suffer, and know that we bear it ill, but we carry this second and heavier cross without impatience. True love goes ever straightforward, not in its own strength, but esteeming itself as nothing. Then indeed we are truly happy. The cross is no longer a cross when there is no self to suffer under it, and to appropriate its good and evil.

Interested & Disinterested Love

Why do the gifts of God confer more pleasure when they exist in ourselves than when they are conferred upon our neighbor, if we are not attached to self? If we prefer to see them in our possession rather than in that of those about us, we shall certainly be afflicted when we see them more perfect in them than they are in ourselves; and this constitutes envy. What is our duty then? We must rejoice that the will of God is done in us, and that it reigns there not for our happiness and perfection, but for his own good pleasure and glory. Now, take notice of two matters. The first is, that this distinction is not an empty subtlety; for God, in his desire to desolate the soul for its own perfection, causes it really to pass through these trials of self, and never lets it alone until He has deprived its love of selfish reflection and support. There is nothing so jealous, so exacting, and so searching as this principle of pure love; it cannot abide a thousand things that were imperceptible in our previous state; and what pious persons would call an unprofitable nicety, seems an essential point to the soul that is desirous of destroying self. As with gold in the furnace, the fire consumes all that is not gold, so it seems necessary that the heart should be melted with fervent heat, that the love of God may be rendered pure. The second remark is, that God does not pursue every soul in this way in the present life. There is an infinite number of truly pious persons whom He leaves in some degree under the dominion of self-love; these remains of self help to support them in the practice of virtue, and serve to purify them to a certain point. Scarce anything would be more injudicious or more dangerous than to deprive them of the contemplation of the grace of God in them as tending to their own personal perfection. The first class exercise disinterested gratitude; they are thankful to God for whatever He does in them, solely because He does it for his own glory; the second are also grateful, but partly because their own perfection is secured at the same time. If the former should endeavor to deprive the latter of this mixed motive and this interior comfort in self, in reference to grace, they would cause them as much injury as they would an infant by weaning it before it was able to eat; to take away the breast, would be to destroy it. We must never seek to deprive a soul of the food which still contains nutriment for it, and which God suffers to remain as a stay to its weakness. To forestall grace is to destroy it. Neither must the latter condemn the former because they do not see them as much concerned as themselves about their own perfection in the grace ministered unto them. God works in every one as he pleases; the wind blows where it wills, and as it wills. The forgetfulness of self in the pure contemplation of God, is a state in which God can do in our souls whatever most pleases Himself. The important point is, that those who are still in a measure supported by self, should not be too anxious about the state of such as are in pure love, nor should these latter endeavor to make the former pass through the trials peculiar to a higher state of grace before God calls them to it.

On True Liberty

When we are no longer embarrassed by the restless reflections of self, we begin to enjoy true liberty. False wisdom, on the other hand, always on the watch, ever occupied with self, constantly jealous of its own perfection, suffers severely whenever it is permitted to perceive the smallest speck of imperfection. Not that the man who is simple minded and detached from self, fails to labor toward the attainment of perfection; he is the more successful in proportion as he forgets himself, and never dreams of virtue in any other light than as something which accomplishes the will of God. The source of all our defects is the love of self; we refer everything to that, instead of to the love of God. Whoever, then, will labor to get rid of self, to deny himself, according to the instructions of Christ, strikes at once at the root of every evil, and finds, in this simple abandonment of self, the germ of every good. Then those words of Scripture are heard within and understood, Where the Spirit of the Lord is, there is liberty. We neglect nothing to cause the kingdom of God to come both within and without; but in the midst of our frailties we are at peace. We would rather die than commit the slightest voluntary sin, but we have no fear for our reputation from the judgment of man. We court the reproach of Christ Jesus, and dwell in peace though surrounded by uncertainties; the judgments of God do not affright us, for we abandon ourselves to them, imploring his mercy according to our attainments in confidence, sacrifice, and absolute surrender. The greater the abandonment, the more flowing the peace; and in such a large place does it set us, that we are prepared for everything; we will everything and nothing; we are as guileless as babes. Our illumination from God discovers the lightest transgressions, but never discourages. We walk before Him; but if we stumble, we hasten to resume our way, and have no watchword but Onward! If we would find God, we must destroy the remains of the old Adam within. The Lord held a little child in his arms, when He declared, of such is the kingdom of Heaven. The sum of the principal directions is this: do not reason too much, always have an upright purpose in the smallest matters, and pay no attention to the thousand reflections by which we wrap and bury ourselves in self, under pretence of correcting our faults.

On The Employment Of Time

I understand perfectly well that you do not ask at my hands any proof that it is incumbent upon us to employ all our time to good purpose; grace has long since convinced you of this. It is a pleasant thing to come in contact with those who can meet us half way; but, notwithstanding this, much remains to be done, and there is a wonderful distance between the conviction of the intellect, even combined with the good intention of the heart, and a faithful and exact obedience. Nothing has been more common in ancient, as well as in modern times, then to meet souls who were perfect and holy, theoretically. You shall know them by their fruits, says the Savior. And this is the only rule that never deceives, when it is properly understood; it is that by which we must judge ourselves. There is a time for everything in our lives; but the maxim that governs every moment, is, that there should be none useless; that they should all enter into the order and sequence of our salvation; that they are all accompanied by duties which God has allotted with his own hand, and of which He will demand an account; for from the first instant of our existence to the last, He has never assigned us a barren moment, nor one which we can consider as given up to our own discretion. The great thing is to recognize his will in relation to them. This is to be effected, not by an eager and restless seeking, which is much more likely to spoil everything, than to enlighten us as to our duty, but by a true submission to those whom God has set over us, and a pure and upright heart which seeks God in its simplicity, and heartily opposes all the duplicity and false wisdom of self, as fast as it is revealed. For we misemploy our time, not only when we do wrong or do nothing, but also when we do something else than what was incumbent on us at the moment, even though it may be the means of good. We are strangely ingenious in perpetually seeking our own interest; and what the world does nakedly and without shame, those who desire to be devoted to God do also, but in a refined manner, under favor of some pretext which serves as a veil to hide from them the deformity of their conduct. The best general means to ensure the profitable employment of our time, is to accustom ourselves to living in continual dependence upon the Spirit of God and his law, receiving, every instant, whatever He is pleased to bestow; consulting Him in every emergency requiring instant action, and having recourse to Him in our weaker moments, when virtue seems to fail; invoking his aid, and rising our hearts to Him whenever we are solicited by sensible objects, and find ourselves surprised and estranged from God, and far from the true road. Happy is the soul that commits itself, by a sincere self-abandonment, into the hands of its Creator, ready to do all his will, and continually crying, Lord, what would You have me do? Teach me to do your will, for You are my God! During our necessary occupations, we need only pay a simple attention to the leadings of Divine Providence. As they are all prepared for us, and presented by Him, our only care should be to receive them with a child-like spirit, and submit everything absolutely to Him; our temper, our own will, our scruples, our restlessness, our self-reflections, our overflowing emotions of hurry, vain joy, or other passions which assault us according as we are pleased or displeased with the different events of the day. Let us be careful, however, not to suffer ourselves to be overwhelmed by the multiplicity of our exterior occupations, be they what they may. Let us endeavor to commence every enterprise with a pure view to the glory of God, continue it without distraction, and finish it without impatience. The intervals of relaxation and amusement are the most dangerous seasons for us, and perhaps the most useful for others; we must, then, be on our guard, that we be as faithful as possible to the presence of God. We must make use of all that Christian vigilance so much recommended by our Lord; raise our hearts to God in the simple view of faith, and dwell in sweet and peaceful dependence upon the Spirit of grace, as the only means of our safety and strength. This is especially necessary for such as are looked up to as in authority, and whose words may be the cause of so much good or evil. Our leisure hours are ordinarily the sweetest and pleasantest for ourselves; we can never employ them better than in refreshing our spiritual strength, by a secret and intimate communion with God. Prayer is so necessary, and the source of so many blessings, that he who has discovered the treasure cannot be prevented from having recourse to it, whenever he has an opportunity. I could add much more concerning these matters, and I may perhaps do so, if my present views do not escape me; but, if they do, it is of little consequence. God gives others when He pleases; if He does not, it is a proof that they are not necessary; and if so, we should be well satisfied with their loss.

MAXIMS OF THE SAINTS

❧

First Article

Of the love of God, there are various kinds. At least, there are various feelings which go under that name. First, There is what may be called mercenary or selfish love; that is, that love of God which originates in a sole regard to our own happiness. Those who love God with no other love than this, love Him just as the miser his money, and the voluptuous man his pleasures; attaching no value to God, except as a means to an end; and that end is the gratification of themselves. Such, love, if it can be called by that name, is unworthy of God. He does not ask it; He will not receive it. In the language of Francis de Sales, "it is sacrilegious and impious." Second, Another kind of love does not exclude a regard to our own happiness as a motive of love, but requires this motive to be subordinate to a much higher one, namely, that of a regard to God's glory. It is a mixed state, in which we regard ourselves and God at the same time. This love is not necessarily selfish and wrong. On the contrary, when the two objects of it, God and ourselves, are relatively in the right position, that is to say, when we love God as He ought to be loved, and love ourselves no more than we ought to be loved, it is a love which, in being properly subordinated, is unselfish and is right.

Second Article

Of the subjects of this mixed love all are not equally advanced.

Mixed love becomes pure love, when the love of self is relatively, though not absolutely, lost in a regard to the will of God. This is always the case, when the two objects are loved in their due proportion. So that pure love is mixed love when it is combined rightly.

Pure love is not inconsistent with mixed love, but is mixed love carried to its true result. When this result is attained, the motive of God's glory so expands itself, and so fills the mind, that the other motive, that of our own happiness, becomes so small, and so recedes from our inward notice, as to be practically annihilated. It is then that God becomes what He ever ought to be - the center of the soul, to which all its affections tend; the great moral sun of the soul, from which all its light and all its warmth proceed. It is then that a man thinks no more of himself. He has become the man of a "single eye." His own happiness, and all that regards himself, is entirely lost sight of in his simple and fixed look to God's will and God's glory.

We lay ourselves at His feet. Self is known no more; not because it is wrong to regard and to desire our own good, but because the object of desire is withdrawn from our notice. When the sun shines, the stars disappear. When God is in the soul who can think of himself? So that we love God, and God alone; and all other things in and for God.

Third Article

In the early periods of religious experience, motives, which have a regard to our personal happiness, are more prominent and effective than at later periods; nor are they to be condemned. It is proper, in addressing even religious men, to appeal to the fear of death, to the impending judgments of God, to the terrors of hell and the joys of heaven. Such appeals are recognized in the Holy Scriptures, and are in accordance with the views and feelings of good men in all ages of the world. The motives involved in them are powerful aids to beginners in religion; assisting, as they do, very much in repressing the passions, and in strengthening the practical virtues. We should not think lightly, therefore, of the grace of God, as manifested in that inferior form of religion which stops short of the more glorious and perfected form of pure love. We are to follow God's grace, and not to go before it. To the higher state of pure love we are to advance step by step; watching carefully God's inward and outward providence; and receiving increased grace by improving the grace we have, till the dawning light becomes the perfect day.

Fourth Article

He who is in the state of pure or perfect love, has all the moral and Christian virtues in himself. If temperance, forbearance, chastity, truth, kindness, forgiveness, justice, may be regarded as virtues, there can be no doubt that they are all included in holy love. That is to say, the principle of love will not fail to develop itself in each of these forms. St. Augustine remarks, that love is the foundation, source, or principle of all the virtues. This view is sustained also by St. Francis de Sales and by Thomas Aquinas. The state of pure love does not exclude the mental state which is called Christian hope. Hope in the Christian, when we analyze it into its elements, may be described as the desire of being united with God in heaven, accompanied with the expectation or belief of being so.

Fifth Article

Souls that, by being perfected in love, are truly the subjects of sanctification, do not cease, nevertheless, to grow in grace. It may not be easy to specify and describe the degrees of sanctification; but there seem to be at least two modifications of experience after persons have reached this state.

The first may be described as the state of holy resignation. Such a soul thinks more frequently than it will, at a subsequent period, of its own happiness.

The second state is that of holy indifference. Such a soul absolutely ceases either to desire or to will, except in cooperation with the Divine leading. Its desires for itself, as it has greater light, are more completely and permanently merged in the one higher and more absorbing desire of God's glory, and the fulfillment of His will. In this state of experience, ceasing to do what we shall be likely to do, and what we may very properly do in a lower state, we no longer desire our own salvation merely as an eternal deliverance, or merely as involving the greatest amount of personal happiness; but we desire it chiefly as the fulfillment of God's pleasure, and as resulting in His glory, and because He Himself desires and wills that we should thus desire and will.

Holy indifference is not inactivity. It is the furthest possible from it. It is indifference to anything and everything out of God's will; but it is the highest life and activity to anything and everything in that will.

Sixth Article

One of the clearest and best established maxims of holiness is, that the holy soul, when arrived at the second state mentioned, ceases to have desires for anything out of the will of God. The holy soul, when it is really in the state called the state of non-desire, may, nevertheless, desire everything in relation to the correction of its imperfections and weaknesses, its perseverance in its religious state, and its ultimate salvation, which it has reason to know from the Scriptures, or in any other way, that God desires. It may also desire all temporal good, houses and lands, food and clothing, friends and books, and exemption from physical suffering, and anything else, so far and only so far, as it has reason to think that such desire is coincident with the Divine desire. The holy soul not only desires particular things, sanctioned by the known will of God; but also the fulfillment of His will in all respects, unknown as well as known. Being in faith, it commits itself to God in darkness as well as in light. Its non-desire is simply its not desiring anything out of God.

Seventh Article

In the history of inward experience, we not infrequently find accounts of individuals whose inward life may properly be characterized as extraordinary. They represent themselves as having extraordinary communications; dreams, visions, revelations. Without stopping to inquire whether these inward results arise from an excited and disordered state of the physical system or from God, the important remark to be made here is, that these things, to whatever extent they may exist, do not constitute holiness. The principle, which is the life of common Christians in their common mixed state, is the principle which originates and sustains the life of those who are truly "the pure in heart," namely, the principle of faith working by love,--existing, however, in the case of those last mentioned, in a greatly increased degree. This is obviously the doctrine of John of the Cross, who teaches us, that we must walk in the night of faith; that is to say, with night around us, which exists in consequence of our entire ignorance of what is before us, and with faith alone, faith in God, in His Word, and in his Providences, for the soul's guide. Again, the persons who have, or are supposed to have, the visions and other remarkable states to which we have referred are sometimes disposed to make their own experience, imperfect as it obviously is, the guide of their life, considered as separate from and as above the written law. Great care should be taken against such an error as this. God's word is our true rule. Nevertheless, there is no interpreter of the Divine Word like that of a holy heart; or, what is the same thing, of the Holy Ghost dwelling in the heart. If we give ourselves wholly to God, the Comforter will take up His abode with us, and guide us into all that truth which will be necessary for us. Truly holy souls, therefore, continually looking to God for a proper understanding of His Word, may confidently trust that He will guide them aright. A holy soul, in the exercise of its legitimate powers of interpretation, may deduce important views from the Word of God which would not otherwise be known; but it cannot add anything to it. Again, God is the regulator of the affections, as well as of the outward actions. Sometimes the state which He inspires within us is that of holy love; sometimes He inspires affections which have love and faith for their basis, but have a specific character, and then appear under other names, such as humility, forgiveness, gratitude. But in all cases there is nothing holy, except what is based upon the antecedent or "prevenient" grace of God. In all the universe, there is not one legitimate Originator. Man's business is that of concurrence. And this view is applicable to all the stages of Christian experience, from the lowest to the highest.

Eighth Article

Writers often speak of abandonment. The term has a meaning somewhat specific. The soul in this state does not renounce everything, and thus become brutish in its indifference; but renounces everything except God's will. Souls in the state of abandonment, not only forsake outward things, but, what is still more important, forsake themselves. Abandonment, or self-renunciation, is not the renunciation of faith or of love or of anything else, except selfishness. The state of abandonment, or entire self-renunciation, is generally attended, and perhaps we may say, carried out and perfected, by temptations more or less severe. We cannot well know, whether we have renounced ourselves, except by being tried on those very points to which our self-renunciation, either real or supposed, relates. One of the severest inward trials is that by which we are taken off from all inward sensible supports, and are made to live and walk by faith alone. Pious and holy men who have been the subjects of inward crucifixion, often refer to the trials which have been experienced by them. They sometimes speak of them as a sort of inward and terrible purgatory. "Only mad and wicked men," says Cardinal Bona, "will deny the existence of these remarkable experiences, attested as they are by men of the most venerable virtue, who speak only of what they have known in themselves." Trials are not always of the same duration. The more cheerfully and faithfully we give ourselves to God, to be smitten in any and all of our idols, whenever and wherever He chooses, the shorter will be the work. God makes us to suffer no longer than He sees to be necessary for us. We should not be premature in concluding that inward crucifixion is complete, and our abandonment to God is without any reservation whatever. The act of consecration, which is a sort of incipient step, may be sincere; but the reality of the consecration can be known only when God has applied the appropriate tests. The trial will show whether we are wholly the Lord's. Those who prematurely draw the conclusion that they are so, expose themselves to great illusion and injury.

Ninth Article

The state of abandonment, or of entire self-renunciation, does not take from the soul that moral power which is essential to its moral agency; nor that antecedent or prevenient grace, without which even abandonment itself would be a state of moral death; nor the principle of faith, which prevenient grace originated, and through which it now operates; nor the desire and hope of final salvation, although it takes away all uneasiness and unbelief connected with such a desire; nor the fountains of love which spring up deeply and freshly within it; nor the hatred of sin; nor the testimony of a good conscience. But it takes away that uneasy hankering of the soul after pleasure either inward or outward, and the selfish vivacity and eagerness of nature, which is too impatient to wait calmly and submissively for God's time of action. By fixing the mind wholly upon God, it takes away the disposition of the soul to occupy itself with reflex acts; that is, with the undue examination and analysis of its own feelings. It does not take away the pain and sorrow naturally incident to our physical state and natural sensibilities; but it takes away all uneasiness, all murmuring; leaving the soul in its inner nature, and in every part of its nature where the power of faith reaches, calm and peaceable as the God that dwells there.

Tenth Article

God has promised life and happiness to His people. What He has promised can never fail to take place. Nevertheless, it is the disposition of those who love God with a perfect heart, to leave themselves entirely in His hands, irrespective, in some degree, of the promise. By the aid of the promise, without which they must have remained in their original weakness, they rise, as it were, above the promise; and rest in that essential and eternal will, in which the promise originated. So much is this the case, that some individuals, across whose path God had spread the darkness of His providences, and who seemed to themselves for a time to be thrown out of His favor and to be hopelessly lost, have acquiesced with submission in the terrible destiny which was thus presented before them. Such was the state of mind of Francis de Sales, as he prostrated himself in the church of St. Stephen des Grez. The language of such persons, uttered without complaint, is, "My God, my God, why have you forsaken me?" They claim God as their God, and will not abandon their love to Him, although they believe, at the time, that they are forsaken of Him. They choose to leave themselves, under all possible circumstances, entirely in the hands of God: their language is, even if it should be His pleasure to separate them forever from the enjoyments of His presence, Not my will, but yours be done." It is perhaps difficult to perceive, how minds whose life, as it were, is the principle of faith, can be in this situation. Take the case of the Savior. It is certainly difficult to conceive how the Savior, whose faith never failed, could yet believe Himself forsaken; and yet it was so. We know that it is impossible for God to forsake those who put their trust in Him. He can just as soon forsake His own word; and, what is more, He can just as soon forsake His own nature. Holy souls, nevertheless, may sometimes, in a way and under circumstances which we may not fully understand, believe themselves to be forsaken, beyond all possibility of hope; and yet such is their faith in God arid their love to Him, that the will of God, even under such circumstances, is dearer to them than anything and everything else.

Eleventh Article

One great point of difference between the First Covenant, or the covenant of works, which said to men, "Do this and live," and the Second Covenant, or the covenant of grace, which says, "Believe and live," is this: The first covenant did not lead men to anything that was perfect. It showed men what was right and good; but it failed in giving them the power to fulfill what the covenant required. Men not only understood what was right and good, but they knew what was evil; but, in their love and practice of depravity, they had no longer power of themselves to flee from it. The new or Christian covenant of grace, not only prescribes and commands, but gives also the power to fulfill. In the practical dispensations of divine grace, there are a number of principles which it may be important to remember.

God being LOVE, it is a part of His nature to desire to communicate Himself to all moral beings, and to make Himself one with them in a perfect harmony of relations and feelings. The position of God is that of giver; the position of man is that of recipient. Harmonized with man by the blood and power of the Cross, he has once more become the infinite fullness, the original and overflowing fountain, giving and ever ready to give.

Such are the relations between God and man, involved in the fact of man's moral agency, that man's business is to receive.

Souls true to the grace given them, will never suffer any diminution of it. On the contrary, the great and unchangeable condition of continuance and of growth in grace is cooperation with what we now have. This is the law of growth, not only deducible from the Divine nature, but expressly revealed and declared in the Scriptures: "For whosoever has, to him shall be given, and he shall have more abundance; but whosoever has not, from him shall be taken away even what he has." A faithful cooperation with grace, is the most effectual preparation for attracting and receiving and increasing grace. This is the great secret of advancement to those high degrees which are permitted; namely, a strict, unwavering, faithful cooperation, moment by moment.

It is important correctly to understand the doctrine of cooperation. A disposition to cooperate, is not more opposed to the sinful indolence which falls behind, than to the hasty and unrighteous zeal which runs before. It is in the excess of zeal, which has a good appearance, but in reality has unbelief and self at the bottom, that we run before God.

Cooperation, by being calm and peaceable, does not cease to be efficacious. Souls in this purified but tranquil state are souls of power; watchful and triumphant against self; resisting temptation; fighting even to blood against sin. But it is, nevertheless, a combat free from the turbulence and inconsistencies of human passion; because they contend in the presence of God, who is their strength, in the spirit of the highest faith and love, and under the guidance of the Holy Ghost, who is always tranquil in His operations.

Twelfth Article

Those in the highest state of religions experience desire nothing, except that God may be glorified in them by the accomplishment of His holy will. Nor is it inconsistent with this, that holy souls possess that natural love which exists in the form of love for themselves. Their natural love, however, which, within its proper degree, is innocent love, is so absorbed in the love of God, that it ceases, for the most part, to be a distinct object of consciousness; and practically and truly they may be said to love themselves IN and FOR God. Adam, in his state of innocence, loved himself, considered as the reflex image of God and for God's sake. So that we may either say, that he loved God in himself, or that he loved himself IN and FOR God. And it is because holy souls, extending their affections beyond their own limit, love their neighbor on the same principle of loving, namely, IN and FOR God, that they may be said to love their neighbors as themselves. It does not follow, because the love of ourselves is lost in the love of God, that we are to take no care, and to exercise no watch over ourselves. No man will be so seriously and constantly watchful over himself as he who loves himself IN and FOR God alone. Having the image of God in himself, he has a motive strong, we might perhaps say, as that which controls the actions of angels, to guard and protect it.

It may be thought, perhaps, that this is inconsistent with the principle in the doctrines of holy living, which requires in the highest stages of inward experience, to avoid those reflex acts which consist in self-inspection, because such acts have a tendency to turn the mind off from God. The apparent difficulty is reconciled in this way. The holy soul is a soul with God; moving as God moves; doing as God does; looking as God looks. If, therefore, God is looking within us, as we may generally learn from the intimations of His providences, then it is a sign that we are to look within ourselves. Our little eye, our small and almost imperceptible ray, must look in, in the midst of the light of His great and burning eye. It is thus that we may inspect ourselves without a separation from God. On the same principle, we may be watchful and careful over our neighbors; watching them, not in our own time, but in God's time; not in the censoriousness of nature, but in the kindness and forbearance of grace; not as separate from God, but in concurrence with Him.

Thirteenth Article

The soul, in the state of pure love, acts in simplicity. Its inward rule of action is found in the decisions of a sanctified conscience. These decisions, based upon judgments that are free from self-interest, may not always be absolutely right, because our views and judgments, being limited, can extend only to things in part; but they may be said to be relatively right: they conform to things so far as we are permitted to see them and understand them, and convey to the soul a moral assurance, that, when we act in accordance with them, we are doing as God would have us do. Such a conscience is enlightened by the Spirit of God; and when we act thus, under its Divine guidance, looking at what now is and not at what may be, looking at the right of things and not at their relations to our personal and selfish interests, we are said to act in simplicity. This is the true mode of action. Thus, in this singleness of spirit, we do things, as some experimental writers express it, without knowing what we do. We are so absorbed in the thing to be done, and in the importance of doing it rightly, that we forget ourselves. Perfect love has nothing to spare from its object for itself, and he who prays perfectly is never thinking how well he prays.

Fourteenth Article

Holy souls are without impatience, but not without trouble; are above murmuring, but not above affliction. The souls of those who are thus wholly in Christ may be regarded in two points of view, or rather in two parts; namely, the natural appetites, propensities, and affections, on the one hand, which may be called the inferior part; and the judgment, the moral sense, and the will, on the other, which may be described as the superior part. As things are, in the present life, those who are wholly devoted to God may suffer in the inferior part, and may be at rest in the superior. Their wills may be in harmony with the Divine will; they may be approved in their judgments and conscience, and at the same time may suffer greatly in their physical relations, and in their natural sensibilities. In this manner, Christ upon the cross, while His will remained firm in its union with the will of His heavenly Father, suffered much through His physical system; He felt the painful longings of thirst, the pressure of the thorns, and the agony of the spear. He was deeply afflicted also for the friends He left behind Him, and for a dying world. But in His inner and higher nature, where He felt Himself sustained by the secret voice uttered in His sanctified conscience and in His unchangeable faith, He was peaceful and happy.

Fifteenth Article

A suitable repression of the natural appetites is profitable and necessary. We are told that the body should be brought into subjection. Those physical mortifications, therefore, which are instituted to this end, denominated austerities, are not to be disapproved. When practiced within proper limits, they tend to correct evil habits, to preserve us against temptation, and to give self-control. The practice of austerities, with the views and on the principles indicated, should be accompanied with the spirit of recollection, of love, and prayer. Christ himself, whose retirement to solitary places, whose prayers and fasting are not to be forgotten, has given us the pattern which it is proper for us to follow. We must sometimes use force against our stubborn nature. "Since the days of John, the kingdom of heaven suffers violence; and the violent take it by force."

Sixteenth Article

The simple desire of our own happiness, kept in due subordination, is innocent. This desire is natural to us; and is properly denominated the principle of self-love. When the principle of self-love passes its appropriate limit, it becomes selfishness. Self-love is innocent; selfishness is wrong. Selfishness was the sin of the first angel, "who rested in himself," as St. Augustine expresses it, instead of referring himself to God. In many Christians a prominent principle of action is the desire of happiness. They love God and they love heaven; they love holiness, and they love the pleasures of holiness; they love to do good, and they love the rewards of doing good. This is well; but there is something better. Such Christians are inferior to those who forget the nothingness of the creature in the infinitude of the Creator, and love God for His own glory alone.

Seventeenth Article

No period of the Christian life is exempt from temptation. The temptations incident to the earlier stages are different from those incident to a later period, and are to be resisted in a different manner. Sometimes the temptations incident to the transition-state from mixed love to pure love are somewhat peculiar, being adapted to test whether we love God for Himself alone. In the lower or mixed state the methods of resisting temptations are various. Sometimes the subject of these trials boldly faces them, and endeavors to overcome them by a direct resistance. Sometimes he turns and flees. But in the state of pure love, when the soul has become strong in the Divine contemplation, it is the common rule laid down by religious writers, that the soul should keep itself fixed upon God in the exercise of its holy love as at other times, as the most effectual way of resisting the temptation, which would naturally expand its efforts in vain upon a soul in that state.

Eighteenth Article

The will of God is the ultimate and only rule of action. God manifests His will in various ways. The will of God may in some cases be ascertained by the operations of the human mind, especially when under a religious or gracious guidance. But He reveals His will chiefly in His written word. And nothing can be declared to be the will of God, which is at variance with His written or revealed will, which may also be called His positive will. If we sin, it is that God permits it; but it is also true, that He disapproves and condemns it as contrary to His immutable holiness. It is the business of the sinner to repent. The state of penitence has temptations peculiar to itself. He is sometimes tempted to murmuring and rebellious feelings, as if he had been unjustly left of God. When penitence is true, and in the highest state, it is free from the variations of human passion.

Nineteenth Article

Among other distinctions of prayer, we may make that of vocal and silent, the prayer of the lips and the prayer of the affections. Vocal prayer, without the heart attending it, is superstitious and wholly unprofitable. To pray without recollection in God and without love, is to pray as the heathen did, who thought to be heard for the multitude of their words. Nevertheless, vocal prayer, when attended by right affections, ought to be both recognized and encouraged, as being calculated to strengthen the thoughts and feelings it expresses, and to awaken new ones, and also for the reason that it was taught by the Son of God to His Apostles, and that it has been practiced by the whole Church in all ages. To make light of this sacrifice of praise, this fruit of the lips, would be an impiety. Silent prayer, in its common form, is also profitable. Each has its peculiar advantages, as each has its place. There is also a modification of prayer, which may be termed the prayer of silence. This is a prayer too deep for words. The common form of silent prayer is voluntary. In the prayer of contemplative silence, the lips seem to be closed almost against the will.

Twentieth Article

The principles of holy living extend to everything. For instance, in the matter of reading, he who has given himself wholly to God, can read only what God permits him to read. He cannot read books, however characterized by wit or power, merely to indulge an idle curiosity, or to please himself alone. In reading this may be a suitable direction, namely, to read but little at a time, and to interrupt the reading by intervals of religious recollection, in order that we may let the Holy Spirit more deeply imprint in us Christian truths. God, in the person of the Holy Ghost, becomes to the fully renovated mind the great inward Teacher. This is a great truth. At the same time we are not to suppose that the presence of the inward teacher exempts us from the necessity of the outward lesson. The Holy Ghost, operating through the medium of a purified judgment, teaches us by the means of books, especially by the word of God, which is never to be laid aside.

Twenty-First Article

One characteristic of the lower states of religious experience is, that they are sustained, in a considerable degree, by meditative and reflective acts. As faith is comparatively weak and temptations are strong, it becomes necessary to gain strength by such meditative and reflective acts, by the consideration of various truths applicable to their situation, and of the motives drawn from such truths. Accordingly, souls array before them all the various motives drawn from the consideration of misery on the one hand, and of happiness on the other; all the motives of fear and hope. It is different with those who have given themselves wholly to God in the exercise of pure or perfect love. The soul does not find it necessary to delay and to meditate, in order to discover motives of action. It finds its motive of action a motive simple, uniform, peaceable, and still powerful beyond any other power, in its own principle of life. Meditation, inquiry, and reasoning, are exceedingly necessary to the great body of Christians; and absolutely indispensable to those in the beginnings of the Christian life. To take away these helps would be to take away the child from the breast before it can digest solid food. Still they are only the props, and not the life itself.

Twenty-Second Article

The holy soul delights in acts of contemplation; to think of God and of God only. But the contemplative state, without any interruption, is hardly consistent with the condition of the present life. It may be permitted to exist, however, and ought not to be resisted, when the attraction towards God is so strong, that we find ourselves incapable of profitably employing our minds in meditative and discursive acts.

Twenty-Third Article

Of the two states, the meditative and discursive on the one hand, which reflects, compares, and reasons, and supports itself by aids and methods of that nature, and the contemplative on the other, which rests in God without such aids, the contemplative is the higher. God will teach the times of both. Neither state is, or ought to be, entirely exclusive of the other.

Twenty-Fourth Article

In some cases God gives such eminent grace, that the contemplative prayer, which is essentially the same with the prayer of silence, becomes the habitual state. We do not mean, that the mind is always in this state; but that, whenever the season of recollection and prayer returns, it habitually assumes the contemplative state, in distinction from the meditative and discursive. It does not follow that this state, eminent as it is, is invariable. Souls may fall from this state by some act of infidelity in themselves; or God may place them temporarily in a different state.

Twenty-Fifth Article

"Whether, therefore," says the Apostle, "you eat or drink, or whatsoever you do, do all thins to the glory of God". And in another passage he says, "Let all thins be done with charity". And again, "By love serve one another," passages which, with many others, imply two things; first, that everything which is done by the Christian ought to be done from a holy principle; and, second, that this principle is love.

Twenty Sixth Article

Our acceptance with God, when our hearts are wholly given to Him, does not depend upon our being in a particular state, but simply upon our being in that state in which God in His providence requires us to be. The doctrine of holiness, therefore, while it recognizes and requires, on its appropriate occasions, the prayer of contemplation or of contemplative silence, is not only not inconsistent with other forms of prayer, but is not at all inconsistent with the practice of the ordinary acts, duties, and virtues of life. It would be a great mistake to suppose, that a man who bears the Savior's image, is any the less on that account a good neighbor or a good citizen; that he can think less or work less when he is called to it; or that he is not characterized by the various virtues, appropriate to our present situation, of temperance, truth, forbearance, forgiveness, kindness, chastity, justice. There is a law, involved in the very nature of holiness, which requires it to adapt itself to every variety of situation.

Twenty-Seventh Article

It is in accordance with the views of Dionysius the Areopagite, to say, that the holy soul in its contemplative state, is occupied with the pure or spiritual Divinity. That is to say, it is occupied with God, in distinction from any mere image of God, such as could be addressed to the touch, the sight, or any of the senses. And this is not all. It does not satisfy the desires of the soul in its contemplative state, to occupy itself merely with the attributes of God; with His power, wisdom, goodness, and the like; but it rather seeks and unites itself with the God of the attributes. The attributes of God are not God himself. The power of God is not an identical expression with the God of power; nor is the wisdom of God identical with the God of wisdom. The holy soul, in its contemplative state, loves to unite itself with God, considered as the subject of His attributes. It is not infinite wisdom, infinite power, or infinite goodness, considered separately from the existence of whom they can be predicated, which it loves and adores; but the God of infinite wisdom, power, and goodness.

Twenty- Eighth Article

Christ is "the way, and the truth, and the life." The grace which sanctifies as well as that which justifies, is by Him and through Him. He is the true and living way; and no man can gain the victory over sin, and be brought into union with God, without Christ. And when, in some mitigated sense, we may be said to have arrived at the end of the way by being brought home to the Divine fold and reinstated in the Divine image, it would be sad indeed if we should forget the way itself, as Christ is sometimes called. At every period of our progress, however advanced it may be, our life is derived from God through Him and for Him. The most advanced souls are those which are most possessed with the thoughts and the presence of Christ. Any other view would be extremely pernicious. It would be to snatch from the faithful eternal life, which consists in knowing the only true God and Jesus Christ His Son, whom he has sent.

Twenty-Ninth Article

The way of holiness is wonderful, but it is not miraculous. Those in it, walk by simple faith alone. And perhaps there is nothing more remarkable nor wonderful in it, than that a result so great should be produced by a principle so simple. When persons have arrived at the state of divine union, so that, in accordance with the prayer of the Savior, they are made one with Christ in God, they no longer seem to put forth distinct inward acts, but their state appears to be characterized by a deep and Divine repose. The continuous act is the act of faith, which brings into moral and religious union with the Divine nature; faith which, through the plenitude of Divine grace, is kept firm, unbroken. The appearance of absolute continuity and unity in this blessed state is increased perhaps by the entire freedom of the mind from all eager, anxious, unquiet acts. The soul is not only at unity with itself in the respects which have been mentioned, but it has also a unity of rest. This state of continuous faith and of consequent repose in God is sometimes denominated the passive state. The soul, at such times, ceases to originate acts which precede the grace of God. The decisions of her consecrated judgment, are the voice of the Holy Ghost in the soul. But if she first listens passively, it is subsequently her business to yield an active and effective cooperation in the line of duty which they indicate. The more pliant and supple the soul is to the Divine suggestions, the more real and efficacious is her own action, though without any excited and troubled movement. The more a soul receives from God, the more she ought to restore to Him of what she has from Him. This ebbing and flowing, if one may so express it, this communication on the part of God and the correspondent action on the part of man, constitute the order of grace on the one hand, and the action and fidelity of the creature on the other.

Thirtieth Article

It would be a mistake to suppose, that the highest state of inward experience is characterized by great excitements, by raptures and ecstasies, or by any movements of feeling which would be regarded as particularly extraordinary. One of the remarkable results in a soul of which faith is the sole governing principle, is, that it is entirely peaceful. Nothing disturbs it. And being thus peaceful, it reflects distinctly and clearly the image of Christ; like the placid lake, which shows, in its own clear and beautiful bosom, the exact forms of the objects around and above it. Another is, that having full faith in God and divested of all selfishness and resistance in itself, it is perfectly accessible and pliable to all the impressions of grace.

Thirty-First Article

It does not follow, that those who possess the graces of a truly sanctified heart, are at liberty to reject the ordinary methods and rules of perception and judgment. They exercise and value wisdom, while they reject the selfishness of wisdom. The rules of holy living would require them every moment to make a faithful use of all the natural light of reason, as well as the higher and spiritual light of grace. A holy soul values and seeks wisdom, but does not seek it in an unholy and worldly spirit. Nor, when it is made wise by the Spirit of wisdom, who dwells in all hearts that are wholly devoted to God, does it turn back from the giver to the gift, and rejoice in its wisdom as its own. The wisdom of the truly holy soul is a wisdom which estimates things in the present moment. It judges of duty from the facts which now are; including, however, those things which have a relation to the present. It is an important remark, that the present moment necessarily possesses a moral extension; so that, in judging of it, we are to include all those things which have a natural and near relation to the thing actually in hand. It is in this manner that the holy soul lives in the present, committing the past to God, and leaving the future with that approaching hour which shall convert it into the present. "Sufficient to the day is the evil thereof." Tomorrow will take care of itself; it will bring, at its coming, its appropriate grace and light. When we live this way, God will not fail to give us our daily bread. Such souls draw on themselves the special protection of Providence, under whose care they live, without a far extended and unquiet forecast, like little children resting in the bosom of their mother. Conscious of their own limited views, and keeping in mind the direction of the Savior, Judge not that you be not judged, they are slow to pass judgment upon others. They are willing to receive reproof and correction; and, separate from the will of God, they have no choice or will of their own in anything. These are the children whom Christ permits to come near Him. They combine the prudence of the serpent with the simplicity of the dove. But they do not appropriate their prudence to themselves as their own prudence, any more than they appropriate to themselves the beams of the natural sun, when they walk in its light. These are the poor in spirit, whom Christ Jesus has declared blessed; and who are as much taken off from any complacency in what others might call their merits, as all Christians ought to be from their temporal possessions. They are the "little ones," to whom God is well pleased to reveal His mysteries, while He hides them from the wise and prudent.

Thirty-Second Article

The children, in distinction from the mere servants of God, have the liberty of children. They have a peace and joy, full of innocence. They take with simplicity and without hesitation the refreshments both of mind and body. They do not speak of themselves, except when called to do it in providence, and in order to do good. And such is their simplicity and truth of spirit, they speak of things just as they appear to them at the moment; and when the conversation turns upon their own works, or characters, they express themselves favorably or unfavorably, much as they would if they were speaking of others. If; however, they have occasion to speak of any good of which they have been the instrument, they always acknowledge, with humble joy, that it comes from God alone. There is a liberty, which might more properly be called license. There are persons who maintain that purity of heart renders pure, in the subjects of this purity, whatever they are prompted to do, however irregular it may be in others. This is a great error.

Thirty-Third Article

It is the doctrine of Augustine, as also of Thomas Aquinas, that the principle of holy love existing in the heart, necessarily includes in itself; or implies the existence, of all other Christian virtues. He who loves God with all his heart, will not violate the laws of purity, because it would be a disregard of the will of God, which he loves above all things. His love, under such circumstances, becomes the virtue of chastity. He has too much love and reverence for the will of God to murmur or repine under the dispensations of His providence. His love, under such circumstances, becomes the virtue of patience. And thus this love becomes by turns, on their appropriate occasions, all the virtues. As his love is perfect, so the virtues which flow out of it, and are modified from it, will not be less so. It is a maxim in the doctrines of holiness, that the holy soul is crucified to its own virtues, although it possesses them in the highest degree. The meaning of this saying is this: The holy soul is so crucified to self in all its forms, that it practices the virtues without taking complacency in its virtues as its own, and even without thinking how virtuous it is.

Thirty-Forth Article

The Apostle Paul speaks of Christians as dead. "You are dead," he says, "and your life is hid with Christ in God." These expressions will apply, in their full import, only to those Christians who are in the state of unselfish or pure love. Their death is a death to selfishness. They are dead to pride and jealousy, self-seeking and envy, to malice, inordinate love of their own reputation, anything and everything which constitutes the fallen and vitiated life of nature. They have a new life, which is "hid with Christ in God."

Thirty-Fifth Article

Some persons of great piety, in describing the highest religious state, have denominated it the state of transformation. But this can be regarded as only a synonymous expression for the state of pure love. In the transformed state of the soul, as in the state of pure love, love is its life. In this principle of love all the affections of the soul, of whatever character, have their constituting or their controlling element. There can be no love without an object of love. As the principle of love, therefore, allies the soul with another, so from that other which is God, all its power of movement proceeds. In itself it remains without preference for anything; and consequently is accessible and pliant to all the touches and guidance of grace, however slight they may be. It is like a spherical body, placed upon a level and even surface, which is moved with equal ease in any direction. The soul in this state, having no preferences of itself, has but one principle of movement, namely, that which God gives it. In this state the soul can say with the Apostle Paul, "I live; Yet not I, but Christ lives in me."

Thirty-sixth Article

Souls which have experienced the grace of sanctification in its higher degrees, have not so much need of set times arid places for worship as others. Such is the purity and the strength of their love, that it is very easy for them to unite with God in acts of inward worship, at all times and places. They have an interior closet. The soul is their temple, and God dwells in it. This, however, does not exempt them from those outward methods and observances which God has prescribed. Besides, they owe something to others; and a disregard to the ordinances and ministrations of the Church could not fail to be injurious to beginners in the religions life.

Thirty-Seventh Article

The practice of confession is not inconsistent with the state of pure love. The truly renovated soul can still say, Forgive us our trespasses. If it does not sin now, deliberately and knowingly, still its former state of sin can never be forgotten.

Thirty-Eighth Article

In the transformed state, or state of pure love, there should be not only the confession of sins, properly so called, but also the confession of those more venial transgressions, termed faults. We should sincerely disapprove such faults in our confession; should condemn them and desire their remission; and not merely with a view to our own cleansing and deliverance, but also because God wills it, and because He would have us to do it for His glory.

Thirty-Ninth Article

It is sometimes the case, that persons misjudge of the holiness of individuals, by estimating it from the incidents of the outward appearance. Holiness is consistent with the existence, in the same person, of various infirmities; (such as an unprepossessing form, physical weakness, a debilitated judgment, an imperfect mode of expression, defective manners, a want of knowledge, and the like.)

Fortieth Article

The holy soul may be said to be united with God, without anything intervening or producing a separation, in three particulars. First.-It is thus united intellectually; that is to say, not by any idea which is based upon the senses, and which of course could give only a material image of God, but by an idea which is internal and spiritual in its origin, and makes God known to us as a Being without form. Second.-The soul is thus united to God, if we may so express it, affectionately. That is to say, when its affections are given to God, not indirectly through a self-interested motive, but simply because He is what He is. The soul is united to God in love without anything intervening, when it loves Him for His own sake. Third.-The soul is thus united to God practically;-and this is the case when it does the will of God, not by simply following a prescribed form, but from the constantly operative impulse of holy love.

Forty-First Article

We find in some devout writers on inward experience, the phrase spiritual nuptials. It is a favorite method with some of these writers, to represent the union of the soul with God by the figure of the bride and the bridegroom. Similar expressions are found in the Scriptures. We are not to suppose that such expressions mean anything more, in reality, than that intimate union which exists between God and the soul, when the soul is in the state of pure love.

Forty-Second Article

We find again other forms of expression, which it is proper to notice. The union between God and the soul is sometimes described by them as an "essential" union, and sometimes as a "substantial" union, as if there were a union of essence, substance, or being, in the literal or physical sense. They mean to express nothing more than the fact of the union of pure love, with the additional idea that the union is firm and established; not subject to those breaks and inequalities, to that want of continuity and uniformity of love which characterize inferior degrees of experience.

Forty-Third Article

It is the holy soul of which St. Paul may be understood especially to speak, where he says, "As many as are led by the Spirit of God, they are the sons of God." Those who are in a state of simple faith, which can always be said of those who are in the state of pure love, are the "little ones" of the Scriptures, of whom we are told that God teaches them. "I thank you," says the Savior, "O Father, Lord of heaven and earth, that you have hid these things from the wise and prudent, and has revealed them to babes." Such souls, taught as they are by the Spirit of God which dwells in them, possess a knowledge which the wisdom of the world could never impart. But such knowledge never renders them otherwise than respectful to religious teachers, docile to the instructions of the Church, and conformable in all things to the precepts of the Scriptures.

Forty-Fourth Article

The doctrine of pure love has been known and recognized as a true doctrine among the truly contemplative and devout in all ages of the Church. The doctrine, however, has been so far above the common experience, that the pastors and saints of all ages have exercised a degree of discretion and care in making it known, except to those to whom God had already given both the attraction and light to receive it. Acting on the principle of giving milk to infants and strong meat to those that were more advanced, they addressed in the great body of Christians the motives of fear and of hope, founded on the consideration of happiness or of misery. It seemed to them, that the motive of God's glory, in itself considered, a motive which requires us to love God for Himself alone without a distinct regard and reference to our own happiness, could he profitably addressed, as a general rule, only to those who are somewhat advanced in inward experience.

Forty-Fifth Article

Among the various forms of expression indicative of the highest experience, we sometimes find that of "Divine union," or "union with God." Union with God, not a physical but moral or religious union, necessarily exists in souls that are in the state of pure love. The state of "Divine union" is not a higher state than that of pure love, but may rather be described as the same state. Strive after it; but do not too readily or easily believe that you have attained to it. The traveler, after many fatigues and dangers, arrives at the top of a mountain. As he looks abroad from that high eminence, and in that clear atmosphere, he sees his native city; and it seems to him to be very near. Overjoyed at the sight, and perhaps deceived by his position, he proclaims himself as already at the end of his journey. But he soon finds that the distance was greater than he supposed. He is obliged to descend into valleys, and to climb over hills, and to surmount rugged rocks, and to wind his tired steps over many a mile of weary way, before he reaches that home and city, which he once thought so near. It is thus in relation to the sanctification of the heart. True holiness of heart is the object at which the Christian aims. He beholds it before him, as an object of transcendent beauty, and as perhaps near at hand. But as he advances towards it, he finds the way longer and more difficult than he had imagined. But if on the one hand we should be careful not to mistake an intermediate stopping place for the end of the way, we should be equally careful on the other not to be discouraged by the difficulties we meet with; remembering that the obligation to be holy is always binding upon us, and that God will help those who put their trust in Him. "Whatsoever is born of God, overcomes the world; and this is the victory that overcomes the world, even our faith."

SPIRITUAL LETTERS

❧

The Advantage Of Humiliation

I pray often to God that He would keep you in the hollow of his hand. The most essential point is lowliness. It is profitable for all things, for it produces a teachable spirit which makes everything easy. You would be more guilty than many others if you made any resistance to God on this point. On the one hand, you have received abundant light and grace on the necessity of becoming like a little child; and on the other, no one has had an experience fitter to humiliate the heart and destroy self-confidence. The great profit to be derived from an experience of our weakness, is to render us lowly and obedient. May the Lord keep you!

How To Bear Suffering So As To Preserve Our Peace

As to our friend, I pray God to bestow upon him a simplicity that shall give him peace. When we are faithful in instantly dropping all superfluous and restless reflections, which arise from a self-love as different as possible from charity, we shall be set in a large place even in the midst of the strait and narrow path. We shall be in the pure liberty and innocent peace of the children of God, without being found wanting either towards God or man. I apply to myself the same counsel that I give to others, and am well persuaded that I must seek my own peace in the same direction. My heart is now suffering; but it is the life of self that causes us pain; that which is dead does not suffer. If we were dead, and our life were hid with Christ in God, we should no longer perceive those pains in spirit that now afflict

us. We should not only bear bodily sufferings with equanimity, but spiritual affliction also, that is to say, trouble sent upon the soul without its own immediate act. But the disturbances of a restless activity, in which the soul adds to the cross imposed by the hand of God, the burden of an agitated resistance, and an unwillingness to suffer, are only experienced in consequence of the remaining life of self. A cross which comes purely from God, and is cordially welcomed without any self-reflective acts, is at once painful and peaceful; but one unwillingly received and repelled by the life of nature, is doubly severe; the resistance within is harder to bear than the cross itself. If we recognize the hand of God, and make no opposition in the will, we have comfort in our affliction. Happy indeed are they who can bear their sufferings in the enjoyment of this simple peace and perfect acquiescence in the will of God! Nothing so shortens and soothes our pains as this spirit of non-resistance. But we are generally desirous of bargaining with God; we would like at least to impose the limits and see the end of our sufferings. That same obstinate and hidden hold of life, which renders the cross necessary, causes us to reject it in part, and by a secret resistance, which impairs its virtue. We have thus to go over the same ground again and again; we suffer greatly, but to very little purpose. The Lord deliver us from falling into that state of soul in which crosses are of no benefit to us! God loves a cheerful giver, according to St. Paul; ah! what must be his love to those who, in a cheerful and absolute abandonment, resign themselves to the entire extent of his crucifying will!

The Beauty Of The Cross

I cannot but wonder at the virtue that lies in suffering; we are worth nothing without the cross. I tremble and am in an agony while it lasts, and all my conviction of its salutary effects vanish under the torture, but when it is over, I look back at it with admiration, and am ashamed that I bore it so ill. This experience of my folly is a deep lesson of wisdom to me. Whatever may be the state of your sick friend, and whatever the issue of her disease, she is blessed in being so quiet under the hand of God. If she die, she dies to the Lord; if she live, she lives to Him. Either the cross or death, says St. Theresa. Nothing is beyond the necessity of the cross but the established kingdom of God; when we bear it in love, it is his kingdom begun, with which we must remain satisfied while it is his pleasure. You have need of the cross as well as I. The faithful Giver of every good gift distributes them to each of us with his own hand, blessed be his name! Ah! how good it is to be chastened for our profit!

The Death Of Self

I cannot express to you, my dear sister, how deeply I sympathize with your afflictions; but my grief is not unmixed with consolation. God loves you, since He does not spare you, but lays upon you the cross of Jesus Christ. Whatever light, whatever feeling we may possess, is all a delusion, if it lead us not to the real and constant practice of dying to self. We cannot die without suffering, neither can we be said to be dead, while there is still any part in us which is alive. That death with which God blesses the soul, pierces even to the dividing asunder of soul and spirit, and of the joints and marrow. He who sees in us what we cannot see, knows full well where the blow should fall; He takes away that which we are most reluctant to give up. Pain is only felt where there is life, and where there is life, is just the place where death is needed. Our Father wastes no time by cutting into parts which are already dead; if He sought to continue life, He would do so, but He seeks to destroy, and this He can only accomplish by cutting into that which is quick and living. You need not expect Him to attack those gross and wicked desires which you renounced forever, when you gave yourself away to Him, but he will prove you, perhaps, by destroying your liberty of soul, and by depriving you of your most spiritual consolations. Would you resist? Ah! no! Suffer all things! This death must be voluntary, and can only be accomplished to that extent to which you are willing it should be. To resist death, and repel its advances, is not being willing to die. Give up voluntarily, then, to the good pleasure of God, all your reliance, even the most spiritual, whenever He may seem disposed to take them from you. What do you fear, O you of little faith? Do you fear that He may not be able to supply to you from Himself, that succor which He takes away on the part of man? And why does He take it away, except to supply it from Himself, and to purify you by the painful lesson? I see that every way is shut up, and that God means to accomplish his work in you, by cutting off every human resource. He is a jealous God; He is not willing you should owe what He is about to perform in you, to any other than to Himself alone. Give yourself up to his plans, be led whither He will by his providences. Beware how you seek aid from man, when God forbids it they can only give you what He gives them for you. Why should you be troubled that you can no longer drink from the aqueduct when you are led to the perennial spring itself from which its waters are derived?

Peace Lies In Simplicity &Obedience

Cultivate peace; be deaf to your too prolific imagination; its great activity not only injures the health of your body, but introduces aridity into your soul. You consume yourself to no purpose; peace and interior sweetness are destroyed by your restlessness. Think you God can speak in those soft and tender accents that melt the soul, in the midst of such a tumult as you excite by your incessant hurry of thought? Be quiet, and He will soon be heard. Indulge but a single scruple; to be scrupulously obedient. You ask for consolation; but you do not perceive that you have been led to the brink of the fountain, and refuse to drink. Peace and consolation are only to be found in simple obedience. Be faithful in obeying without reference to your scruples, and you will soon find that the rivers of living water will flow according to the promise. You will receive according to the measure of your faith; much, if you believe much; nothing, if you believe nothing and continue to give ear to your empty imaginations. You dishonor true love by the supposition that it is anxious about such trifles as continually occupy your attention; it goes straight to God in pure simplicity. Satan is transformed into an angel of light; he assumes the beautiful form of a scrupulous love and a tender conscience; but you should know by experience the trouble and danger into which he will lead you by vehement scruples. Everything depends upon your faithfulness in repelling his first advances. If you become ingenuous and simple in your desires, I think you will have been more pleasing to God than if you had suffered a hundred martyrdoms. Turn all your anxieties toward your delay in offering a sacrifice so right in the sight of God. Can true love hesitate when it is required to please its well-beloved?

The True Source Of Peace Is In The Surrender Of The Will

Remain in peace; the fervor of devotion does not depend upon yourself; all that lies in your power is the direction of your will. Give that up to God without reservation. The important question is not how much you enjoy religion, but whether you will whatever God wills. Humbly confess your faults; be detached from the world, and abandoned to God; love Him more than yourself, and his glory more than your life; the least you can do is to desire and ask for such a love. God will then love you and put his peace in your heart.

True Good Is Only Reached By Abandonment

Evil is changed into good when it is received in patience through the love of God; while good is changed into evil when we become attached to it through the love of self. True good lies only in detachment, and abandonment to God. You are now in the trial; put yourself confidently and without reserve into his hand. What would I not sacrifice to see you once more restored in body, but heartily sick of the love of the world! Attachment to ourselves is a thousand times more infectious than a contagious poison, for it contains the venom of self. I pray for you with all my heart.

Knowledge Puffs Up; Charity Edifies

I am happy to hear of your frame of mind, and to find you communicating in simplicity everything that takes place within you. Never hesitate to write me whatever you think God requires. It is not at all surprising that you have a sort of jealous ambition to advance in the spiritual life, and to be intimate with persons of distinction who are pious. Such things are by nature very flattering to our self-love, and it eagerly seeks them. But we should not strive to gratify such an ambition by making great progress in the religious life, and by cultivating the acquaintance of persons high in honor; our aim should be to die to the flattering delights of self-love, by becoming humble and in love with obscurity and contempt, and to have a single eye to God. We may hear about perfection without end, and become perfectly familiar with its language, and yet be as far from its attainment as ever. Our great aim should be, to be deaf to self, to hearken to God in silence, to renounce every vanity, and to devote ourselves to solid virtue. Let us speak but little and do much, without a thought as to whether we are observed or not. God will teach you more than the most experienced Christians, and better than all the books that the world has ever seen. And what is your object in such an eager chase after knowledge? Are you not aware that all we need is to be poor in spirit, and to know nothing but Christ and Him crucified? Knowledge puffs up; it is only charity that can edify. Be content with charity, then, alone. What! is it possible that the love of God, and the abandonment of self for his sake, is only to be reached through the acquisition of so much knowledge? You have already more than you use, and need further illuminations much less than the practice of what you already know. O how deceived we are, when we suppose we are advancing, because our vain curiosity is gratified by the enlightenment of our intellect! Be humble, and expect not the gifts of God from man.

We Are Not To Choose How Our blessings Are Bestowed

You know what God requires of you; will you refuse? You perceive that your resistance to the drawings of his grace, arises solely from self-love: will you suffer the refinements of pride, and the most ingenious inventions of self, to reject the mercies of God? You who have so many scruples in relation to the passing thought, which is involuntary and therefore innocent, who confess so many things that should rather be dismissed at once, have you no scruples about your long-continued resistance to the Holy Spirit, because He has not seen fit to confer the benefits you desire, by a channel which was flattering to your self-love? What matter if you received the gifts of grace as beggars receive bread? The gifts themselves would be neither less pure nor less precious. Your heart would only be the more worthy of God, if, by its humility and annihilation, it attracted the succor that He was disposed to send. Is this the way you put off self? Is this the view that pure faith takes of the instrument of God? Is it thus that you die to the life of self within? To what purpose are your readings about pure love, and your frequent devotions? How can you read what condemns the very depths of your soul? You are influenced not only by self-interest, but by the persuasions of pride, when you reject the gifts of God, because they do not come in a shape to suit your taste. How can you pray? What is the language of God in the depths of your soul? He asks nothing but death, and you desire nothing but life. How can you put up to Him a prayer for his grace, with a restriction that He shall only send it by a channel demanding no sacrifice on your part but ministering to the gratification of your carnal pride?

The Discovery & Death Of Self

Yes, I joyfully consent that you call me your father! I am so and will be always; there needs only on your part a full and confident persuasion of it, which will come when your heart is enlarged. Self-love now shuts it up. We are in a strait place, indeed, when we are enclosed in self, but when we emerge from that prison, and enter into the immensity of God and the liberty of his children, we are set at large. I am rejoiced to find that God has reduced you to a state of weakness. Your self-love can neither be convinced nor vanquished by any other means, ever finding secret resources and impenetrable retreats in your courage and ingenuity. It was hidden from your eyes, while it fed upon the subtle poison of an apparent generosity, by which you constantly sacrificed yourself for others. God has forced it to cry aloud, to come forth into open day, and display its excessive jealousy. O how painful, but how useful, are these seasons of weakness? While any self-love remains, we are afraid of its being revealed, but so long as the least symptom of it lurks in the most secret recesses of the heart, God pursues it, and by some infinitely merciful blow, forces it into the light. The poison then becomes the remedy; self-love, pushed to extremity, discovers itself in all its deformity by a transport of despair, and disgraces all the refinements, and dissipates the flattering illusions of a whole life. God sets before your eyes your idol, self. You behold it, and cannot turn your eyes away; and as you have no longer power over yourself, you cannot keep the sight from others. Thus to exhibit self-love without its mask is the most mortifying punishment that can be inflicted. We no longer behold it wise, discreet, polite, self-possessed, and courageous in sacrificing itself for others; it is no longer the self-love whose nourishment consisted in the belief that it had need of nothing, and the persuasion that its greatness and generosity deserved a different name. It is the selfishness of a silly child, screaming at the loss of an apple; but it is far more tormenting, for it also weeps from rage that it has wept; it cannot be still, and refuses all comfort, because its venomous character has been detected. It beholds itself foolish, rude, and impertinent, and is forced to look its own frightful countenance in the face. It says with Job: For the thing which I greatly feared has come upon me, and that which I was afraid of is come unto me. For precisely that which it most fears is the most necessary means of its destruction. We have no need that God should attack in us what has neither life nor sensibility. It is the living only that must die, and all the rest is nothing. This, then, is what you needed, to behold a self-love convinced, sensitive, gross, and palpable. And now all you have to do, is to be quietly willing to look at it as it is; the moment you can do this, it will have disappeared. You ask for a remedy, that you may get well. You do not need to be cured, but to be slain; seek not impatiently for a remedy, but let death come. Be careful, however, lest a certain courageous resolve to avail yourself of no remedy, be itself a remedy in disguise, and give aid and comfort to this cursed life. Seek no consolation for self-love, and do not conceal the disease. Reveal everything in simplicity and holiness, and then suffer yourself to die. But this is not to be accomplished by any exertion of strength. Weakness has become your only possession; all strength is out of place; it only serves to render the agony longer and more distressing. If you expire from exhaustion, you will die so much the quicker and less violently. A dying life must of necessity be painful. Cordials are a cruelty to the sufferer on the wheel; he only longs for the fatal blow, not food, nor sustenance. If it were possible to weaken him and hasten his death, we should abridge his sufferings; but we can do nothing; the hand alone that tied him to his torture can deliver him from the remains of suffering life. Ask, then, neither remedies, sustenance, nor death; to ask death, is impatience; to ask food or remedies, is to prolong our agony. What, then, shall we do? Let alone; seek nothing, hold to nothing; confess everything, not as a means of consolation, but through humility and desire to yield. Look to me, not as a source of life, but as a means of death. As an instrument of life would belie its purpose, if it did not minister to life, so an instrument of death would be falsely named, if, in lieu of slaying, it kept alive. Let me, then, be, or at least seem to you to be, hard, unfeeling, indifferent, pitiless, wearied, annoyed, and contemptuous. God knows how far it is from the truth; but he permits it all to appear; and I shall be much more serviceable to you in this false and imaginary character than by my affection and real assistance, for the point is not, how you are to be sustained and kept alive, but how you are to lose all and die.

The Sight Of Our Imperfections

There is something very hidden and very deceptive in your suffering; for while you seem to yourself to be wholly occupied with the glory of God, in your inmost soul it is self alone that occasions all your trouble. You are, indeed, desirous that God should be glorified, but that it should take place by means of your perfection, and you thus cherish the sentiments of self-love. It is simply a refined pretext for dwelling in self. If you would truly derive profit from the discovery of your imperfections, neither justify nor condemn on their account, but quietly lay them before God, conforming your will to his in all things that you cannot understand, and remaining at peace; for peace is the order of God for every condition whatever. There is, in fact, a peace of conscience which sinners themselves should enjoy when awakened to repentance. Their suffering should be peaceful and mingled with consolation. Remember the beautiful word which once delighted you, that the Lord was not in noise and confusion, but in the still, small voice.

Living By The Cross And By Faith

Everything is a cross; I have no joy but bitterness; but the heaviest cross must be borne in peace. At times it can neither be borne nor dragged; we can only fall down beneath it, overwhelmed and exhausted. I pray that God may spare you as much as possible in apportioning your suffering; it is our daily bread; God alone knows how much we need; and we must live in faith upon the means of death, confident, though we see it not, that God, with secret compassion, proportions our trials to the unperceived succor that He administers within. This life of faith is the most penetrating of all deaths.

Despair At Our Imperfection Is A Greater Obstacle

Be not concerned about your defects. Love without ceasing, and you shall be much forgiven, because you have loved much. We are apt to seek the delights and selfish supports of love, rather than love itself. We deceive ourselves, even in supposing we are endeavoring to love, when we are only trying to see that we love. We are more occupied with the love, says St. Francis of Sales, than with the Well-beloved. If He were our only object, we should be all taken up with Him; but when we are employed in obtaining an assurance of his love, we are still in a measure busy with self. Our defects, regarded in peace and in the spirit of love, are instantly consumed by love itself; but considered in the light of self, they make us restless, and interrupt the presence of God and the exercise of perfect love. The chagrin we feel at our own defects, is ordinarily a greater fault than the original defect itself. You are wholly taken up with the less of the two faults, like a person whom I have just seen, who, after reading the life of one of the saints, was so enraged at his own comparative imperfection, that he entirely abandoned the idea of living a devoted life. I judge of your fidelity by your peace and liberty of soul; the more peaceful and enlarged your heart, the nearer you seem to be to God.

Pure Faith Sees God Alone

Be not anxious about the future; it is opposed to grace. When God sends you consolation, regard Him only in it, enjoy it day by day as the Israelites received their manna, and do not endeavor to lay it up in store. There are two peculiarities of pure faith; it sees God alone under all the imperfect envelopes which conceal Him, and it holds the soul incessantly in suspense. We are kept constantly in the air, without being suffered to touch a foot to solid ground. The comfort of the present instant will be wholly inappropriate to the next; we must let God act with the most perfect freedom, in whatever belongs to Him, and think only of being faithful in all that depends upon ourselves. This momentary dependence, this darkness and this peace of the soul, under the utter uncertainty of the future, is a true martyrdom, which take place silently and without any stir. It is death by a slow fire; and the end comes so imperceptibly and interiorly, that it is often almost as much hidden from the sufferer himself, as from those who are unacquainted with his state. When God removes his gifts from you, He knows how and when to replace them, either by others or by Himself. He can raise up children from the very stones. Eat then your daily bread without thought for the morrow; sufficient unto the day is the evil thereof. Tomorrow will take thought for the things of itself. He who feeds you today, is the same to whom you will look for food tomorrow; manna shall fall again from heaven in the midst of the desert, before the children of God shall want any good thing. The man that looks on glass, On it may stay his eye; Or, if he pleases, through it pass, And then the heavens espy. Pure faith cannot see the neighbor that succeeds, as he blindly thinks, in injuring us, nor the disease that attacks our bodies; that would be to stay its eye upon the glass, in which it would see a thousand flaws and imperfections that would annoy it and destroy its peace; it looks right through and discovers God; and what He permits, it cannot but joyfully acquiesce in.

Knowledge Stands In Our Way Of Becoming Wise

Live in peace, my dear young lady, without any thought for the future; perhaps there will be none for you. You have no present, even, of your own, for you must only use it in accordance with the designs of God, to whom it truly belongs. Continue the good works that occupy you, since you have an attraction that way, and can readily accomplish them. Avoid distractions, and the consequences of your excessive vivacity, and, above all things, be faithful to the present moment, and you will receive all necessary grace. It is not enough to be detached from the world; we must become lowly also; in detachment, we renounce the things without, in lowliness, we abandon self. Every shadow of perceptible pride must be left behind, and the pride of wisdom and virtue is more dangerous than that of worldly fortune, as it has a show of right, and is more refined. We must be lowly-minded in all points, and appropriate nothing to ourselves, our virtue and courage least of all. You rest too much in your own courage, disinterestedness, and uprightness. The babe owns nothing; it treats a diamond and an apple alike. Be a babe; have nothing of your own; forget yourself; give way on all occasions; let the smallest be greater than you. Pray simply from the heart, from pure love, and not from the head, from the intellect alone. Your true instruction is to be found in spoliation, deep recollection, silence of the whole soul before God, in renouncing your own spirit, and, in the love of lowliness, obscurity, feebleness, and annihilation. This ignorance is the accomplished teacher of all truth; knowledge cannot attain to it, or can reach it but superficially.

Those Who Endeavor To Injure Us Are To Be Loved

I sympathize, as I ought, in all your troubles, but I can do nothing else except pray God that He would console you. You have great need of the gift of his Spirit to sustain you in your difficulties, and to restrain your natural vivacity under the trials which are so fitted to excite it. As to the letter touching your birth, I think you should lay it before God alone, and beg his mercy upon him who has sought to injure you. I have always perceived, or thought that I perceived, that you were sensitive on that point. God always attacks us on our weak side; we do not aim to kill a person by striking a blow at his insensible parts, such as the hair or nails, but by endeavoring to reach at once the noble organs, the immediate seats of life. When God would have us die to self, he always touches the most tender spot, that which is fullest of life. It is thus that he distributes crosses. Suffer yourself to be humbled. Silence and peace under humiliation are the true good of the soul; we are tempted, under a thousand specious pretexts, to speak humbly; but it is far better to be humbly silent. The humility that can yet talk, has need of careful watching; self-love derives comfort from its outward words. Do not suffer yourself to get excited by what is said about you. Let the world talk; do you strive to do the will of God; as for that of men, you could never succeed in doing it to their satisfaction, and it is not worth the pains. A moment of silence, of peace, and of union to God, will amply recompense you for every calumny that shall be uttered against you. We must love our fellows, without expecting friendship from them; they leave us and return, they go and come; let them do as they will; it is but a feather, the sport of the wind. See God only in them; it is He that afflicts or consoles us, by means of them, according as we have need.

Quietness In God Our True Resource

Warmth of imagination, ardor of feeling, acuteness of reasoning, and fluency of expression, can do but little. The true agent is a perfect abandonment before God, in which we do everything by the light which He gives, and are content with the success which He bestows. This continual death is a blessed life known to few. A single word, uttered from this rest, will do more, even in outward affairs, than all our most eager and officious care. It is the Spirit of God that then speaks the word, and it loses none of its force and authority, but enlightens, persuades, moves, and edifies. We have accomplished everything, and have scarce said anything. On the other hand, if left to the excitability of our natural temperament, we talk forever, indulging in a thousand subtle and superfluous reflections; we are constantly afraid of not saying or doing enough; we get angry, excited, exhausted, distracted, and finally make no headway. Your disposition has an especial need of these maxims; they are as necessary for your body as your soul, and your physician, and your spiritual adviser should act together. Let the water flow beneath the bridge; let men be men, that is to say, weak, vain, inconstant, unjust, false, and presumptuous; let the world be the world still; you cannot prevent it. Let everyone follow his own inclination and habits; you cannot recast them, and the best course is, to let them be as they are and bear with them. Do not think it strange when you witness unreasonableness and injustice; rest in peace in the bosom of God; He sees it all more clearly than you do, and yet permits it. Be content to do quietly and gently what it becomes you to do, and let everything else be to you as though it were not.

True Friendships Are Founded Only In God

We must be content with what God gives, without having any choice of our own. It is right that his will should be done, not ours; and that his should become ours without the least reservation, in order that it may be done on earth as it is done in heaven. This is a hundred times more valuable an attainment than to be engaged in the view or consolation of self. O how near are we to each other when we are all united in God! How well do we converse when we have but a single will and a single thought in Him who is all things in us! Would you find your true friends, then? Seek them only in Him who is the single source of true and eternal friendship. Would you speak with or hear from them? Sink in silence into the bosom of Him who is the word, the life, and the soul of all those who speak and live the truth. You will find in Him not only every want supplied, but everything perfect, which you find so imperfect in the creatures in whom you confide.

The Cross A Source Of Our Pleasure

I sympathize with all your distresses; but we must carry the cross with Christ in this transitory life. We shall soon have no time to suffer; we shall reign with God our consolation, who will have wiped away our tears with his own hand, and from before whose presence pain and sighing shall forever flee away. While this fleeting moment of trial is permitted us, let us not lose the slightest portion of the worth of the cross. Let us suffer in humility and in peace; our self-love exaggerates our distresses, and magnifies them in our imagination. A cross borne in simplicity, without the interference of self-love to augment it, is only half a cross. Suffering in this simplicity of love, we are not only happy in spite of the cross, but because of it; for love is pleased in suffering for the Well-beloved, and the cross which forms us into his image is a consoling bond of love.

The Absence Of Feeling And The Revelation Of Self

I pray God that this new year may be full of grace and blessing to you. I am not surprised that you do not enjoy recollection as you did on being delivered from a long and painful agitation. Everything is liable to be exhausted. A lively disposition, accustomed to active exertion, soon languishes in solitude and inaction. For a great number of years you have been necessarily much distracted by external activity, and it was this circumstance that made me fear the effect of the life of abandonment upon you. You were at first in the fervor of your beginnings, when no difficulties appear formidable. You said with Peter, it is good for us to be here; but it is often with us as it was with him, that we know not what we say. In our moments of enjoyment, we feel as if we could do everything; in the time of temptation and discouragement, we think we can do nothing, and believe that all is lost. But we are alike deceived in both. You should not be disturbed at any distraction that you may experience; the cause of it lay concealed within even when you felt such zeal for recollection. Your temperament and habits all conduce to making you active and eager. It was only weariness and exhaustion that caused you to relish an opposite life. But, by fidelity to grace, you will gradually become permanently introduced into the experience of which you have had a momentary taste. God bestowed it that you might see whither He would lead you; He then takes it away, that we may be made sensible that it does not belong to us; that we are neither able to procure nor preserve it, and that it is a gift of grace that must be asked in all humility. Be not amazed at finding yourself sensitive, impatient, haughty, self-willed; you must be made to perceive that such is your natural disposition. We must bear the yoke of the daily confusion of our sins, says St. Augustine. We must be made to feel our weakness, our wretchedness, our inability to correct ourselves. We must despair of our own heart, and have no hope but in God. We must bear with ourselves, without flattering, and without neglecting a single effort for our correction. We must be instructed as to our true character, while waiting for Gods time to take it away. Let us become lowly under his all-powerful hand; yielding and manageable as often as we perceive any resistance in our will. Be silent as much as you can. Be in no haste to judge; suspend your decisions, your likes and dislikes. Stop at once when you become aware that your activity is hurried, and do not be too eager even for good things.

The Imperfection Of Others To Be Borne In Love

It is a long while since I renewed the assurance of my attachment to you in our Lord. It is, nevertheless, greater than ever. I desire with all my heart that you may always find in your household the peace and consolation which you enjoyed in the beginning. To be content with even the best of people, we must be contented with little and bear a great deal. Those who are most perfect, have many imperfections, and we have great faults, so that between the two, mutual toleration becomes very difficult. We must bear one another's burdens, and so fulfill the law of Christ, thus setting off one against the other in love. Peace and unanimity will be much aided by frequent silence, habitual recollection, prayer, self-abandonment, renunciation of all vain criticisms, and a faithful departure from the vain reflections of a jealous and difficult self-love. To how much trouble would this simplicity put an end! Happy he who neither listens to self nor to the tales of others! Be content with leading a simple life, according to your condition. Be obedient, and bear your daily cross; you need it, and it is bestowed by the pure mercy of God. The grand point is to despise self from the heart, and to be willing to be despised, if God permits it. Feed upon Him alone; St. Augustine says that his mother lived upon prayer; do you likewise, and die to everything else. We can only live to God by the continual death of self.

The Fear Of Death Not Taken Away By Our Own Courage

I am not in the least surprised to learn that your impression of death becomes more lively, in proportion as age and infirmity bring it nearer. I experience the same thing. There is an age at which death is forced upon our consideration more frequently, by more irresistible reflections, and by a time of retirement in which we have fewer distractions. God makes use of this rough trial to undeceive us in respect to our courage, to make us feel our weakness, and to keep us in all humility in his own hands. Nothing is more humiliating than a troubled imagination, in which we search in vain for our former confidence in God. This is the crucible of humiliation, in which the heart is purified by a sense of its weakness and unworthiness. In his sight shall no man living be justified; yea, the heavens are not clean in his sight, and in many things we offend all. We behold our faults and not our virtues; which would be dangerous to behold, if they are real. We must go straight on through this deprivation without interruption, just as we were endeavoring to walk in the way of God, before being disturbed. If we should perceive any fault that needs correction, we must be faithful to the light given us, but do it carefully, lest we be led into false scruples. We must then remain at peace, not listening to the voice of self-love, mourning over our approaching death, but detach ourselves from life, offering it in sacrifice to God, and confidently abandon ourselves to Him. St. Ambrose was asked, when dying, whether he was not afraid of the judgments of God; We have a good master, said he, and so must we reply to ourselves. We need to die in the most impenetrable uncertainty, not only as to Gods judgment upon us, but as to our own characters. We must, as St. Augustine has it, be so reduced as to have nothing to present before God but our wretchedness and his mercy. Our wretchedness is the proper object of his mercy, and his mercy is all our merit. In your hours of sadness, read whatever will strengthen your confidence and establish your heart. Truly God is good to Israel, even to such as are of a clean heart. Pray for this cleanness of heart, which is so pleasing in his sight, and which renders Him so compassionate to our failings.

Sensitiveness Under Reproof

I greatly desire that you may have interior peace. You know that it cannot be found, except in lowliness of mind, and lowliness is not real, except it be produced by God upon every proper occasion. These occasions are chiefly when we are blamed by someone who disapproves of us, and when we experience inward weakness. We must accustom ourselves to bearing both these trials. We are truly lowly when we are no longer taken by surprise at finding ourselves corrected from without and incorrigible within. We are then like little children, below everything, and are willing to be so; we feel that our reprovers are right, but that we are unable to overcome ourselves, in order to correct our faults. Then we despair of ourselves, and expect nothing except from God; the reproofs of others, harsh and unfeeling as they may be, seem to us less than we deserve; if we cannot bear them, we condemn our sensitiveness more than all our other imperfections. Correction cannot then make us more humble than it finds us. The interior rebellion, far from hindering the profit of the correction, convinces us of its absolute necessity; in truth, the reproof would not have been felt, if it had not cut into some living part; had death been there, we should not have perceived it; and thus the more acutely we feel, the more certainly we know that the correction was necessary. I beg your forgiveness if I have said anything too harsh; but do not doubt my affection for you, and count as nothing everything that comes from me. See only the hand of God, which makes use of the awkwardness of mine, to deal you a painful blow. The pain proves that I have touched a sore spot. Yield to God, acquiesce in all his dealings, and you will soon be at rest and in harmony within. You know well enough how to give this advice to others; the occasion is important, critical. O what grace will descend upon you, if you will bear, like a little child, all the means God employs to humiliate and dispossess you of your senses and will!

I pray that he may so diminish you that you can no longer be found at all.

Imperfection Only Is Intolerant Of Imperfection

It has seemed to me that you have need of more enlarging of heart in relation to the defects of others. I know that you cannot help seeing them when they come before you, nor prevent the opinions you involuntarily form concerning the motives of some of those about you. You cannot even get rid of a certain degree of trouble which these things cause you. It will be enough if you are willing to bear with those defects which are unmistakable, refrain from condemning those which are doubtful, and not suffer yourself to be so afflicted by them as to cause a coolness of feeling between you. Perfection is easily tolerant of the imperfections of others; it becomes all things to all men. We must not be surprised at the greatest defects in good souls, and must quietly let them alone until God gives the signal of gradual removal; otherwise we shall pull up the wheat with the tares. God leaves, in the most advanced souls, certain weaknesses entirely disproportioned to their eminent state. As workmen, in excavating the soil from a field, leave certain pillars of earth which indicate the original level of the surface, and serve to measure the amount of material removed, in the same way, leaves pillars of testimony to the extent of his work in the most pious souls. Such persons must labor, each one in his degree, for his own correction, and you must labor to bear with their weaknesses. You know from experience the bitterness of the work of correction; strive then to find means to make it less bitter to others. You have not an eager zeal to correct, but a sensitiveness that easily shuts up your heart. I pray you more than ever not to spare my faults. If you should think you see one, which is not really there, there is no harm done; if I find that your counsel wounds me, my sensitiveness demonstrates that you have discovered a sore spot; but if not, you will have done me an excellent kindness in exercising my humility, and accustoming me to reproof. I ought to be more lowly than others in proportion as I am higher in position, and God demands of me a more absolute death to everything. I need this simplicity, and I trust it will be the means of cementing rather than of weakening our attachment.

We Should Listen To God And Not To Self-Love

I beseech you not to listen to self. Self-love whispers in one ear and the love of God in the other; the first is restless, bold, eager, and impetuous; the other is simple, peaceful, and speaks but a few words in a mild and gentle voice. The moment we attend to the voice of self crying in our ear, we can no longer hear the modest tones of holy love. Each speaks only of its single object. Self-love entertains us with self, which, according to it, is never sufficiently well attended to; it talks of friendship, regard, esteem, and is in despair at everything but flattery. The love of God, on the other hand, desires that self should be forgotten, that it should be trodden under foot and broken as an idol, and that God should become the self of espoused souls, and occupy them as others are occupied by self. Let the vain, complaining babbler, self-love, be silenced, that in the stillness of the heart we may listen to that other love that only speaks when addressed.

Absolute Trust The Shortest Road To God

I have no doubt but that God constantly treats you as one of his friends, that is, with crosses, sufferings, and humiliations. The ways and means of God to draw souls to Himself, accomplish his design much more rapidly and effectually than all the efforts of the creature; for they destroy self-love at its very root, where, with all our pains, we could scarce discover it. God knows all its windings, and attacks it in its strongest holds. If we had strength and faith enough to trust ourselves entirely to God, and follow Him simply wherever He should lead us, we should have no need of any great effort of mind to reach perfection. But as we are so weak in faith, as to require to know all the way without trusting in God, our road is lengthened and our spiritual affairs get behind. Abandon yourself as absolutely as possible to God, and continue to do so to your latest breath, and He will never desert you.

During Temptation & Distress

Your excessive distress is like a summer torrent, which must be suffered to run away. Nothing makes any impression upon you, and you think you have the most substantial evidence for the most imaginary states; it is the ordinary result of great suffering. God permits you, notwithstanding your excellent faculties, to be blind to what lies immediately before you, and to think you see clearly what does not exist at all. God will be glorified in your heart, if you will be faithful in yielding to his designs. But nothing would be more injudicious than the forming of resolutions in a state of distress, which is manifestly accompanied by an inability to do anything according to God. When you shall have become calm, then do in a spirit of recollection, what you shall perceive to be nearest the will of God respecting you. Return gradually to devotion, simplicity, and the oblivion of self. Commune and listen to God, and be deaf to self. Then do all that is in your heart, for I have no fear that a spirit of that sort will permit you to take any wrong step. But to suppose that we are sane when we are in the very agony of distress, and under the influence of a violent temptation of self-love, is to ensure our being led astray. Ask any experienced adviser, and he will tell you that you are to make no resolutions until you have re-entered into peace and recollection. You will learn from him that the readiest way to self-deception is, to trust to ourselves in a state of suffering, in which nature is so unreasonable and irritated. You will say that I desire to prevent you doing as you ought, if I forbid your doing it at the only moment when you are capable of it. God forbid! neither desire to permit nor hinder: my only wish is so to advise you that you shall not be found wanting toward God. Now it is as clear as day, that you would fall in that respect, if you took counsel at the hands of a self-love wounded to the quick, and an irritation verging upon despair. Would you change anything to gratify your self-love, when God does not desire it? God forbid! Wait, then, until you shall be in a condition to be advised. To enjoy the true advantages of illumination, we must be equally ready for every alternative, and must have nothing which we are not cheerfully disposed at once to sacrifice for His sake.

Who Has Love, Has All

I have thought frequently, since yesterday, on the matters you communicated to me, and I have increasing confidence that God will sustain you. Though you take no great pleasure in religious exercises, you must not neglect to be faithful in them, as far as your health will permit. A convalescent has but little appetite, but he must eat to sustain life. It would be very serviceable to you, if you could occasionally have a few minutes of Christian converse with such of your family as you can confide in, and, as to the choice, be guided in perfect liberty by your impressions at the moment. God does not call you by any lively emotions, and I heartily rejoice at it, if you will but remain faithful; for a fidelity, unsustained by delights, is far purer, and safer from danger, than one accompanied by those tender feelings, which may be seated too exclusively in the imagination. A little reading and recollection every day, will be the means of insensibly giving you light and strength for all the sacrifices God will require of you. Love Him, and I will acquit you of everything else; for everything else will come by love. I do not ask from you a love tender and emotional, but only that your will should lean towards love, and that, notwithstanding all the corrupt desires of your heart, you should prefer God before self and the whole world.

Weakness Preferable To Strength

I am told, my dear child in our Lord, that you are suffering from sickness. suffer with you, for I love you dearly; but I cannot but kiss the hand that smites you, and I pray you to kiss it lovingly with me. You have heretofore abused your health and the pleasures derived from it; this weakness and its attendant pains are the natural consequence of such a course. I pray God only that He may depress your spirit even more than your body, and while He comforts the latter according to your need, that He may entirely vanquish the former. O how strong we are when we begin to perceive that we are but weakness and infirmity! Then we are ever ready to believe that we are mistaken, and to correct ourselves while confessing it; our minds are ever open to the illumination of others; then we are authoritative in nothing, and say the most decided things with simplicity and deference for others; then we do not object to be judged, and submit without hesitation to the censure of the first comer. At the same time, we judge no one without absolute necessity; we speak only to those who desire it, mentioning the imperfections we seem to have discovered, without dogmatism, and rather to gratify their wishes than from a desire to be believed or create a reputation for wisdom. I pray God that He may keep you faithful to his grace, and that He who has begun a good work in you will perform it until the day of Jesus Christ. We must bear with ourselves with patience and without flattery, and remain in unceasing subjection to every means of overcoming our thoughts and inward repugnance; we shall thus become more pliable to the impressions of grace in the practice of the gospel. But let this work be done quietly and peacefully, and let it not be entered upon too eagerly, as though it could all be accomplished in a single day. Let us reason little, but do much. If we are not careful, the acquisition of knowledge will so occupy this life that we shall need another to reduce our acquirements into practice. We are in danger of believing ourselves advanced towards perfection in proportion to our knowledge of the way; but all our beautiful theories, far from assisting in the death of self, only serve to nourish the life of Adam in us by a secret delight and confidence in our illumination. Give up trusting in your own power and in your own knowledge of the way, and you will make a great stride towards perfection. Humility and self-distrust, with a frank ingenuousness, are fundamental virtues for you. This seems one of the most common as well as most serious mistakes to which spiritual persons are liable. God gives the knowledge and desires us to put it in practice; but the moment we see it, we are so carried away with delight, that we forget that there is anything else to be done; whereas we have comparatively slender reason to rejoice until it is put in vital operation in the life. You see, says the Savior, but do not perceive; you hear, but do not understand. Food, lying undigested in the stomach, is not only of no service to the body, but, if not removed, will become a serious injury; it is only when it is assimilated and mingled with the blood, and when it appears by its good effects in our hands, feet, head, and trunk, that it can be said to have become our own. To have a divine truth in the intellect, is indeed matter of thanksgiving; but it will avail only to our condemnation, if it be not also loved in the heart and acted in the life. Let us remember that it is not the knowledge of the way that God desires in us, but the practice of it; not light, but love. For though I understand all mysteries, and all knowledge, and have not charity, I am nothing.

Beware Of Pride Of Reasoning

Your mind is too much occupied with exterior things, and still worse, with argumentation, to be able to act with a frequent thought of God. I am always afraid of your excessive inclination to reason; it is a hindrance to that recollection and silence in which He reveals Himself. Be humble, simple, and sincerely abstracted with men; be recollected, calm, and devoid of reasoning before God. The persons who have heretofore had most influence with you, have been infinitely dry, reasoning, critical, and opposed to a true interior life. However little you might listen to them, you would hear only endless reasoning and a dangerous curiosity, which would insensibly draw you out of Grace and plunge you into the depths of Nature. Habits of long standing are easily revived; and the changes which cause us to revert to our original position are less easily perceived, because they are natural to our constitution. Distrust them, then; and beware of beginnings which, in fact, include the end. It is now four months since I have had any leisure for study; but I am very happy to forego study, and not to cling to anything, when providence would take it away. It may be that during the coming winter I shall have leisure for my library, but I shall enter it then, keeping one foot on the threshold, ready to leave it at the slightest intimation. The mind must keep fasts as well as the body. I have no desire to write, or speak, or to be spoken about, or to reason, or to persuade any. I live every day aridly enough, and with certain exterior inconveniences which beset me; but I amuse myself whenever I have an opportunity, if I need recreation. Those who make almanacs upon me, and are afraid of me, are sadly deceived. God bless them! I am far from being so foolish as to incommode myself for the sake of annoying them. I would say to them as Abraham said to Lot: Is not the whole land before you? If you go to the east, I will go to the west. Happy he who is indeed free! The Son of God alone can make us free; but He can only do it by snapping every bond; and how is this to be done? By that sword which divides husband and wife, father and son, brother and sister. The world is then no longer of any account; but, as long as it is anything to us, so long our freedom is but a word, and we are as easily captured as a bird whose leg is fastened by a thread. He seems to be free; the string is not visible; but he can only fly its length, and he is a prisoner. You see the moral. What I would have you possess is more valuable than all you are fearful of losing. Be faithful in what you know, that you may be entrusted with more. Distrust your intellect, which has so often misled you. My own has been such a deceiver, that I no longer count upon it. Be simple, and firm in your simplicity. The fashion of this world passes away. We shall vanish with it, if we make ourselves like it by reason of vanity; but the truth of God remains forever, and we shall dwell with it if it alone occupies our attention. Again I warn you, beware of philosophers and great thinkers. They will always be a snare to you, and will do you more harm than you will know how to do them good. They linger and pine away in discussing exterior trifles, and never reach the knowledge of the truth. Their curiosity is an insatiable spiritual avarice. They are like those conquerors who ravage world without possessing it. Solomon, after a deep experience of it, testifies to the vanity of their researches. We should never study but on an express intimation of Providence; and we should do it as we go to market, to buy the provision necessary for each days wants. Then, too, we must study in the spirit of prayer. God is, at the same time, the Truth and the Love. We can only know the truth in proportion, as we love it, we understand it well. If we do not love, we do not know Love. He who loves much, and remains humble and lowly in his ignorance, is the well-beloved one of the Truth; he knows what philosophers not only are ignorant of, but do not desire to know. Would that you might obtain that knowledge which is reserved for babes and the simple-minded, while it is hid from the wise and prudent.

The Gifts Of God Can Come From Strange Places

I am glad you find in the person of whom you speak, the qualities you were in search of. God puts what He pleases where He pleases. Naaman could not be healed by all the waters of Syria, but must apply to those of Palestine. What does it matter from what quarter our light and help come? The source is the important point, not the conduit; that is the best channel which most exercises our faith, puts to shame our human wisdom, makes us simple and humble, and undeceives us in respect to our own power. Receive, then, whatever He bestows, in dependence upon the Spirit that blows where it will. We know not whence it comes nor whither it goes. But we need not seek to know the secrets of God; let us only be obedient to what He reveals. Too much reasoning is a great distraction. Those who reason, the in devout wise, quench the inward spirit as the wind extinguishes a candle. After being with them for awhile, we perceive our hearts dry, and our mind off its centre. Shun intercourse with such men; they are full of danger to you. There are some who appear recollected, but whose appearance deceives us. It is easy to mistake a certain warmth of the imagination for recollection. Such persons are eager in the pursuit of some outward good, to which they are attached; they are distracted by this anxious desire; they are perpetually occupied in discussions and reasoning, but know nothing of that inward peace and silence, that listens to God. They are more dangerous than others, because their distraction is more disguised. Search their depths, and you will find them restless, fault-finding, eager, constantly occupied without, harsh and crude in all their desires, sensitive, full of their own thoughts, and impatient of the slightest contradiction; in a word, spiritual busy-bodies, annoyed at everything, and almost always annoying.

Poverty & Spoliation The Way Of Christ

Everything contributes to prove you; but God who loves you, will not suffer your temptations to exceed your strength. He will make use of the trial for your advancement. But we must not look inwards with curiosity to behold our progress, our strength, or the hand of God, which is not the less efficient because it is invisible. Its principal operations are conducted in secrecy, for we should never die to self, if He always visibly stretched out his hand to save us. God would then sanctify us in light, life, and the possession of every spiritual grace; but not upon the cross, in darkness, privation, nakedness and death. The directions of Christ are not, if anyone will come after me, let him enjoy himself, let him be gorgeously appareled, let him be intoxicated with delight, as was Peter on the mount, let him be glad in his perfection in me and in himself, let him behold himself, and be assured that he is perfect; on the contrary, his words are; If any one will come after me, I will show him the road he must take; let him deny himself, take up his cross and follow me in a path beside precipices, where he will see nothing but death on every hand. St. Paul declares that we desire to be clothed upon, and that it is necessary, on the contrary, to be stripped to very nakedness, that we may then put on Christ. Suffer Him, then, to despoil self-love of every adornment, even to the inmost covering under which it lurks, that you may receive the robe whitened by the blood of the Lamb, and having no other purity than his. O happy soul, that no longer possesses anything of its own, nor even anything borrowed, and that abandons itself to the Well-beloved, being jealous of every beauty but his? O spouse, how beautiful you are, when you have no longer anything of your own! You shall be altogether the delight of the bridegroom, when He shall be all your comeliness! Then He will love you without measure, because it will be Himself that He loves in you. Hear these things and believe them. This pure truth shall be bitter in your mouth and belly, but it shall feed your heart upon that death which is the only true life. Give faith to this, and listen not to self; it is the grand seducer, more powerful than the serpent that deceived our mother. Happy the soul that hearkens in all simplicity to the voice that forbids its hearing or compassionating self!

The Will Of God Our Only Treasure

I desire that you may have that absolute simplicity of abandonment that never measures its own extent, nor excepts anything in the present life, no matter how dear to our self-love. All illusions come, not from such an abandonment as this, but from one attended by secret reservations. Be as lowly and simple in the midst of the most exacting society as in your own closet. Do nothing from the reasoning of wisdom, nor from natural pleasure, but all from submission to the Spirit of life and death; death to self, and life in God. Let there be no enthusiasm, no search after certainty within, no looking forwards for better things, as if the present, bitter as it is, were not sufficient to those whose sole treasure is the will of God, and as if you would indemnify self-love for the sadness of the present by the prospects of the future! We deserve to meet with disappointment when we seek such vain consolation. Let us receive everything in lowliness of spirit, seeking nothing from curiosity, and withholding nothing from a disguised selfishness. Let God work, and think only of dying to the present moment without reservation, as though it were the whole of eternity.

Abandonment Is Not A Heroic Sacrifice

Your sole task, my dear daughter, is, to bear your infirmities both of body and mind. When I am weak, says the Apostle, then am I strong; strength is made perfect in weakness. We are only strong in God in proportion as we are weak in ourselves; your feebleness will be your strength if you accept it in all lowliness. We are tempted to believe that weakness and lowliness are incompatible with abandonment, because this latter is represented as a generous act of the soul by which it testifies its great love, and makes the most heroic sacrifices. But a true abandonment does not at all correspond to this flattering description; it is a simple resting in the love of God, as an infant lies in its mothers arms. A perfect abandonment must even go so far as to abandon its abandonment. We renounce ourselves without knowing it; if we knew it, it would no longer be complete, for there can be no greater support than a consciousness that we are wholly given up. Abandonment consist, not in doing great things for self to take delight in, but simply in suffering our weakness and infirmity, in letting everything alone. It is peaceful, for it would no longer be sincere, if we were still restless about anything we had renounced. It is thus that abandonment is the source of true peace; if we have not peace, it is because our abandonment is exceedingly imperfect.

Daily Dying Takes The Place Of Final Death

We must bear our crosses; self is the greatest of them; we are not entirely rid of it until we can tolerate ourselves as simply and patiently as we do our neighbor. If we die in part every day of our lives, we shall have but little to do on the last. What we so much dread in the future will cause us no fear when it comes, if we do not suffer its terrors to be exaggerated by the restless anxieties of self-love. Bear with yourself, and consent in all lowliness to be supported by your neighbor. O how utterly will these little daily deaths destroy the power of the final dying!

Suffering Belongs To The Living, Not The Dead

Many are deceived when they suppose that the death of self is the cause of all the agony they feel, but their suffering is only caused by the remains of life. Pain is seated in the living, not the dead parts; the more suddenly and completely we expire, the less pain do we experience. Death is only painful to him who resist it; the imagination exaggerates its terrors; the spirit argues endlessly to show the propriety of the life of self; self-love fights against death, like a sick man in the last struggle. But we must die inwardly as well as outwardly; the sentence of death has gone forth against the spirit as well as against the body. Our great care should be that the spirit die first, and then our bodily death will be but a falling asleep. Happy they who sleep this sleep of peace!

The Limits Of Our Grace Are Those Of Our Temptation

I sympathize sincerely with the sufferings of your dear sick one, and with the pain of those whom God has placed about her to help her bear the cross. Let her not distrust God, and He will proportion her suffering to the patience which He will bestow. No one can do this but He who made all hearts, and whose office it is to renew them by his grace. The man in whom He operates, knows nothing of the proper proportions; and, seeing the extent, neither of his future trials, nor of the grace prepared to meet them, he is tempted to discouragement and despair. Like a man who had never seen the ocean, he stands, at the coming in of the tide, between the water and an impassable wall of rock, and thinks he perceives the terrible certainty that the approaching waves must surely engulf him; he does not see that he stands within the point, at which God, with unerring finger, has drawn their boundary line, and beyond which they shall not pass. God proves the righteous as with the ocean; he stirs it up, and makes its great billows seem to threaten our destruction, but He is always at hand to say, thus far shall you go and no farther. God is faithful, who will not suffer you to be tempted above what you are able.

Resisting God, An Effectual Bar To Grace

You perceive, by the light of God, in the depth of your conscience, what grace demands of you, but you resist Him. Hence your distress. You begin to say within, it is impossible for me to undertake to do what is required of me; this is a temptation to despair. Despair as much as you please of self, but never of God; He is all good and all powerful, and will grant you according to your faith. If you will believe all things, all things shall be yours, and you shall remove mountains. If you believe nothing, you shall have nothing, but you alone will be to blame. Look at Mary, who, when the most incredible thing in the world was proposed to her, did not hesitate, but exclaimed; be it unto me according to your word. Open, then your heart. It is now so shut up, that you not only have not the power to do what is required of you, but you do not even desire to have it; you have no wish that your heart should be enlarged, and you fear that it will be. How can grace find room in so straitened a heart? All that I ask of you is, that you will rest in a teachable spirit of faith, and that you will not listen to self. Simply acquiesce in everything with lowliness of mind, and receive peace through recollection, and everything will be gradually accomplished for you; those things which, in your hour of temptation, seemed the greatest difficulties, will be insensibly smoothed away.

God Speaks More Effectually In The Soul, Than To It

Nothing gives me more satisfaction than to see you simple and peaceful. Simplicity brings back the state of Paradise. We have no great pleasures, and suffer some pain; but we have no desire for the former, and we receive the latter with thanksgiving. This interior harmony, and this exemption from the fears and tormenting desires of self-love, create a satisfaction in the will, which is above all the joys of intoxicating delights. Dwell, then, in your terrestrial paradise, and take good care not to leave it from a vain desire of knowing good and evil. We are never less alone than when we are in the society of a single faithful friend; never less deserted, than when we are carried in the arms of the All-powerful. Nothing is more affecting than the instant succor of God. What He sends by means of his creatures, contracts no virtue from that foul and barren channel; it owes everything to the source. And so, when the fountain breaks forth within the heart itself, we have no need of the creature. God, who at sundry times and in divers manners, spoke in time past unto the fathers by the prophets, has, in these last days, spoken unto us by his Son. Shall we then feel any regret that the feeble voice of the prophets has ceased? O how pure and powerful is the immediate voice of God in the soul! It is certain whenever Providence cuts off all the channels.

The Circumcision Of The Heart

Our eagerness to serve others, frequently arises from mere natural generosity and a refined self-love; it may soon turn into dislike and despair. But true charity is simple, and ever the same towards the neighbor, because it is humble, and never thinks of self. Whatever is not included in this pure charity, must be cut off. It is by the circumcision of the heart that we are made children and inheritors of the faith of Abraham, in order that we may, like him, leave our native country without knowing where we go. Blessed lot! to leave all and deliver ourselves up to the jealousy of God, the knife of circumcision! Our own hand can effect nothing but superficial reforms; we do not know ourselves, and cannot tell where to strike; we should never light upon the spot that the hand of God so readily finds. Self-love arrests our hand and spares itself; it has not the courage to wound itself to the quick. And besides, the choice of the spot and the preparation for the blow, deaden its force. But the hand of God strikes in unexpected places, it finds the very joint of the harness, and leaves nothing unscathed. Self-love then becomes the patient; let it cry out, but see to it that it does not stir under the hand of God, lest it interfere with the success of the operation. It must remain motionless beneath the knife; all that is required is fidelity in not refusing a single stroke. I am greatly attached to John the Baptist, who wholly forgot himself that he might think only of Christ; he pointed to Him, he was but the voice of one crying in the wilderness to prepare the way, he sent Him all his disciples, and it was this conduct, far more than his solitary and austere life, that entitled him to be called the greatest among them that are born of women.

FENELON BIOGRAPHY

A celebrated French bishop and author, b. in the Château de Fénelon in Périgord (Dordogne), 6 August, 1651; d. at Cambrai, 7 January, 1715. He came of ancient family of noble birth but small means. Fénelon was the second of the three children of Pons de Salignac, Count de La Mothe-Fénelon, by his second wife, Louise de La Cropte. Owing to his delicate health Fénelon's childhood was passed in his father's château under a tutor, who succeeded in giving him a keen taste for the classics and a considerable knowledge of Greek literature, which influenced the development of his mind in marked degree. At the age of twelve he was sent to the neighbouring University of Cahors, where he studied rhetoric and philosophy, and obtained his first degrees. As he had already expressed his intention of entering the Church, one of his uncles sent him to Paris and placed him in the Collège du Plessis, whose students followed the course of theology at the Sorbonne. There Fénelon showed such decided talent that at the age of fifteen he was chosen to preach a public sermon, in which he acquitted admirably. To facilitate his preparation for the priesthood, the marquis sent his nephew to the Séminaire de Saint-Sulpice (about 1672), then under the direction of Monsieur Tronson, but the young man was placed in the small community reserved for ecclesiastics whose health did not permit them to follow the excessive exercises of the seminary. In this famous school, of which he always retained affectionate memories. Fénelon was grounded not only in the practice of piety and priestly virtue, but above all in solid Catholic doctrine, which saved him later from Jansenism and Gallicanism.

Thirty years later, in a letter to Clement XI, he congratulates himself on his training by M. Tronson in the knowledge of his faith and the duties of the ecclesiastical life. About 1675 he was ordained priest and for a while thought of devoting himself to the Eastern missions. This was, however, only a passing inclination. Instead he joined the commuity of Saint Sulpice and gave himself up to the works of the priesthood especially preaching and catechizing.

In 1678 Harlay de Champvallon, Archbishop of Paris, entrusted Fénelon with the direction of the house of "Nouvelles-Catholiques", a community founded in 1634 by Archbishop Jean-François de Gondi for Protestant young women about to enter the Church or converts who needed to be strengthened in the Faith. It was a new and delicate form of apostolate which thus offered itself to Fénelon's zeal and required all the resources of his theological knowledge, persuasive eloquence, and magnetic personality.

When Louis XIV revoked the Edict of Nantes, by which Henry IV had granted freedom of public worship to the Protestants, missionaries were chosen from among the greatest orators of the day, and were sent to those parts of France where heretics were most numerous, to labour for their conversion. At the suggestion of his friend Bossuet, Fénelon was sent with five companions to Santonge, where he manifested great zeal, though his methods were always tempered by gentleness. According to Cardinal de Bausset, he induced Louis XIV to remove all troops and all evidences of compulsion from the places he visited, and it is certain that he proposed and insisted on many methods of which the king did not approve. "When hearts are to be moved", he wrote to Seignelay," force avails not. Conviction is the only real conversion". Instead of force he employed patience, established classes, and distributed New Testaments and catechisms in the vernacular. Above all, he laid especial emphasis on preaching provided the sermons were by gentle preachers who have a faculty not only for instructing but for winning the confidence of their hearers". It is doubtless true, as recently published documents prove, that he did not altogether repudiate measures of force, but he only allowed them as a last resource.

Even then his severity was confined to exiling from their villages a few recalcitrants and to constraining others under the small penalty of five sous to attend the religious instructions in the churches. Nor did he think that preachers ought to advocate openly even these measures; similarly he was unwilling to have known the Catholic authorship of pamphlets against Protestant ministers which he proposed to have printed in Holland. This was certainly an excess of cleverness; but it proves at least that Fénelon was not in sympathy with that vague tolerance founded on scepticism which the eighteenth century rationalists charged him with. In such matters he shared the opinions of all the other great Catholics of his day. With Bossuet and St. Augustine he held that "to be obliged to do good is always an advantage and that heretics and schismatics, when forced to apply their minds to the consideration of truth, eventually lay aside their erroneous beliefs, whereas they would never have examined these matters had not authority constrained them."

The Duchesse de Beauvilliers, mother of eight daughters, asked Fénelon for advice concerning their education. His reply was the "Traité de l'education des filles", in which he insists on education begining at an early age and on the instruction of girls in all the duties of their future condition of life. The religious teaching he recommends is one solid enough to enable them to refute heresies if necessary. He also advises a more serious course of studies than was then customary. Girls ought to be learned without pedantry; the form of instruction should be concrete, sensible, agreeable, and prudent, in a manner to aid their natural abilities. In many ways his pedagogy was ahead of his time, and we may yet learn much from him.

The Duc de Beauvilliers, was in 1689 named governor of the grandchildren of Louis XIV. He hastened to secure Fénelon as tutor to the eldest of these princes, the Duke of Burgundy. It was a most important post, seeing that the formation of the future King of France lay in his hands; but it was not without great difficulties, owing to the violent, haughty, and character of the pupil. Fénelon brought to his task a whole-hearted zeal and devotion. Everything down to, the Latin themes and versions, was made to serve in the taming of this impetuous spirit. The results of this training were wonderful. When the prince grew to man's estate, his piety seemed often too refined; he was continually examining himself, reasoning for and against, till he was unable to reach a definite decision, his will being paralyzed by fear of doing the wrong thing. However, these defects of character, against which Fénelon in his letters was the first to protest, did not show themselves in youth.

To reward the tutor, Louis XIV gave him, in 1694, the Abbey of Saint-Valéry, with its annual revenue of fourteen thousand livres. The Académie had opened its doors to him and Madame de Maintenon, the morganatic wife of the king, began to consult him on matters of conscience, and on the regulation of the house of Saint-Cyr, which she had just established for the training of young girls. Soon afterwards the archiepiscopal See of Cambrai, one of the best in France, fell vacant, and the king offered it to Fénelon, at the same time expressing a wish that he would continue to instruct the Duke of Burgundy. Nominated in February, 1696, Fénelon was consecrated in August of the same year by Bossuet in the chapel of Saint-Cyr. The future of the young prelate looked brilliant, when he fell into deep disgrace.

The cause of Fénelon's trouble was his connection with Madame Guyon, whom he had met in the society of his friends, the Beauvilliers and the Chevreuses. In exaggerated language characteristic of her visionary mind, she presented a system too evidently founded on the Quietism of Molinos, that had just been condemned by Innocent XI in 1687.

Fénelon refused to sign articles, on the plea that his honor forbade him to condemn a woman who had already been condemned. To explain his own views, he hastened to publish the "Explication des Maximes des Saints", a rather arid treatise in forty-five articles. Each article was divided into two paragraphs, one laying down the true, the other the false, teaching concerning the love of God. In this work he undertakes to distinguish clearly every step in the upward way of the spiritual life. The final end of the Christian soul is pure love of God, without any admixture of self-interest, a love in which neither fear of punishment nor desire of reward has any part. The means to this end, Fénelon points out, are those long since indicated by the Catholic mystics, i.e. holy indifference, detachment, self-abandonment, passiveness, through all of which states the soul is led by contemplation. Fénelon's book was scarcely published when it aroused much opposition. The king, in particular, was angry. He distrusted all religious novelties, and he reproached Bossuet with not having warned him of the ideas of his grandsons' tutor. He appointed the Bishops of Meaux, Chartes, and Paris to examine Fénelon's work and select passages for condemnation, but Fénelon himself submitted the book to the judgment of Holy See (27 April, 1697). A vigorous conflict broke out at once, particularly between Bossuet and Fénelon. Attack and reply followed too fast for analysis here. The works of Fénelon on the subject fill six volumes, not to speak of the 646 letters relating to Quietism, the writer proving himself a skillful polemical writer, deeply versed in spiritual things, endowed with quick intelligence and a mental suppleness not always to be clearly distinguished from quibbling and a straining of the sense. After a long and detailed examination by the consulters and cardinals of the Holy Office, lasting over two years and occupying 132 sessions, "Les Maxims des Saints" was finally condemned (12 March, 1699) as containing propositions which, in the obvious meaning of the words, or else because of the sequence of the thoughts, were "temerarious, scandalous, ill-sounding, offensive to pious ears, pernicious in practice, and false in fact". Twenty-three propositions were selected as having incurred this censure, but the pope by no means intended to imply that he approved the rest of the book. Fénelon submitted at once. "We adhere to this brief", he wrote in a pastoral letter in which he made known Rome's decision to the flock, "and we accept it not only for the twenty three propositions but for the whole book, simply, absolutely, and without a shadow of reservation." Most of his contemporaries found his submission adequate, edifying and admirable. In recent times, however, scattered letters have enabled a few critics to doubt its sincerity. In our opinion a few words written impulsively, and contradicted by the whole tenor of the writer's life, cannot justify so grave a charge. It must be remembered, too, that at the meeting of the bishops held to receive the Brief of condemnation, Fénelon declared that he laid aside his own opinion and accepted the judgment of Rome, and that if this act of submission seemed lacking in any way, he was ready to do whatever Rome would suggest. The Holy See never required anything more than the above-mentioned spontaneous act.

Louis XIV, who had done all he could to bring the condemnation of the "Maximes des Saints", had already punished its author by ordering him to remain within the limits of his diocese. Fénelon submitted without complaint or regret, and gave himself up entirely to the care of his flock. With a revenue of two hundred thousand livres and eight hundred parishes, some of which were on Spanish territory, Cambrai, which had been regained by France only in 1678, was one of the most important sees in the kingdom. Every year he gave a Lenten course in one or other important parish of his diocese, and on the principal feasts he preached in his own cathedral. His sermons were short and simple composed after a brief meditation, and never committed to writing; with the exception of some few preached on more important occasions, they have not been preserved. His dealings with his clergy were always marked by condescension and cordiality. "His priests", says Saint-Simon, "to whom he made himself both father and brother, bore him in their hearts." He took a deep interest in their seminary training, assisted at the examination of those who were to be ordained, and gave them conferences during their retreat. He presided over the concursus for benefices and made inquiries among the pastors concerning the qualifications of each candidate.

Fénelon was always approachable, and on his walks often conversed with those he chanced to meet. He loved to visit the peasants in their houses, interested himself in their joys and sorrows, and, to avoid paining them, accepted the simple gifts of their hospitality. During the War of the Spanish Succession the doors of his palace were open to all the poor who took refuge in Cambrai. The rooms and stairways were filled with them, and his gardens and vestibules sheltered their live stock. He is yet remembered in the vicinity of Cambrai and the peasants still give their children the name Fénelon, as that of a saint.

In spite of the multiplicity of his labours, Fénelon found time to carry on an absorbing correspondence with his relatives, friends, priests, and in fact every one who sought his advice. It is in this mass of correspondence, ten volumes of which have reached us, that we may see Fénelon as a director of souls. People of every sphere of life, men and women of the work, religious, soldiers, courtiers, servants, are here met with, not forgetting the Duke of Burgundy. Fénelon shows how well he possessed all the qualities he required from directors, patience, knowledge of the human heart and the spiritual life, equanimity of disposition, firmness, and straightforwardness, "together with a quiet gaiety" altogether removed from any stern or affected austerity". In return he required docility of mind and entire submission of will. He aimed at leading souls to the pure love of God, as far as such a thing is humanly possible, for though the errors of the "Maximes des Saints" do not reappear in the letters of direction, it is still the same Fénelon, with the same tendencies, the same aiming at self-abandonment and detachment from all personal interests, all kept, however, within due limits; for as he says "this love of God does not require all Christians to practice austerities like those of the ancient solitaries, but merely that they be sober, just, and moderate in the use of all things expedient"; nor does piety, "like temporal affairs, exact a long and continuous application"; "the practice of devotion is in no way incompatible with the duties of one's state in life". The desire to teach his disciples the secret of harmonizing the duties of religion with those of everyday life suggests to Fénelon all sorts of advice, sometimes most unexpected from the pen of a director, especially when he happens to be dealing with his friends at court. This has given occasion to some of his critics to accuse him of ambition, and of being as anxious to control the state as to guide souls.

Fénelon's last years were saddened by the death of his best friends. Towards the end of 1710 he lost Abbe de Langeron, his lifelong companion; in February, 1712, his pupil, the Duke of Burgundy, died. A few months later the Duc de Chevreuse was taken away, and the Duc de Beauvilliers followed in August, 1714. Fénelon survived him only a few months, making a last request to Louis XIV to appoint a successor firm against Jansenism, and to favor the introduction of Sulpicians into his seminary.

CPSIA information can be obtained at www.ICGtesting.com
Printed in the USA
BVOW04s0432150615

404084BV00002B/114/P